Theories in Criminology

CONSULTING EDITOR:

LEONARD SAVITZ

TEMPLE UNIVERSITY

THEORIES IN CRIMINOLOGY

PAST AND PRESENT PHILOSOPHIES
OF THE CRIME PROBLEM

STEPHEN SCHAFER

NORTHEASTERN UNIVERSITY

RANDOM HOUSE / NEW YORK

To the memory of my father

Acknowledgments

The author of any book written primarily for students should be, to some extent, the student of his students. Over the years my students, both abroad and in the United States, have given me invaluable help through their questions and comments in developing the ideas expressed in this book. To them I wish to express my thanks.

No less is my debt to Professor Leonard Savitz, consulting editor, who generously read and commented on the manuscript and offered most helpful suggestions. I am deeply obligated to Mr. Theodore Caris, senior editor, who throughout the preparation of the book offered his support with enthusiastic and warm encouragement. I am no less grateful to Miss Leona Huberman, manuscript editor, who helped shape the final version of this book.

However, my chief gratitude is due to my late father, who taught me that skepticism is the guiding light in science and thinking.

S. S.

Preface

Interest in crime, perennial in human history, has not diminished over the years. In addition to the scientific, pseudoscientific, and lay discussions of countless meetings and committees, an almost alarming flood of books, articles, television and radio talks, films, and plays has been produced on the subject. The problem of crime and delinquency invariably excites the public's curiosity and concern. One might ask how aroused they are about, say, rheumatic fever, which takes some 20,000 lives a year in this country, or the 60,000 deaths caused yearly by pneumonia. But the 10,000 mortal homicides provoke keen attention. Crime and punishment, once the concern only of flower-hatted spinsters, today attracts the interest of the man on the street. The public is almost preoccupied with the problem of crime.

Theories in Criminology is meant to be a retrospective exposition of man's struggle for an insight into the problem of crime and a hint of its perspectives and prospects. The essential history of criminological theory covers barely a century and shows a massive effort by many brave thinkers. Although none of these men achieved what they hoped for, they are remembered for their distinguished theoretical contributions to the understanding of crime.

The history of criminological theory is a depressing one, for the problem of crime is too complex to yield to simple solutions and the search for an answer leads inevitably to the use of inter-related approaches. Criminal offenses are defined by the law. But the most persuasive theories demand an understanding of the legal definition as drawn from many branches of human inquiry. It is no wonder, then, that half a century ago Birkmeyer, a gallant defender of the German classical school of criminal law, challenged the criminologically oriented Franz von Liszt: *"Was lässt von Liszt vom Strafrecht übrig?"* (What is left for criminal law?) Indeed, criminal behavior today is more perplexing than ever.

Hypotheses on crime are legion, and ever since the first crude scientific attempts to study crime and delinquency we have witnessed a continuing battle between conceptualists and empiricists. Some empiricists seem to be carried away by statistical euphoria and occasionally base their conclusions on a tortuous process of analysis after, seemingly, having already prejudged the issue. Conversely, the conceptualist theorists sometimes manipulate elusive assumptions devoid of any empirical evidence. Some have found comfort in building their system on loans from other theories or other disciplines. Other theorists claim novelty for their product, but they only present new ways of thinking about old speculations. The disarray in criminological theory becomes more painfully obvious every day.

If supported by truths, how easy it is for one to devaluate these theories just because they fail to answer the question of crime. How easy it is to pass judgment on them—usually by those who cannot offer a better proposition. Much can be said about the vulnerability of many criminological theories, but theorists dauntlessly persist in their attempts to construct a viable model. The immense amount of information gathered in this century does not seem to have brought us closer to a final solution.

All criminological theories try to fathom why laws are obeyed and, more important, why they are violated. Thus theories in criminology inevitably draw on and tangle with criminal justice. One major obstacle is that "justice" means only what those who are using the term agree to make it mean, and therefore the concept of crime is relative and changing. The evolution of the concept of justice is rooted in the evolution of the concept of responsibility; justice may be thought of as a philosophy of responsibility. That is why the central theme of this work is to describe some major theories in criminology primarily insofar as they describe the conducts, characteristics, and conditions that they propose are related to criminal responsibility.

This volume is just a short and sketchy account of many, but not all, theories that have helped shape contemporary criminological thought; the author does not claim to have exhausted all hypotheses or every aspect of crime and delinquency worthy of study. The limited space permits only an adumbration of the strengths and weaknesses of these theories. Anyone proposing to work through the theories in criminology with such a slim volume must be ready for an intellectual forced march, as much material has been necessarily compressed and, on occasion, perhaps oversimplified.

The author does not mean this book to stand without additional readings, for it is hardly more than hints, snatches, and gaps. He has to rely on the willingness and ability of his readers to complete their acquaintance with criminological theories. This is also necessary because the author has found himself unable to solve any of the problems.

This is not a defense, but the apology of the author.

S. S.

Boston, 1968

Contents

Theories in Criminology

I

The Dual Responsibility

Criminological Theories

What constitutes a criminological theory and what is its appropriate scope are extremely difficult questions. The delimitation of theories in criminology is no less difficult than in general philosophy, and any attempt at delimiting cannot avoid considerable arbitrariness. Criminology, like the other social sciences, is primarily a research-oriented discipline and therefore its theories are accepted as valid only if verified by existing data. Even the law, which objectively defines the necessary conditions of crime, and which seems to be abstract before applied practically, is increasingly predicated on observation. In criminology a "pure theory" cannot be profitably employed, unless, as a last resort, purely abstract thinking aids in the understanding of the empirical material.

However, if verification is fundamental to any theory and proof is as rigorously interpreted as it is in the natural sciences, hardly any current set of propositions in criminology could correctly be labeled a theory. The vision of most theorists is not always based on mathematical-statistical evidence, a fate also true of almost every social science theory. No criminological theory has established the "truth" or shown us the causes of crime. This is not a matter of judgment, but a statistical fact: a panoramic study and appraisal of criminological theories and related action programs clearly demonstrates that crime rates have not dropped and criminal recidivism has not been reduced. A cynical judgment may be that these ideas are hypotheses rather than theories.

It may be that no criminological theory can ever be verified fully; most criminological truths have a transitional character. Crimes and criminals change in definition, by time and place; what is a crime today may not be a crime tomorrow. Nicholas S. Timasheff suggests that a theory is verified "if no known fact or generalization seems to contradict it."[1] But at present there is little likelihood of creating any generalizations with universal validity, that is, fully conforming to all existing information. Most issues in criminology are so complex that often there are several alternative explications and conceptualizations simultaneously available. Indeed many of them tolerate the plausibility of other models of explanation.

Of the several approaches to formulating a criminological theory, some include so many criteria that any theory becomes overly rigid. Marvin E. Wolfgang and Franco Ferracuti, for example, claim an elaborate number of sets and subsets to meet their standard of theory construction.[2] Not content with Talcott Parsons' suggestions for conceptual clarity, precision, and logical integration,[3] they add to Clarence Schrag's list of testability, logical adequacy, generality, comprehensiveness, informative content, fertility, parsimony, credibility, predictability, and significance.[4] These many requirements indicate that much disagreement prevails regarding the acceptance of a creative proposition as a theory. Certainly George Vold is right in suggesting that "No present scheme of theoretical concepts is entirely valid or entirely sufficient to account for the full range and complexity of human behavior."[5] In the present confusing, changing, and challenging state of crime and responsibility, more than reasonability, probability, and flexibility can hardly be expected from a speculative-explaining proposition that should justifiably be called a criminological theory.

We are faced with a curious duality in criminological theories. There are theories that attempt to explain the causes of criminal behavior and independent propositions dealing with the rehabilitation of criminals and the efficiency of the penal system. Theories of causes are coupled with "theories" of treatment. As Leslie Wilkins states, "Scientific methods may be concerned with the advancement of knowledge, but this does not restrict the range of the problems to which they are applied."[6] In other words, crime, like other social problems, requires manipulation and "solution" regardless of whether the full causal nexus is understood. "For the administrator an understanding of human behavior is unnecessary, or it is necessary only as a means to an end."[7] Wilkins uses medicine as an analogy: doctors often cure an ailment without knowing its etiology and gladly accept the favorable results without diminishing the problem itself. Daniel Glaser similarly contends that correctional problems could be most adequately solved by controlled experiments and that by and large correctional research "has not been designed primarily to test theories of crime causation and contribute to the academic debates on that topic, but to evaluate correctional practices."[8] There is an increasing number of those who respond to crime with recommendations for what can be done with the criminals, rather than seeking an explanation of why criminals violate the law. Much relief may come from therapies, correctional methods, operational decisions and actions; perhaps the only barrier between them and the criminological theories is that the treatment propositions want to treat something that is not known and is yet to be found by the theories.

Crime and Responsibility

When Xerxes, son of the great Darius, caned the furious waves for their disobedience, he was not entirely correct. A case could have been made for holding them responsible and punishing them for their rebellious lack of response to his order; but he should have paid closer attention to the nature of their resistance. Most criminological theories approach crime in a reverse direction of thinking; they try to explicate criminal conduct but pay little attention to why certain acts are defined as crimes and why criminal responsibility is attached to some actions. Actually, the crime problem presents two interconnected elements: the types of behavior defined in the law as crimes and the forces that impel some people to engage in conduct labeled criminal by the law. Both pose the problem of responsibility, but from two different angles.

The former deals with the responsibility of individuals who have engaged in certain acts and are thereby threatened with punishment under the law. Misappropriation or misapplication of money entrusted to one's care may involve his being held responsible for embezzlement. A person who willfully or maliciously burns something, even without the intent to defraud, may be responsible for arson. The law threatens anyone who takes anything of value from a person by force or violence with the responsibility for the crime of robbery. Lawmakers select, define, and imbue these and other acts with responsibility. Penal sanctions remain only abstract threats so long as the law is respected.

The other type of responsibility involves the forces that motivate one's conduct against the law. Why does a person become an embezzler, an arsonist, or a robber? What factors are responsible for his disrespect for the legal threat of punishment? Is it his biological makeup, his psychiatric condition, his social or economic environment that is responsible for his criminal conduct?

Or did he simply "want" to engage in a crime and, in a sense, accepted responsibility by his "free will"?

Who can be made responsible for what, and who is responsible and why—these are the two crucial issues in criminological thought. The answer to both issues is certainly ever changing, mirroring the values of the social, cultural, and political conditions of the given era. Both responsibilities are changing.

The concept of responsibility as used here is not the individual legal accountability or culpability for having engaged in punishable conduct. This responsibility may be classified as "answerability," for it involves the lawmaker defining crime and the individual reacting to the law by breaking it—both are elements of a single continuum.[9] Crime factors cannot be understood without an intimate knowledge of the law. Criminal law similarly cannot be fully comprehended without some understanding of the etiology of crime. Without this dual understanding of responsibility, crime may remain unknown.

The two responsibilities are interrelated and cannot be disconnected. This twofold concept seems to be the heart of the crime problem; its crux is the drama between the threatening responsibility and the counterresponsibility. Without the former we would have a lawless and, necessarily, a "crimeless" society; with it we may only hope for some miraculous disappearance of crime. Changes in the law are not inevitably followed by changes in human conduct. A new law requires adjustment in individual behavior, but this may not always be made by all members of the society. Changes in law are variables of a composite and complicated relationship. Two variables are almost never perfectly correlated; in the case of extremely complex phenomena, such as the law and criminal behavior, any number of contributory, contingent, and alternative conditions may sharply affect the relationship between the two. Yet, in crude generalization, the criminal conduct may be viewed as the dependent variable. Crime is committed by man, but crime is defined by law; the supreme tragedy of the drama is that the law, too, is made by man.

Since no one has yet invented a system of absolute justice, every society has produced its own unique system of control. But the systems are continually changing. A constant and eternal natural law would be possible only if all social phenomena, and all lawmaking powers, recurred with unchanging uniformity. Thus, an accurate description of the causes of crime could be determined only if an immutable natural law existed. Raffaele Garofalo's exciting pursuit of "natural" crime is never ultimately convincing.[10] In most criminological analyses the question of causes—in other words, the "responsibility" for the criminal conduct—has become so central that it is easy to lose sight of the changing criminal law.

Because the law is in a constant state of flux, an individual's frame of reference cannot be "naturally" consistent with his society's demands. His conduct has to be adjusted to changes in the system of control. Even if the laws of two different control systems seem to resemble one another, invariably they differ in the interpretation and application of the law, largely because of variation in the use of the lawmaking powers. The concept of responsibility fluctuates bewilderingly from society to society and from one generation to the next. In all periods of human history man has been aware of its inconsistencies, for herein lies the distinction between conformists and criminals. As the legal philosopher Morris Cohen put it, "The legal system of any country has a definite history which helps us to understand its provisions and shows how it changes according to varying social conditions, and even according to the will of certain powerful individuals."[11]

Responsibility is determined by an ever changing formula. It might be said that crime does not change but responsibility does. Some individuals may enjoy a lifetime without being frustrated by significant changes of law, while others may be exposed to painful changes in the system of responsibilities that require severe changes in their behavior. The reason for changes in law is inherent in the reason for the law itself. A system of law might be understood without reference to crime, but the meaning of crime can hardly be perceived without understanding its relationship with the responsibility-making law.

Responsibility and Law

The source of responsibility-making law is "social power." Only support for such power makes it possible for a law to become "the law." Inversely, from the law we can discover its source; a given concept of responsibility usually reflects the lawmaking power. John Austin contended that the law is the "command of the sovereign."[12] Gustav Radbruch, in a sense, extended Austin's statement by contending that absolute justice is undiscoverable.[13] A combination of Austin's dictate with Radbruchian relativism would imply that lawmaking power is not necessarily in the hands of a king or a dictator. Any group or particular individual may, at a given moment of time, acquire such power. E. Adamson Hoebel contends that Sir Henry Maine[14] was wrong in suggesting that early legal prohibitions seemed similar to a "despotic father's commands."[15] Morris Cohen also addressed himself to this question: "Doubtless, the law will never, so long as it is administered by human beings, be free from arbitrary will and brute force."[16] And this is probably true for all of human history, regardless of the form of the sovereign authority or social power that designed the concept of responsibility.

Edward Westermarck, after reviewing and analyzing the origin and development of the moral ideas, finally concluded that the simple historical fact is that the "law expresses a rule of duty by making an act or omission which is regarded as wrong a crime."[17] All laws are formulated on the assumption that they are just. They are "just" at least insofar as they are defined by the ruling social power and so long as the existing social power prevails. This social power knows what is right and wrong, and in the form of the commands raises the law to the level of "truth." Cicero told the story of a captured pirate who defended himself before Alexander the Great by saying that he did exactly what the great conqueror did but that he was to be punished as a pirate rather than a conqueror just because he operated with only a small boat rather than with a large armada.[18]

Of course, the case of the pirate is not as simple as that. The question of who or what has the right to declare what right is has been seriously studied by legal philosophers as well as by sociologists. Perhaps one of the reasons for the long-standing disagreement in finding an answer is that the lawyers are too close to the problem and the sociologists are too distant from it. Max Weber, in describing power and legitimacy, doubted that the "absurd" would arise in practice,[19] but it should be remembered that he did not witness the revolutionary changes of the last half a century, when throughout the world traditional patterns of legitimacy and old truths have been demolished and new "truths" have been declared.

In his somewhat naturalist search for the morality of law, Lon Fuller contended, "There is no doubt that a legal system derives its ultimate support from a sense of being 'right.' "[20] But, understandably, his stand is based on what he or we think is "right." Dennis Lloyd, another modern philosopher of law, suggests that whoever requires the obedience of others should be entitled to do so.[21] In other words, he seems to opt for a law to enable the lawmaker to make the law. Perhaps Herbert Hart came closest to the truth when, in one of his generalizing "issues," he proposed that a penal statute declaring certain conduct as criminal and specifying the punishment to which the criminal is liable "may appear to be the gunman situation writ large."[22] Certainly the lawmaker cannot be identified with a gunman simply by virtue of having the coercive power of making others obey his commands, yet there are intrinsic similarities between the two situations. The death penalty and the first-degree murder differ only in their legality, as determined by conventional society.

Although from the Justinian Law to our time many laws were born in dictatorial situations, the gunman circumstances are not typical in the responsibility-making processes. The lawmaker is not necessarily a gunman, but he may be. Nicholas Timasheff finds that "A law of revolutionary origin may exist as well as a law of traditional origin."[23] However, this is just a procedural issue. In both variations of the origin of law, John Austin's claim, that in the last analysis the law is the command of the sovereign, may well be a terrifying truth. Austin, a disciple of Jeremy Bentham, may have oversimplified the essence of the lawmaking, but his tenet offers little shelter for those who abandon the real world for the comfort of illusions. Indeed, there is much more involved in the idea of law than sheer obedience, but "The factor of obedience is nevertheless a crucial one."[24] Usually a rich and complex interplay between individuals, groups, and conflicting values takes place before a law is created. Questions as to who has this sovereign power, what legalities or formalities must be observed, and what behavior is demanded, do not alter the fundamental structure of lawmaking. Hans Kelsen's theory on the identity of state and law[25] would be closer to John Austin's thinking if the state were equated with power.

One may assume that the puzzle of what power exists, and the related questions of "legitimacy" of this power, leads inevitably to the problem of the "rightness" of law. Perhaps the greatest obstacle to settling this apparently interminable argument is our reluctance to accept the fact that what we think of as right does not necessarily represent the only correct view. We tend to think in terms of a single immutable truth and conclude that therefore there is only one possible system of justice. The claim that the law is moral or ethical rests upon the dubious hypothesis that there is only one moral or ethical code. The law makes objective rather than absolute judgments; it is right or wrong only in the way it interprets actions. The social power of the group defines values to be learned; it defines the rightness or wrongness of some modes of human conduct. Whatever is defined by this social power as right or wrong must be accepted by those who are required to obey so long as the power is a "power."

Lon Fuller suggests that the continuity of law "is so obvious that everyone normally assumes this continuity as a matter of course."[26] The picturesque example of a woman who was convicted in 1944 in England for telling fortunes in violation of the Witchcraft Act of 1735 is certainly not too encouraging as evidence for hailing the stationary nature of legal commands.[27] Changes take different form and speed in different cultures and under the rule of different "sovereigns." It is inherent in the dynamics of totalitarian powers that changes in the law are generally faster and more abrupt than in democracies. But it is difficult to agree with Rudolf Stammler, who, in his quest for a "just" law expressing a "social ideal," hypothesized despotic control systems where the commands of the rulers were not binding on the rulers.[28] Most dictatorships make no less effort to maintain the continuity of law than do democracies. Whether the rulers are bound by their own commands is hardly a distinguishing characteristic of authoritarian systems. Even in democracies, where the "supreme legal authority [is] the constitution itself,"[29] behind legitimacy lies authority, and behind authority, power. It is not true that the continuity of law is preserved simply because a constitution is written. The English are constitutionalists and therefore have a constitution, even though it is an unwritten one; "certain other peoples have written constitutions but are not constitutionalists."[30]

Clearly legislative apparatus and lawmaking in totalitarian systems differ from those in democracies. Dictatorial powers monopolize lawmaking; in democracies, "There is a great variety of interactions between social evolution and legal change."[31]

However distinct the two lawmaking processes are, it does seem that essentially both remain "commands of the sovereign." Howard Becker's "outsiders," who are deviants because they failed "to obey group rules,"[32] are simply those who failed in their obligation to obey Austin's "sovereign." As Becker says, "Before any act can be viewed as deviant . . . someone must have made the rule which defines the act as deviant."[33]

The lawmaking power may be a single man or many men; it may be a despotic dictator or a democratic parliament; "The source of authority may be . . . the words of a prophet or a saint."[34] But man makes the law and defines responsibility, and thus they vary with changing ideas and transfers in power. The idea of the continuity of law seems weakened by the discontinuity in the source of law. The inevitable changes in the participants of the lawmaking process alone account for unavoidable changes in the definition of crimes and punishments. *Lex posterior derogat priori;* the law of yesterday may not be the law of today if it is no longer supported by the ultimate power in the society. The later law derogates earlier ones. Sometimes the "continuity" of the law involves a legal code of great stability with only minor changes; but upon examination this continuity is proved a fiction. It is therefore impossible to speak about "causes" of crime or crime "in general" without an awareness of the forces that create and enforce the law and the manner in which the forces themselves change.

The test of a man is how he responds to the system of control in his society that aims to establish or fortify an ideal social order. Studying "criminal" behavior relative to the changing law may lead to a balanced assessment of the crime problem. It is a highly complex relationship, and the correlation between legal prohibition and criminal action is much too intricate to be measured by conventional methods; the frame of reference the observer is using is vital to the judgment. Yet a balanced perspective seems to be the cornerstone of any meaningful etiology of crime. The correlation between making people responsible for engaging in crime and the factors that produce noncompliance largely determines the relative significance of crime and the success of the social order. The irony of the man-committed crime is that it is so dependent upon the man-made law.

NOTES

1. Nicholas S. Timasheff, *Sociological Theory, Its Nature and Growth* (3rd ed., New York, 1967), p. 10.
2. Marvin E. Wolfgang and Franco Ferracuti, *The Subculture of Violence, Towards an Integrated Theory in Criminology* (London, 1967), p. 64.
3. Talcott Parsons, "Comment" to L. Gross, "Preface to a Metatheoretical Framework," *American Journal of Sociology*, 67, September 1961, 136–140.
4. Wolfgang and Ferracuti, *op. cit.*, pp. 64–65.
5. George B. Vold, *Theoretical Criminology* (New York, 1958), p. 4.
6. Leslie T. Wilkins, *Social Deviance, Social Policy, Action, and Research*, XII (Englewood Cliffs, N.J., 1965).
7. Leslie T. Wilkins, "Operational Research and Administrative Problems," *O & M Bulletin*, Vol. 14, No. 6 (London, n.d.), p. 4.
8. Daniel Glaser, *The Effectiveness of a Prison and Parole System* (New York, 1964), p. 7.
9. H. L. A. Hart in his *Punishment and Responsibility* (Oxford, 1968), pp. 211–212, called attention to the wide range of ideas covered by the term "responsibility" in and out of the law. Hart distinguished among role responsibility, causal responsibility, liability responsibility, and capacity responsibility. In the present context, liability responsibility is the one charged by the lawmaking power (it is role responsibility only in its moral sense as a general obligation of all members of the society), and causal responsibility refers to crime factors. Capacity responsibility, as concrete accountability, is merely a legal and often technical question and thus outside the scope of the present topic.

10. Raffaele Garofalo, *Criminology*, Robert Wyness Millar (tr.) (Boston, 1914).

11. Morris Raphael Cohen, *Reason and Law* (New York, 1961), p. 12.

12. John Austin, *Lectures on Jurisprudence or the Philosophy of Positive Law* (London, 1861). Austin's first six lectures were published in his lifetime under the title *The Province of Jurisprudence Determined* (1832); the rest were published with the assistance of his widow.

13. Gustav Radbruch, *Rechtsphilosophie* (3rd ed., Berlin, 1932).

14. Sir Henry Sumner Maine, *Ancient Law, Its Connection with the Early History of Society and Its Relation to Modern Ideas* (1861), with Introduction and Notes by Sir Frederick Pollock (London, 1906).

15. E. Adamson Hoebel, *The Law of Primitive Man, A Study in Comparative Legal Dynamics* (Cambridge, Mass., 1954), pp. 258–259.

16. Cohen, *op. cit.*, p. 112.

17. Edward Westermarck, *The Origin and Development of the Moral Ideas* (2nd ed., London, 1912), Vol. I, p. 168.

18. Cicero, *De republica*, III, 12.

19. Max Weber, *Grundriss der Sozialökonomie, III. Abteilung, Wirtschaft und Gesellschaft* (Tübingen, 1922), p. 28, and *infra*.

20. Lon L. Fuller, *The Morality of Law* (New Haven and London, 1964), p. 138.

21. Dennis Lloyd, *The Idea of Law* (Baltimore, 1964), pp. 27–28.

22. Herbert Lionel Adolphus Hart, *The Concept of Law* (Oxford, 1961), pp. 6–7.

23. Nicholas S. Timasheff, *An Introduction to the Sociology of Law* (Cambridge, Mass., 1939), p. 214.

24. Lloyd, *op. cit.*, p. 27.

25. Hans Kelsen, *Allgemeine Staatslehre* (Berlin, 1925).

26. Fuller, *op. cit.*, p. 149.

27. Hart, *op. cit.*, p. 60.

28. Rudolf Stammler, *Wirtschaft und Recht nach der materialistischen Geschichtsanfassung* (5th ed., Leipzig, 1924).

29. Stanley I. Benn and Richard S. Peters, *The Principles of Political Thought* (London and New York, 1965), p. 302.

30. Alfred De Grazia, *The Elements of Political Science, II* (London and New York, 1965), 49.

31. Wolfgang Friedmann, *Law in a Changing Society* (Baltimore, 1964), p. 34.

32. Howard S. Becker, *Outsiders, Studies in the Sociology of Deviance* (New York, 1963), pp. 7–8.

33. *Ibid.*, p. 162.

34. Karl Mannheim, *Systematic Sociology, An Introduction to the Study of Society*, J. S. Erös and W. A. C. Stewart (eds.) (New York, 1957), p. 126.

II

The Nature of Law

What Is Law?

Law is the formal expression of the value system of the prevailing social power. It is present in all its positive and negative aspects in man's life even before his birth. He is as much surrounded by it as by the air he breathes, and it follows him in all circumstances to the end of his life, and even after that. One may not realize his perdurable ties with the law until he comes into violent contact with it. Everybody living in a civilized society has at some time been told "to do something, or to refrain from doing something, because there is a law requiring it, or because it is against the law."[1] The law is coercive and negative, but it is also positive in that it affirms the values of the ruling social power. As such it is not always concerned with reality: not what is but what should be is its central concern.

The law consists of specific rules for human behavior. Although it disciplines conduct, it is not exclusively a regulative tool. It is perhaps first of all a teleological instrument in the service of the existing power structure. As such, the law is not concerned with justifications as to why particular types of behavior are required or prohibited. The law attempts to achieve certain ends established by the reigning "sovereign." Human rights as defined by the law can be understood only in the mirror of this power-established value system. In other words, whenever the law attempts to attain specific goals it must at the same time take a position in favor of certain values; thereby it enables society to distinguish between right and wrong. The values that the law supports are not the result of the law but the reason for its existence. Laws can be interpreted as right or wrong and argued accordingly, but they always represent what "should be"—what is regarded as right by the prevailing social power. In Gustav Radbruch's relativistic and skeptical philosophy, a value is never right just because it is or because it was, or even because it is going to be.[2]

Legal codes, statutes, and precedents acquaint us with the law, giving us reliable information about how the law organizes, arranges, and settles the conditions of life. Family relationships, contracts, property, insurance, civil rights, price controls, administration of justice, and every other segment of organized life are governed by legal norms. The criminal law advises us what acts we may take only at the peril of being classed and punished as criminals. At a glance, law is practice oriented. Thus one may raise the question, why philosophize on the nature of law? It has been suggested that "It is unquestionably possible to be a good lawyer or jurist without being clear about one's legal philosophy."[3] But one might inquire how much credit is due a conductor who leads the orchestra after he has meticulously memorized all the notes without understanding what the composer meant to express in his music.

In order to examine the question "What is law?" we have to step out from the world of law and view legal norms from a larger perspective. In point of fact, perhaps the question What is law? is not well phrased to express the real problem. Although Herbert Hart suggests that "What is the nature of law?" and "What is the essence of law?" are "more obscurely framed questions,"[4] he himself could not avoid using these terms; indeed he seems to prefer an even more elusive phrase, "the concept of law."[5]

Law is a social and political phenomenon, and any examination of its nature cannot dispense with historical and sociological analyses. Talcott Parsons rightly contends that "Law and sociology have an unusually wide area of overlapping interests."[6] The question What is the nature of law? inevitably leads us to philosophy. Is law a "natural" idea born with us? Is it an *a priori* form of thinking that is independent of experience? Can law be separated from morality? Is it perhaps a "superstructure" arising out of the economic structure of the society? Is law the command of a limitless sovereign to be used for his particular utilitarian ends? For these and other questions we have to turn to the philosophy of law, or jurisprudence. Nevertheless, even in the philosophy of law one cannot hope to find crystallized tenets. On none of the major issues is there an agreement of views. The nature of law, as Roscoe Pound described it, "has been the chief battleground of jurisprudence since the Greek philosophers began to argue" about it.[7]

Law as a Superstitious Command

Credulity regarding the supernatural has been present in one form or another throughout human history. Edward Westermarck observed that "Men not only believe in the existence of supernatural beings, but enter into frequent relations with them."[8] In primitive societies much of the profound reverence for the gods is due to the deities having been garbed in the same sanctity as the human sovereign; the authority to distinguish between right and wrong is also attributed to them. They alone define the responsibilities with which certain human conducts are charged; they define crimes and their punishment, for crime is a challenge to them.

The concept of crime merged with the notion of sin. Sir Henry

Maine's theory that law has its origin in religion[9] has not been disproved.[10] There seems to be general agreement that early in human history law and religion were indistinguishable; they appeared together in an intricate mixture.

The Ten Commandments, perhaps mankind's first criminal code, is essentially an expression of religious law or legalistic religion, and almost every other primitive legal code similarly represents legal elements in combination with religious ideas and rituals. In his monumental Hindu code, Manu (about the 5th century B.C.) presented the rules of proper behavior as they were revealed to him in the form of fundamental truths by *Brahma.* Yajnavalkya, another important jurist of Manu's time, similarly based his *Institutes* on religious precepts. Narada was perhaps the first divine sage of Hindu jurisprudence who, in his 4,000 verses of law, attempted to free his *Naradasmriti* "from a crowding of religious and moral principles."[11] Islamic law was no less religious; the Prophet Mohammed, founder of the Moslem religion, promulgated many of the Arabian legal customs in the Holy Koran (A.D. 622–632). After the death of the Prophet, liberalizing trends developed in Moslem law, and under the Shütes the imam became the final interpreter of law, but, of course, his authority was based on divine command. The Zoroastrian books in Persia, the mysterious doctrines of the Egyptian Hermes Trismegistus, and the Babylonian Code of Hammurabi all embody laws heavily shaped by religious doctrines.

Ancient Judaism played "a decisive role in shaping the origins of Western concepts of law."[12] The Old Testament's staggering conceptualizations and penetrating legal philosophy are unparalleled in world literature and represent the noblest monument of the rendezvous of law with religion. The one God gave His law to His chosen people; He "called Moses, and spoke to him from the tent of meeting, saying, 'Speak to the people of Israel, and say to them' . . ."[13] Moses merely communicated the law to the people, for it was not his law but God's.

The notion of dual responsibility embraced two different spheres. Responsibility for certain human behaviors was defined and charged in the heavenly sphere; responsibility for man's conduct contrary to divine law was born on earth. Why, then, did the supernatural not intervene to make humans obey their commands? Or, if everything was controlled by a supernatural force, why were humans held responsible for what had been ordered by the divine power? These are problems left to the province of theology. However, the "rightness" of law and the ultimate justice of the legal commands were beyond argument. Belief in the supernatural marked the "nature of law."

Law as the Representation of Justice

The idea of "earthly" justice as the essence of the nature of law emerged rather early in Greek philosophy. One factor that may have contributed to this mode of thought was the extreme harshness of the laws, which were drawn or compiled by the celebrated Draco in about 621 B.C. and which, according to contemporary Athenians, were written not in ink but in blood.[14] The Draconian code, together with the laws of Solon, Klysthenes, and Zeleukos, represented "justice" as retribution by the state against law violators. The continuing public controversies and the rather frequent changes in law stimulated Greek philosophers to concern themselves with such questions as What is law? What is a "right" or "good" law? What is the moral basis that should govern human behavior? and the ultimate question, What is justice?

The Sophists (*circa* fifth century B.C.) were early involved in the question of changing human law versus eternal natural law. The Greek world was alive with speculations about reason and justice in law. In *Eumenides* (about 458 B.C.) the dramatist Aeschylus took a bold stand for peace and social harmony to be secured by law. Sophocles, the Athenian tragic poet, in his play *Antigone* (c. 441 B.C.), presented natural law as if it were a divine rule, both omniscient and unchangeable. The Sophists' view, dismissed by Plato as basically dishonest, held that justice and morality in the natural law were given to man by a divine force, as contrasted to man-made law, which serves only the interests of its human creators.

Following the practical philosophy of the Sophists, which was sharply critical of the existing laws, Socrates (c. 469–399 B.C.) tried to develop a rational ethics and politics. He devoted himself to the search for the "general good," and this led him to examine some basic ethical issues.

In his rather utopian dream Plato (about 428–348 B.C.), perhaps the greatest of all the idealists of the ancient world, visualized law within the context of an ideal state.[15] In his dialogue *Politeia*[16] the questions "What is justice?" and "Is the just life happier than the unjust?" are the central theme. Plato placed the interest of the state above that of the individual. Because of his belief in the omnipotence of the state, those who are unfamiliar with the totalitarian rule of justice would make of him the intellectual father of dictatorial systems. But in Plato's *Utopia* only sages and philosophers are qualified to rule the people. His ideal world is ruled by philosopher-kings who provide justice to every man and woman, who, in return, are required to obey their decisions. The distinguishing characteristic of Plato's political philosophy is its aristocratic nature: rule by a few outstanding leaders. However, the rulers exercise power not for their own ends but in the interest of the people. The concept of responsibility is embodied in the people's interest.

Perhaps Plato realized the overly idealistic design of his utopia, because toward the end of his life he prepared his dialogue *Laws*, in which alternative ideal states are depicted. Here he emphasized the idea that the law "cannot, of course, be in conflict with the idea of justice."[17] The law should rule the rulers, but the "right" law would be recognized as offering the greatest "good" to the people. His law remains in essence a system of natural law.

Against Plato's idealism, Aristotle, who studied at Athens under Plato, followed a more practical path in his search for justice. If the Sophists had advocated false doctrines, "Plato would have been a Sophist in the eyes of Aristotle, and vice versa."[18] Aristotle's method of philosophical analysis involved what we would today call a comparison of political institutions. By contrasting development of different political systems, he attempted in *Politics* to find what led to "bright" or "dark" periods in human history. Using the material of 158 city constitutions, he sought for "the ideal aim of men as individuals and as associated in states."[19]

Whereas Aristotle's *Rhetoric* deals primarily with contemporary legal procedures and court practices, the idea of justice is more fully developed in his *Nichomachean Ethics*. To Aristotle, "Justice in its most general sense is voluntary obedience to law";[20] he quotes with approval the proverb, "Justice is the summary of all virtue." One of his focal points is that equal men should have equal justice. Justice has two elements, it must be lawful and it must be fair. If, as was the case, people are not considered equal, they cannot have an equal share of justice. Aristotle thus distinguished between "distributive" and "corrective" justice; distributive justice is concerned with everybody getting his just deserts, and corrective justice tries to right every wrong.

Regarding the nature of law, Aristotle distinguished natural justice from legal justice. Natural justice is universally valid and is independent of individual opinions; legal justice exists only when it has been laid down. By placing heavy emphasis on the necessity of all citizens observing the law, Aristotle called attention to the law's teleological nature: it is the lawgiver's task to make man "good" by means of the law.

The Socratic-Platonic and the Aristotelian views of natural law were developed to some extent in the teachings of Zeno (about 334–262 B.C.) and other Stoics.[21] While Plato and Aristotle conceptualized in terms of local city laws (*polis*), the Stoics based their philosophy on a universal city (*cosmopolis*). Their cosmopolitan theories were based on the superiority of reason-derived universal laws over man-made local laws; they accepted justice only if local law was not in conflict with universal law. In the eighteenth century Rousseau and Kant furthered the Stoic rationale as it relates to the law.

Another Greek school of philosophy, the Epicureans,[22] "had much in common with utilitarian positivism."[23] Epicureanism, a rather materialistic philosophy, held human happiness to be the highest good and pleasure to be the most rational satisfaction of the mind. Their "nature of law" resembles that of the later contract theories.

The Roman contribution to the philosophical analysis of law was largely derivative and notably lacking in originality. Even Cicero, Rome's greatest orator, writer, statesman, and lawyer, demonstrates a strong Greek influence throughout his works. His *De republica* (54 B.C.) and *De legibus* (52 B.C.) reflect the cosmopolitan Stoic natural law. The famous distinction he makes among *ius civile, ius gentium,* and *ius naturale* lacks clarity. The *ius civile* is derived from special conditions and the spirit of the nation (*civilis ratio*); it actually means the law of Rome. The *ius gentium* is *naturalis ratio inter omnes homines constituit,* based on natural reason; it developed into the practice of the "recuperators" and resulted in the jurisdiction of the *praetor peregrinus*. The *ius naturale* is *quod natura omnia animalia docuit,* universal and unchanging. The *ius naturale* defines man's rights and duties, limits the powers of the legislators, and is the ideal toward which lawmakers should strive. It essentially is the principle, *Honeste vivere, neminem laedere, suum cuique tribuere*.[24]

Law as the Order of the Divine World

Greek philosophy had considerable influence upon medieval philosophers. However, whereas the Greeks examined and constructed earthly communities, the great Christian philosophers of the Middle Ages deliberately turned away from the world around them to dream of a heavenly kingdom.

St. Augustine (354–430) expressed this concern in the title of his greatest work, *City of God*. In contrasting the kingdom of God with the state of men, he gave his views about human societies. He "recognized that even in the imperfect states of this world there was need for justice as decreed by God."[25] This justice is part of the law in the divine world, insofar as it becomes natural law within the *civitas Dei*, the community of God. "To believe in God, to venerate and adore him, to give to his church its proper place in the community, all this is now included in the concept of justice."[26]

Medieval legal philosophy reached its zenith in the work of the memorable Christian theologian Thomas Aquinas (1225–1274). Aristotle's influence on him is apparent not only in his comments on Aristotle's *Politics*, but also in his *Tractatus de regimine principum*, a treatise dealing with the basic principles of governing a state.[27]

In his masterwork, *Summa theologica*, Aquinas reflects on the existence and nature of God, rules of morality, and his concept of law. He distinguished among three laws: *Lex aeterna*, eternal law, the divine wisdom that governs the world (*ratio divinae sapientiae*); *lex naturalis*, natural law, which directs human behavior for the common good; and *lex humana*, man-made law, which forces adherence even if people do not wish to obey. Man-made law can never be contrary to the eternal and natural laws; it represents justice only if completely subordinated to the heavenly order.

Law as the Order of the Secular World

The waning of the Middle Ages saw the rise of theories of secular power. The doctrine of a divine legal order was subordinated to a more worldly law. In this philosophy the site of responsibility making descended to earth.

Dante (1265–1321), the Italian poet, expounded his political theories in *Convivio* and later in *Monarchia*. Arguing for the independence of the emperor from the pope, he proposed the establishment of a world state. Perhaps the outstanding advocate of the independence of the secular power was the Franciscan monk William of Occam, or Ockham (about 1280–1349), known as the "Invincible Doctor," who was imprisoned at Avignon on charges of heresy. In his *Dialogus inter clericum et militem super dignitate papali et regia* he established (or, better, revived) the "nominalistic" orientation. In his view, general universalistic concepts do not represent reality but are merely names (*nominalia*). Only real laws are in force, since they are based on real authority. A similar approach is seen in the *Defensor pacis* of Marsilius of Padua (about 1270–1342) and in the *Concordantia catholica* of Nicholas of Cusa (1401–1464), the German cardinal and scholar.

Law as the Representation of the Sovereign

Belief in the independence of secular powers was furthered by the concept of the sovereign as the supreme legislator. Some strong positivist thought viewed the law as a system not dependent on anything else for its validity and thus detached from the rule of superhuman forces.

Sir Thomas More (1478–1535), whose brilliant public career under Henry VIII ended on the gallows, in *De optimo reipublicae statu sive de nova insula Utopia,* like Plato in his *Republic,* attempted to construct an ideal state. He rejected monarchy and advocated a republican form of government. His system, he contended, would reduce, though not eliminate, crime. Legally stipulated punishment would not in itself prevent crime; rather, conditions that give rise to crime should be changed. The law in his utopia tried to eliminate socially undesirable conditions.

At the time Thomas More voiced his democratic and even socialistic aspirations, Niccolo Machiavelli (1469–1527) was proclaiming his nationalistic ideas. An Italian statesman who was imprisoned on a charge of conspiracy, Machiavelli has been characterized as a ruthless realist. After having been released and exiled, he completed *Il Principe*, dedicated to Lorenzo de Medici, in which he rejected the impractical and visionary and viewed the state, history, and man in their crude realities. Power is the prime objective if the state is to be great, and techniques should be selected insofar as they further this objective. Machiavelli's "sovereignty," the Prince's law, is not limited by morality, nor by justice—it is the life and freedom of the nation that dictate the action. How far Baruch Spinoza, almost two centuries later, derived his philosophy from Machiavelli's ideas is still debatable.

Between More's republic and Machiavelli's prince stands the sovereignty of the legislative power as advanced by the French political thinker Jean Bodin (1530–1597). In *Six livres de la république* he proposed that the state is the supreme power, with an unlimited right to create and enforce laws. The state cannot be restricted by any conditions; the law is the will of the sovereign power. The command of the sovereign, and an understanding of the law as refined some three centuries later by John Austin, is Bodin's focal idea; but how far the sovereign power is governed by divine laws is not quite clear in Bodin's conception.

This claim for the autonomy of the secular powers foreshadows later demands against absolute monarchy. These dissenters might be regarded the pioneers of the "monarchomachs" or "tyrannomachs." One of these was the Scottish humanist, George Buchanan (1506–1582),[28] who was forced to flee to France but later returned and became the tutor of Queen Mary. Another,

Johannes Althusius (1557–1638), in *Politica methodice digesta* advanced his theory of the ultimate sovereignty of the people and the social contract. As Carl Friedrich says, "It is the defense of such an order, rather than merely the concern with the prescriptions of natural law, which the right, indeed the duty, of resistance implies for Athusius and his precursors."[29]

Law as the Order of the Dual Sovereignty

Two basic ideas run through in the philosophy of Hugo Grotius (1583–1645), the Dutch jurist. As a republican, he was arrested and sentenced to life imprisonment, but he succeeded in escaping to France, where he composed his *De iure belli ac pacis*, a classic of international law. Grotius suggests that natural law exists outside the positive law;[30] for example, the concept of private property is the product of the positive law, but as soon as this concept developed, the concept of theft emerged as a transgression of the natural law. In other words, he expounded the theory of "a purely secular natural law based upon Stoic doctrine and freed from all ecclesiastical authority."[31] He started with a sociable human nature, the *appetitus societatis*, which permits this man-made natural law. He segregated natural law from religious sovereignty.

William Archibald Dunning suggests that Grotius' natural law had its origins in the philosophy of Richard Hooker.[32] Hooker (1554–1600), a theologian and a strongly conservative philosopher, had based his theory on the scholastic doctrines and teachings of Thomas Aquinas.[33] In *Laws of Ecclesiastical Polity* and primarily in the first volume, *Concerning Laws and their several kinds in general,* he analyzed law in its broadest sense ("any kind of rule or canon"). In addition to the laws of men, the laws of reason drawn by "voluntary agents," he distinguished three types of divine laws: eternal law, drawn by God for himself; superhuman law, the law of the angels to rule the heavens; and natural law, for the "natural agents." Like Sir Thomas Smith, Hooker found the "nature of law" in the constitutional order as ultimately directed by divine law.

"What is law and not what ought to be law" was the *leitmotif* of Sir Francis Bacon (1561–1626) in his struggle to determine supremacy in the battle between natural law and common law—the question of dual or single sovereignty. Bacon, who served as Lord Chancellor under James I (1566–1625) and whose views reflect Buchanan's, leaned toward a limitless sovereignty. He criticized philosophers who admire the law but talk about it only with a "remote use" (*ab usu remota*) and those who are only jurists and whose sole contribution to the philosophy of law is a chain of legal rules. In *Advancement of Learning* he analogizes kings ruling by their laws with God ruling by his natural law.

Sir Edward Coke (1552–1634) took a contrary view. During his splendid legal career he was the Speaker of the House of Commons, the prosecutor against the Gunpowder Plot conspirators, and finally Lord Chief Justice of England. The four volumes of his *Institutes*, particularly the first, *Coke upon Littleton*, have become legal classics. A defender of the English tradition, he did not advocate dual sovereignty but argued for the rule of common law.

Law as a Utilitarian Command

The basic tenet of the utilitarians is that human conduct depends on the balance between pain and pleasure. Happiness is the diminishment of pain and maximization of pleasure. Natural laws cannot guarantee such progress, but man-made laws can; if men recognized the utility of laws, which might result in greater happiness, they would obey.

The first major legal philosophy built on utility came from Thomas Hobbes (1588–1679), a strong royalist, tutor to the exiled Prince Charles, and author of the *Leviathan*, often referred to as a portrait of a totalitarian society. His first legal work, *The Elements of Law Natural and Politic,* was in defense of the king. The second was *De Cive,* which contains a considerable part of his legal philosophy. Leo Strauss contends that Hobbes's most profound work, the *Leviathan,* "is by no means an adequate source for an understanding of Hobbes's moral and political ideas."[34] His last work in law, the *Dialogue of the Common Laws of England,* prepared in his advanced age, is an argument with Edward Coke against the common-law doctrines.

Basically, Hobbes' philosophy is one of "nominalistic materialism." It is nominalistic because he considered terms or names as symbols of concepts rather than the concepts themselves; as he put it in the *De Cive: Nomina signa sunt conceptuum non signa ipsarum rerum* ("Names signify concepts, not the thing itself"). And it is materialistic because Hobbes attempted to reduce everything to its mechanical state; to him, not only the material of the body but also the state is a functioning mechanism.

Hobbes held that the early stages of human history were characterized by *bellum omnium in omnes*—everybody warring against everybody. The reason for this is that all men are equal; they are equal in power. Power is the means of achieving future good. Law, in Hobbes' understanding, is our liberty to use our power with reason. A coercive power is necessary to compel men by the terror of punishment to perform their "covenants"; the law is simply a forceful guide to reasonable conduct.

The lawmaker is the sole sovereign; he decides right and wrong, defines responsibility, and is himself beyond punishment. In the *Leviathan* Hobbes emphasized that in "natural" conditions there is no justice; where there is no common power justice cannot exist. Justice means that everybody is assured of his own particular rights, but then the question becomes, On what grounds can anyone claim a right as his own? To Hobbes no claim could be derived from nature, since whatever nature "gave" has been divided by men among themselves, and has caused war among them. Only the lawmaker can make order in these hostile conditions, and this, to Hobbes, is justice. Barna Horváth suggests that this is the most delicate point in Hobbes' philosophy, since one cannot help assuming that the sovereign alone is in a "natural" state, as opposed to the "legal state," wherein are all other members of the community.[35] Nevertheless, although Hobbes' portrayal of the natural conditions is not the first "satire of the golden ages,"[36] the brilliant logic of his philosophical structure is without parallel.

Utility as a source of both praise and approbation is the focal idea in the philosophy of David Hume (1711–1776), the Scottish historian whose critique of miracles and other Christian dogmas aroused Immanuel Kant's admiration. His chief work was *A Treatise of Human Nature,* later rewritten and simplified under the title *An Enquiry Concerning Human Understanding.* Another important work is *An Enquiry Concerning the Principles of Morals.*

To Hume "justice" is right only if it is socially useful. He suggested that if men had sufficient sagacity to perceive the interest that binds them to the "observance of justice" and if they were determined to adhere to their general interest against the temptation of petty advantages, there would be no need for government or other political organization. The stability of private property, its transfer by consent, and the "performance of promises" are the basic rules of a peaceful and secure human society. However, men and their "benevolent" emotions are not strong enough to achieve this by themselves, so, in their own best interests, law must lead them. The concept of responsibility for violating the law appears here to involve liability for not wanting or not being capable of rational conduct.

Hume based his understanding of utility on the concept of causality, but he failed to find a full answer to the law of causality, being unable to verify empirically the connection between cause and effect. His difficulties regarding causality made him skeptical about the natural law; nevertheless, Wilhelm Windelband was probably correct in calling Hume the real father of positivism.[37]

Sir William Blackstone (1723–1780), a professor of law at Oxford and a justice of the English Court of Common Pleas, may not have been an original thinker, but one would be remiss in failing to mention him, not only because certain conceptual distinctions were "embodied in Anglo-American legal thought by Blackstone"[38] but also because his work served as a starting point for Jeremy Bentham's utilitarian philosophy. The chapter entitled "Of the Nature of Laws in General" in his *Commentaries on the Laws of England* contains his concept of law.

To Blackstone the law is "a rule of action dictated by some superior being." The natural law is, of course, the will of the Creator. However, man must seek his own happiness, and to this end human laws are created, but they must not contradict the law of the Creator. Thus he seems to derive the positive law from the natural law.

The most formidable critic of Blackstone's heterogeneous theory was one of his students, Jeremy Bentham (1748–1832), whose *A Fragment on Government* probably marks the true birth of utilitarianism. Horváth suggests that Bentham's *Fragment,* the American Declaration of Independence, and Adam Smith's *Wealth of Nations,* which all appeared in 1776, show a significant historical harmony of philosophic endeavor.[39]

To Bentham the utility of the law is measured by the extent to which it promotes the pleasure, good, and happiness of the people. The object of all legislation should be the greatest happiness for the greatest number. Bentham contended that nature had placed man under two distinct sovereigns, pain and pleasure, and that the interaction of the two structures determines human behavior. The art of politics consists of governing people toward their own best interests by creating such artifices that, despite avarice and ambition, all are compelled to cooperate for the public good. Friedrich sees here "a massive restatement of Hobbes's pessimistic view of human nature."[40]

It can be assumed that Helvétius, John Locke, Joseph Priestley, Montesquieu, and Cesare Beccaria strongly influenced Bentham's philosophy.

Bentham contended that a political community can survive only if there is a "habit of obedience" by subjects toward rulers. Law is the expression of the will of a person or several persons whom, at a given time and in a given matter, the members of the community will obey. Bentham used this concept of law in many of his works,[41] but perhaps most clearly in his *Chrestomathia* and *Pannomial Fragments*.

For Bentham the law is a command, and it presupposes possible punishment; without the threat of punishment, obedience would be like an effect without a cause. Whether the law is based on obedience or obedience is derived from the law is a critical point in Bentham's theory. His philosophy also has difficulties in resolving punishment and reward. A reward cannot influence will and cannot secure obedience, as will a threatening command. The threat of loss of a reward can prompt obedience, but this "reward" is really a form of punishment.

One of those who influenced Bentham's views was James Mill (1773–1836), a long-time friend. Mill was interested in philosophy and law, and his published papers include *Liberty, Jurisprudence,* and, his most important, *Government*. It is said he guided Bentham's philosophy in a radical direction. James Mill's son, John Stuart Mill (1806–1873), whose education was directed personally by his father, started his career as the greatest promise of the utilitarians. In *Utilitarianism* he accepted the importance of happiness; however, in *On Liberty* he departed from Bentham's precepts by emphasizing individual life styles.

Bentham's true heir, perhaps greater than his testator, was John Austin (1790–1859), the founder of the "analytical" school of jurisprudence. The son of an Ipswich flour miller, who helped John Stuart Mill's education, he taught as professor of jurisprudence at the University of London. His frequent sojourns in Germany afforded him the opportunity of meeting German philosophers, and he spent several years in Paris. His *Lectures on Jurisprudence, or the Philosophy of Positive Law,* in part a posthumous work, expressed his strictly imperative philosophy of law and submitted the general legal concepts to an unparalleled analysis.

To Austin a law is a rule laid down for the guidance of an intelligent being by another intelligent being having power over him. It is a law because of the difference in their relative positions. All laws are commands, and what the command means is the key problem of legal and ethical philosophies. The essence of the command lies in the power of the commander to inflict wrongs or pains upon the disobedient. This wrong is the "sanction" with which disobedience is threatened.

Austin's concept of command necessarily includes the concept of superiority. Whoever can oblige another to comply with his wishes is the superior, while the one who is supposed to obey the superior is called by Austin the "inferior." Austin admitted that the terms are relative; but this is not, as suggested by some critics, a weakness in his theory. Rather, it can be seen as a strength of Austin's thinking because it calls attention to the changing basis of the power structure.[42] As he said, the relation of superior and inferior, and the relation of inferior and superior, are relative; one may be viewed as the superior from one aspect and as the inferior from another.

Nevertheless, whoever is the sovereign cannot be restricted by legal barriers, for he has no legal obligations. If the sovereign had any legal obligation, this would mean that he himself would be inferior to a higher power. Austin firmly stated that to think of a supreme power limited by positive law is "a flat contradiction in terms." Austin accepted constitutional law only in restricted areas, and in his view the sovereign is morally obliged to follow only those principles and maxims approved by the larger society. Consequently, any act of the sovereign may be "unconstitutional" without infringing on the law itself. The command itself is a fact; thus, according to Austin, general jurisprudence should be concerned only with law as it *is* rather than as it *ought* to be.

In his *Province of Jurisprudence Determined* Austin does not accept the assumption of an original "contract" as the basis of governing a society. It is an agreement only in the sense that we agree with something even if it is bad so to avoid something worse.

Austin clearly rejects the existence of natural law and accepts the law only if it is issued by an intelligent and powerful human. The real sovereign is not truly visible, and as soon as we try to approach him he disappears. Barna Horváth raised the question whether such a sovereign actually exists at all.[43] The greatest, and perhaps the only, difficulty with Austin's philosophy is that it cannot be refuted simply because it cannot be proved.

The theorist Karl Bergbohm maintained that the principles and concepts in law are closely interrelated.[44] He thought that a legal philosophy could be built on a compilation of existing positive laws. A similar mode of thought can be seen in the works of Adolf Merkel and Rudolf Ernst Bierling.[45] Bierling, however, attempted to extend his analyses in a search for legal concepts independent of the positive contents of laws.

Law as a Derivative of the Constitutional Order

The philosopher John Locke (1632–1704) used elements of Hobbes' thinking to construct a very different theory. Locke, who originally practiced medicine, can be regarded as the dominant representative of classical naturalism. *An Essay Concerning Human Understanding* contains his general philosophy, while his *Two Treatises of Government* presents his philosophy of law, including a criticism of Sir Robert Filmer's work,[46] and his own theoretical beliefs. In general, he did not accept that man's natural condition is a continual state of war. Locke strongly believed in the idea of legislation and proposed that governments derive their authority from the people's consent. Governmental rule gives organized form and substance to natural conditions. Thus for Locke legislative power is restricted to the issues involving the public good, which is a reflection of the natural law.

To Locke the law "in its true nature" is not so much its "direction of a free and intelligent agent to his proper interest," but its ceasing to control people when it is beyond the general good or public welfare.

Locke's naturalistic idea about the origin of positive law has also been expressed by the Italian G. Vico (1688–1744), who in both *De universi iuris uno principio et fine uno liber unus* and *Principi di una scienza nuova d'intorno alla commune natura delle nazioni* suggested that the development of human history is not based on random chance but takes place in accordance with eternal laws.

Charles Louis Secondat, Baron de la Brède et de Montesquieu (1689–1755), the magnificent French historian and author of the *Lettres persanes,* the *Considérations sur les causes de la grandeur des Romains et de leur décadence,* and, most important, *De l'esprit des lois (The Spirit of Laws),* analyzed the factors that influence the spirit of the positive law. To Montesquieu law was the expression of justice.

This system of justice, however, can be only approached, never fully achieved. Montesquieu proposed that every society adjust justice to its own "spirit." He believed in the importance of constitutional law and did not accept the rule of tyranny. He believed that law was derived from nature.

Law as the Expression of Man's Natural Reason

Although "in a way, we are face to face here with a particular German development,"[47] among the first to profess man's nature as the dominant force was the Dutch philosopher Benedict (or Baruch) Spinoza (1632–1677). Abandoning Judaism for a rationalistic pantheism, he was persecuted by the Jews and had to leave Amsterdam. He then settled in The Hague, where he made a living by polishing optical glasses. In *Tractatus theologico-politicus*, a critique of the Bible, he states that the origin of law is power. Although he mentions the power of nature to determine human behavior, he cannot without qualification be listed among the adherents of natural law. To him the establishment of the state ends natural law and replaces it with the positive law. Man is a "natural" creature, strongly motivated by preservation but who nevertheless exercises power with reason.

Man's natural reason is emphasized in a different context by Samuel Pufendorf (1632–1694), born in the year of Spinoza's birth. He tried to combine Grotius' *appetitus societatis* with Hobbes' *bellum omnium in omnes*. Pufendorf thought that man's egotistic instincts dominate his sociability. In his *De jure naturae et gentium libri octo* he proposed that the state developed because men did not trust themselves—that their original incapacity (*imbecillitas*) drove them to organize their community. This "imbecility" is part of man's basic nature and lies at the origin of the natural law. Roscoe Pound suggests that Pufendorf "rests his whole theory upon an original pact" and that "he argues that there was in the beginning a 'negative community,' " which was abolished by the mutual agreement of men when they established the state.[48]

Friedrich says that, in its recognition of this contradiction in man, Pufendorf's doctrine makes it possible "to see crime and punishment as necessary consequences of man's freedom."[49]

Man's moral nature is the starting point of the philosophy of

Gottfried Wilhelm Leibniz (1646–1716), whose versatile genius showed itself when at the age of twenty he was offered a university professorship in Germany. His basic interest was mathematics; while meditating on the nature of law (*Nova methodus docendi discendique juris*) or the reunion of the Protestant and Catholic churches (*Systema theologicum*), he invented a calculating machine and devised a new form of differential and integral calculus. He believed in a universe consisting of a number of monads in harmony with one another and with God, a universe where faith and reason do not conflict.

To Leibniz, man's nature is that of a sage whose heart is full with love. The moral idea is an eternal idea, like justice that is derived from reason. To him law is a natural law, combining a wise love of mankind with the unchangeable dictates of reason.

Leibniz' contemporary, Christian Thomasius (1655–1728), a highly respected philosopher of the Enlightenment, claimed that human reason recognizes the law of nature and obliges everyone to do whatever good his reason tells him. Thomasius, in *Fundamenta juris naturae in quibus decernuntur principia honesti, justi ac decori*, based his philosophy on man's moral nature. He discussed inborn rights and inborn obligations, and, by distinguishing between *honestum* and *justum*, he separated morality from law and ethics from natural law.

A synthesis of the philosophies of Leibniz and Thomasius was attempted by Christian Wolff (1679–1754), but he lacked the depth of Leibniz and the passion of Thomasius. He identified man's striving for perfection with his striving for happiness; to him perfection is happiness. Wolff's *Ius naturae methodo scientifico pertractum* presents an intriguing picture of a welfare state that is also a police state, which was established by a "contract" among men to maximize happiness.

Whereas Wolff believed in the moral necessity of striving for perfection, Jean Jacques Rousseau (1712–1778) focused on man's natural ability to attain perfection. His somewhat disarranged course of life led him to live for a time in England under the patronage of Hume. Except for his romance, *La nouvelle Héloïse*, all his other works, including *Confessions*, a description of his wanderings, the revolutionary *Du contrat social*, and *Émile*, an educational treatise, demonstrate Rousseau's belief in the supreme importance of the law.

Man in nature was originally "good," but civilization perverted this goodness. Man should listen to his natural sentiments and reason, for they will always direct him toward his own good. But he does not always understand what his will is, and therefore a constitution or state structure that fulfills the principles of the social contract is necessary to secure equality and freedom.

These attempts to reconcile man's natural reason with his moral nature, and which seem to introduce utilitarian elements in the concept of morality, were rejected by the great thinker of Königsberg, Immanuel Kant (1724–1804), who believed that the supreme source of all morality is pure reason. His *Thoughts on the True Estimates of Living Forces* and *Theory of the Heavens* (a defense of the existence of God) were published before he was appointed professor of logic and metaphysics. Best known of his works is the *Critique of Pure Reason*, followed by the *Prolegomena to [Any] Future Metaphysics*, *Foundations of the Metaphysics of Ethics*, *Metaphysics of Nature*, *Critique of Practical Reason*, *Critique of Judgment*, and the *Metaphysics of Morals*, actually his philosophy of law, which he prepared after ill health led to his retirement. He distinguished between noumenon (an object of purely intellectual intuition) and phenomenon (an object of perception or experience); phenomena, however, are not independent and exist only in relation to the mind. A command of the moral law, a universally and unconditionally binding rule, is a "categorical imperative." Kant's law is basically an ethical system: no society can pride itself on its system of justice or morality if the categorical imperative is not a moral imperative.

Kant's views on criminal law are emphatically retributive. Morris Raphael Cohen wrote, "A little more regard for human experience which Kant so cavalierly rejects in this field suggests that most of Kant's assertions are as weak logically as they are defective in human sympathy and understanding."[50] The idea of retributive punishment fits in with Kant's absolutist concepts: he believed not only in the moral nature of law, but also in the right and necessity of the state to enforce this system of law.

The thinking is somewhat Kantian in the works of Johann Gottlieb Fichte (1762–1814), a professor at Jena who was accused of atheism and forced to resign. In his *Critique of Religious Revelation* Fichte deduced his belief in natural law from "unconditional" pure reason. In his *Theory of Politics* human activity is the starting point of his metaphysical thinking; in describing a utopian state he arrived from an individualistic to an anti-individualistic concept.

Friedrich Wilhelm Joseph von Schelling (1775–1854), professor of philosophy at Erlangen and Berlin, expounded a system of objective idealism: natural law did not originate in the subjective human reason but within some objective world view. In this respect perhaps Victor von Cathrein, with his *Recht, Naturrecht und positives Recht,* is Schelling's modern counterpart, although his is a theologizing philosophy.

Law as an Order of the Utopias

One characteristic common to both utopias and philosophies of natural law is that they try to portray an ideal state or legal order and claim it as the only right system. The name "Utopia" was given by Sir Thomas More to his imaginary commonwealth and hence has been applied to similar dream countries of other writers. Gyula Moór rightly classifies utopian literature as a branch of natural-law philosophy;[51] the search for a law that is permanently right and "true" is really a utopian quest.

Among the utopians the French satirist François Rabelais (1483–1553) should be mentioned. In *La vie inestimable de Gargantua* he describes a totally free, anarchic society. The members of this society, the "Thelemites," do not know time, since reason controls man, not the ticking of the clock.

Sir Francis Bacon described in his *Nova Atlantis* a scientific utopia where the inhabitants of a little island control the forces of nature in the service of human happiness.

Tommaso Campanella (1568–1639) in *Civitas Solis* described the State of Sun, where pure communistic rules regulate every phase of human life, including sexual activities.

James Harrington (1611–1677) portrayed his model state in *Oceana,* a rather imperialistic society built along the lines of a club in which members argue over vital issues.

William Godwin (1756–1836), husband of the feminist Mary Wollstonecraft, described his peculiar anarchic-utopian society in *Enquiry Concerning Political Justice and Its Influence on Morals and Happiness*. Interestingly, Godwin was basically a utilitarian and the foundation of his theory is not essentially different from Bentham's, yet he arrives at very different conclusions.

François Charles Marie Fourier (1772–1834), a naïve petty clerk in France, in *Le nouveau monde industriel* describes his utopia as a place of the highest perfection of man. In his "new world" he would transform even the natural forces; thus his is a cosmographic utopia.

Etienne Cabet (1788–1856) described his dream state in his utopian romance, *Voyage en Icarie*.

All these theorists believed in the basically "good" nature of man, all professed a belief in natural law, and most proposed a more or less communistic structure for their imaginary societies. Some of them denied any justification for law and proposed lawless communities. It may be that modern anarchism can be traced to utopian writings. At any rate, one can say that both have their origin in natural-law thinking.

Law as an Agent of the Right Purpose

The emergence of sociology in the nineteenth century, coupled with utilitarianism in legal philosophy, directed attention to the search for a better understanding of law and its societal role.

This quest is expressed in the title of the monumental work of Rudolf von Jhering (1818–1892), *Der Zweck im Recht* (*The Purpose in Law*). Jhering's central idea—that the purpose is the creator of law—is also expressed in his other major writings, published earlier: *Der Geist des römischen Rechts auf den verschiedenen Stufen seiner Entwicklung,* on the spirit of the Roman law, and *Der Kampf ums Recht,* on the struggle over the law.

In Jhering the law serves as a means of reconciling conflicting interests. Since in his theory the individual is for himself, the individual is for the society, and the society is for the individual, a three-directional purpose has to guide the law. All interests are closely linked, and the law can be understood only within the mirror of "purpose." Since Jhering's purpose, or better, "social purpose," borders the concept of values, his thinking is close to the theories focusing on the rightness of law.

The problem of the "right" law has also been analyzed by Rudolf Stammler (1856–1938), the founder of the Neo-Kantian school of thought. His thorough and detailed analysis, *Wirtschaft und Recht nach der materialistischen Geschichtsauffassung,* deals essentially with three basic problems: the rightness of law, the question of anarchism, and the concept of law. Stammler analyzed the "right" law again in *Die Lehre von dem richtigen Rechte* (*The Study of the Right Law*). His *Theorie der Rechtswissenschaft* more or less repeats what he said in his earlier writings, but also offers some thoughts on methodology. His *Lehrbuch der*

Rechtsphilosophie is not simply a textbook of jurisprudence but, mainly in the chapter "Das Werden des Rechtes" ("The Development of Law"), a treatise on the sociology of law.

Stammler sought for a method of measuring the "rightness" of law, that is, the best possible definition of law and the correct assignment of responsibility. To him the law is a kind of natural law with changing content; but this, of course, contradicts the concept of natural law, which by definition is unchangeable. The law is a coercive attempt to achieve, in Stammler's phrase, the "social ideal." His demand for obedience to the law entangles his natural law with positive law.

A similar kind of purposeful right law was the philosophical target of Bódog Somló (1873–1920). In *Jogbölcseleti Elöadások* (*Lectures on Jurisprudence*) he attempted to approach the nature of law from a sociological perspective. Later, however, in *Das Verhältnis von Soziologie und Rechtsphilosophie,* he took a strong stand against the overuse of sociology in the philosophy of law. In his chief work, *Juristische Grundlehre,* he accepted an "absolute morality" as the basis from which one may arrive at the "right" law; however, the untimely end of his life prevented his further analysis.

Law as a Reflection of History

The outstanding figure in the so-called historical school of law, which proposed to find the source of law, state, and ethics in historical development, was Georg Wilhelm Friedrich Hegel (1770–1831), professor of philosophy at Heidelberg and Berlin, to whom "Marx was so much indebted."[52] Dennis Lloyd remarked, "The melancholy part that this historicist philosophy has played in the modern cults of nationalist totalitarianism is sufficiently well known to require no further elaboration here."[53] Hegel's statement in his *Grundlinien der Philosophie des Rechts oder Naturrecht und Staatswissenschaft im Grundrisse,* that the task of the philosopher is to be acquainted with the existing state rather than to construe a new state, is characteristic of his way of thinking. In Hegel, whatever is rational is real and whatever is real is rational.

Like Schelling, his contemporary, Hegel assumed an objective world reason or world spirit as the only existing force; all else can be understood as the projection of this force. The world spirit, the "whole," is alone real; the state and the law are only parts of this force and represent channels through which the spirit becomes "real."

The world as it is expresses Hegel's "absolute" idea. This absolute has an internal necessity to develop itself, and the progress of development can be witnessed in the course of history. This unfolding process can be understood through the dialectical relationship of concepts (in the Hegelian term "categories"), which directs them to meet each other as a reconciliation of their contradictions. So law too submits to historical development.

Ethics is not missing from Hegel's philosophy. It too is treated as a reality, for it is present in the concepts of "good" and "freedom." To Hegel the state and the law represent the ethical idea. His state is an ethical state; it is the realization of the good and the freedom. "It is not an institution for the realization of ethics but is this realization itself" and Friedrich warns, "if one does not grasp this basic position of Hegel, Hegel's legal philosophy remains incomprehensible."[54] Neither does Hegel make clear on what grounds the individual member of a society can be charged with responsibility for violating the law of the world spirit.

The original idea of the historical basis of the law can be traced to Edmund Burke (1727–1797), the conservative English statesman. The significance of his legal philosophy can best be judged if seen as the forerunner of the romantic German orientation of Hegel and Savigny. Burke believed in traditions and customs and proposed that the "prescription" is not a product but the "master" of positive law.

Gustav Hugo (1764–1861), by virtue of his *Lehrbuch des Naturrechts als eine Philosophie des Positiven Rechts*, can also be listed as one of the founders of the historical school, which was developed greatly in Friedrich Carl von Savigny's (1779–1861) *Vom Beruf unserer Zeit für Gesetzgebung und Rechtswissenschaft*, on the task of the legislation and legal sciences. For Savigny the law is an organic result of the people's spirit (*Volksgeist*) as it unfolds in a historical process.

The historical school in general refused to accept the unchangeable nature of natural law. The law is in a constant state of flux. Since the law is essentially the product of a collective national spirit, it changes as the character of the nation changes in the course of history.

Sir Henry James Sumner Maine (1822–1888), professor of jurisprudence at Oxford and of international law at Cambridge, was perhaps the most renowned representative of the English historical school. In his *Ancient Law, Its Connection with the Early History of Society and Its Relation to Modern Ideas*, and later in *Village Communities, Lectures on the Early History of Institutions, Dissertations on Early Law and Custom*, and other works, he demonstrated his opposition to Bentham's utilitarianism. Maine's works are heavily loaded with historical details that have but little interest to legal philosophy. The essence of his thinking is that the developmental changes in law show a historical sequence; from the commands of Themis (the goddess of law and justice) through the development of social customs, we arrived at contemporary laws. Roscoe Pound rightly pointed out that Maine presented a Hegelian theory in identifying the development of law with the historical development of ideas.[55]

Maine may have been the most eminent thinker of the English historical school, but its origin might be traced to the Russian Paul Vinogradoff (1854–1925), who a year after he arrived in England, in 1884, found Bracton's original notes.[56] These were published by Frederic William Maitland (1850–1906), professor of English law at Cambridge, but the discovery secured for Vinogradoff a chair at Oxford and collaboration with Maitland. Maitland, with Sir Frederick Pollock (1845–1937), professor of jurisprudence at Oxford, published about this time *The History of English Law*.[57] The revived and profound study of English legal history, which culminated in Holdsworth's monumental work,[58] was largely due to the triumvirate of Pollock, Maitland, and Vinogradoff.[59] Although Pollock had an Aristotelian orientation, Maitland was attracted to a theory of political pluralism, and Vinogradoff leaned toward a sociological approach, all their philosophies were basically historical. Maitland was especially attracted to the work of Otto von Gierke (1844–1921), the outstanding proponent of the German historical school of thought.

A neo-Hegelian school, involving a kind of ethnological-historical jurisprudence, developed under Joseph Kohler (1849–1919), who attempted to advance the idea of objective values in the dominant role of historical developments. In his *Lehrbuch der Rechtsphilosophie* he suggested that the law and its development should be traced to earlier stages of cultural development. Kohler, together with Friedrich Berolzheimer, accepted the Hegelian view of history but did not agree with the dialectic method or the "unconditional logic" of world history.

Law as an Instrument of Class Ideology

Hegel's philosophy contributed in part to what has been called historical materialism, originally formulated by the formidable speculative energy of Karl Heinrich Marx (1813–1883), son of a German lawyer, in collaboration with his lifelong friend, Friedrich Engels (1820–1895), another German, son of a wealthy manufacturer. The historical approach to economic conditions and the significance of the class struggle was recognized well before Marx. The works of the French socialist Claude Henri Saint-Simon (1760–1825) and his disciple Louis Blanc (1811–

1882) already advocated the establishment of cooperative work-shops (*ateliers nationaux*) and other socialist schemes. The theory of "surplus value" and other socialist thinking could already be found in the works of William Thompson (1785–1833) and Karl Johann Rodbertus (1805–1875). Ferdinand Lassalle (1825–1864) propagated socialist doctrines as related to the class struggle of the proletariat. The materialistic notions of Ludwig Andreas Feuerbach (1804–1872) undoubtedly strongly influenced Marx. And many of the Marxist elements were present in the early utopian-socialist literature.

No one, however, can deny the originality of Marx's theory. It was he who brought together and structured the thoughts, and from his shabby study sent his gigantic system off on its world-conquering way. "Fame and acknowledgment came slowly to Marx, and when he died in 1883 a few outside of the circle of his political followers were aware of his work and stature."[60] It took another generation before his social and economic theories shook the world, and an enormous saint empire has been transformed to bring Marx's philosophy to life.

Marx and Engels did not expound their full social philosophy in any single treatise, and their thinking is reflected in a number of writings. Perhaps their most important works are *Communist Manifesto* (1847) and *Deutsche Ideologie*. Best known of Marx's works are *Das Kapital, Kritik der Hegelschen Rechtsphilosophie, Die Heilige Familie, Zur Kritik der politischen Ökonomie*, and *La misère de la philosophie, réponse à la philosophie de la misère de M. Proudhon*; Engels' most important work is the *Condition of the Working Class in England*.

There is much truth in Harold Berman's remark that Marxism offers only a critique of law, and "in seeking to explain law, it explains it away."[61] Law is not even a part of the communist ideology; rather, it is its instrument.

To Marx the mode of production in material life determines the general character of the social, political, and spiritual processes of life. They are an *Überbau* (superstructure) built upon the basic economy, and thus they change as the economic structure changes. Law, political institutions, religion, philosophy, and all other conceptions are parts of this superstructure and can be explained only by understanding the economic base.

This is why the Marxist law is not oriented toward justice, as justice is interpreted in non-Marxist legal systems. In criticizing Proudhon's theory, Marx rejected the possibility of an "eternal justice" and dismissed any such abstraction as the meaning or nature of law. The essence of law, as Imre Szabó interprets the Marxist view, is neither an abstraction deduced from the typical characteristics of the positive law nor an *a priori* idea from which legal institutions may be derived.[62] Law is created to defend particular interests, and these interests cannot be understood outside the particular society. "Since law originates in economics, it is necessary to change the whole economy before any fundamental reform of law can be achieved."[63]

The particular interest to be defended by the law is that of the "proletariat."[64] The state is a product of economic forces, a tool in the hands of the ruling classes to exploit the working classes. The process of "historical materialism" through the inevitable operations of the capitalist economy must inevitably lead to the liberation of the proletariat. However, the proletariat should attempt to assume political power by use of force. Then the working classes would replace the exploiting bourgeois classes and the interest of the proletariat would be served by the law. Thus the law becomes an instrument of the ideology.

Ferdinand Lassalle's social democracy, Karl Kautsky's orthodox Marxism, Edouard Bernstein's revisionism, Mikhail Bakunin's syndicalism, the Bolshevism as professed by Trotsky, Bukharin, and Radek, not to mention Lenin, have all modified or revised the original Marxist theories, but none have proposed a theory of law significantly different from the ideas of Marx and Engels.

The definition of a Marxist-Leninist political and legal science has fallen to the lot of the jurists of the Soviet Union, the first nation to establish the rule of this ideology.[65] The philosophical study of law first diverged from orthodox Marxism in the works of E. B. Pashukanis, who attempted to build a positive law upon a Marxist scheme.[66] A. Ia. Vyshinsky analyzed the normative elements of law and accepted positive law only to the extent that it conforms with socialist principles.[67]

Although strongly based on Vyshinsky's orientation, the work of S. A. Golunskii and M. S. Strogovich embraced more of the problems. In addition to a historical account, they touched upon the concept of law and identified the socialist law with the Soviet law.[68] More forceful endeavors appeared in the field toward the end of the 1950s; however, these were without apparent qualitative change, except that the scope of the problems was expanded. M. P. Kareva and G. I. Fedjkin's textbook on the theories of state and law, published in 1955, went so far as to discuss the problem of law and morality.[69] D. A. Kerimov, A. J. Koroliev, and M. D. Shargorodskii's textbook in 1961 separated the question of socialist legal norms from natural socialist law and dealt with the general characteristics of the socialist concept of responsibility;[70] P. S. Romashkin, M. S. Strogovich, and V. A. Tumanov's textbook of 1962 was very similar.[71]

Perhaps O. S. Joffe and M. D. Shargorodskii have gone deepest in Marxist-Leninist legal philosophy in their work on legal theories, published in 1961.[72] They are close to Austin's approach; in socialist legal philosophy they recognize the Marxist counterpart of the positive law. However, they conclude by returning to what has been affirmed many times by those who entered the world of law via Marxist ideology: the philosophy of law is to analyze the nature of law and its regularities as they are determined by history, economy, and class.

Law as the Expression of Relative Values

Gustav Radbruch (1878–1949) was perhaps the most inspiring advocate of the relativity of law in the recent history of legal philosophy. In *Rechtsphilosophie* he utilized Kant's skepticism to support his own doubts about absolute values. He distinguished between "is" (*sein*) and "ought" (*sollen*), and found it was impossible to infer from the "is" the "valuable," the "right," or what "ought to be." Nothing is right merely because it exists.

In his culturally relativistic philosophy Radbruch accepted any value judgment as correct if it is related to a higher value or world view, while not necessarily accepting the "rightness" of the assumed higher value. His skepticism finally led him to doubt even the source of law. To Radbruch law itself is the reality that serves the idea of law, which, again, *is* justice. In his thinking only the "actual" is relevant to values; law should be seen as a social norm to regulate the life of the society.

The autonomous and self-contained nature of law is even more emphasized by Hans Kelsen (1881–), who was mentioned by Radbruch as one of the representatives of relativism. His "pure theory of law" was expounded in *Reine Rechtslehre, Der juristische und der soziologische Staatsbegriff*, and many of his other works.[73]

To Kelsen the law is a hypothetical (or conditional) judgment. It is the judgment of the state and indicates how the state would react under certain circumstances, but it does not tell what the subjects of the state should do. As Dennis Lloyd remarked, the validity of law "has to be conceived in legal terms and not in terms of morals or of any other extraneous system of norms or values."[74] Kelsen's concept of law relates to social norms rather than to human conduct. Although he seemed to reject Austin's command theory, he could not ultimately avoid the use of coercion for the legal system to be effective.

In Kelsen these social norms are based on a single basic norm, which he called the *Grundnorm*. What this *Grundnorm* means is never made quite clear. But this is probably where Kelsen's relativism lies: the *Grundnorm* is a matter of choice in a given society, and it is dependent upon the actual circumstances. This is why it is rather difficult to find where responsibility rests.

Law as a Societal Phenomenon

The French socialist Saint-Simon was perhaps the first who, in *Du système industriel* and *Nouveau christianisme,* proposed the necessity of a political science that would analyze the patterns and trends of social developments. He contended that our world view increasingly involves theology and metaphysics.

Auguste Comte (1798–1857), who started to call positive philosophy "sociology," in his *Cours de philosophie positive* and *Système de politique positive* was obviously inspired by Saint-Simon. He viewed society as if it were an organism and, following Saint-Simon's way of thinking, found theological, metaphysical, and positive trends as historical developmental stages.

The philosophy of Herbert Spencer (1820–1903) more logically related sociology to the other "positive" sciences. Spencer was an editor of *The Economist* and had practiced engineering before entering journalism. Barna Horváth called him an autodidact and a dilettante philosopher,[75] but this should just enhance his significance. The beginnings of his approach to law can be seen in his early work *The Proper Sphere of Government.* In *Social Statics* and *The Developmental Hypothesis* he established the basic ideas of his philosophy. In *Principles of Psychology* and *First Principles* he elaborated on his synthetic philosophy. Poor health delayed the publication of his *Principles of Biology* and *Principles of Sociology,* in which he presented the full scope of his thinking. He contended that society is an organism made up of men, and thus its development can be observed by use of psychology and biology. Evolution and freedom are his two basic beliefs.

Spencer was not emancipated from utilitarian influences, and this is probably why his thoughts on law are not well integrated in his general philosophy. He accepted the justification of divine and human commands based on unequal power, but he dreamed of law based on consensus and equality.

The Italian M. A. Vaccaro's biological, and almost ecological, approach to the sociological understanding of law,[76] the Russian L. Petrazhitsky's[77] and the American L. Ward's[78] psychological orientation, as well as E. Ross' concept of "social control,"[79] attempted to build a bridge to the sociology of law. Emile Durkheim, the renowned French sociologist, focused primarily on social integration and social disorganization, but he contributed relatively little to the philosophy of the nature of law.[80] Vilfredo Pareto discussed some legal philosophical points but never dealt with "What is law?"[81] William Graham Sumner[82] and Edward Alexander Westermarck, the Finnish anthropologist and professor of sociology at the University of London,[83] also analyzed the origin of laws and customs.

Georg Jellinek, however, greatly advanced the study of the sociology of law;[84] he was, with Hans Kelsen and Max Weber, one of the trio described by Radbruch as relativists. Léon Duguit's ideas about the collective conscience of people resemble Durkheim's concept of solidarity and lean strongly toward acceptance of natural law.[85]

The development of a sociology of law was forcefully advanced by A. H. Post and Hermann Kantorowicz. Post tried to transform traditional jurisprudence into a discipline in which the methods of enthnological and natural science would be appropriate. No one before him related sociology and law so closely.[86] Kantorowicz, who first wrote under the pseudonym Gnaeus Flavius, urged that the law be studied within the framework of social relations. He fought against words and formalism. Kantorowicz established the foundations of his philosophy on "meanings," or, as he called it, on the *Freirechstlehre* ("the study of free law").[87]

Despite admiration for their contribution to the analysis of law in society, it is perhaps erroneous to treat Eugen Ehrlich and Max Weber as the founders of the sociology of law.

The Austrian Eugen Ehrlich (1862–1922), in *Grundlegung einer Soziologie des Rechts*,[88] somewhat after Kantorowicz, emphasized the importance of social processes in the relationship between social norms and the law. The state is of little importance in the creation of law. He analyzed the "forms of life" in order to find what he called "juristic law" and pointed to the "central gravity" of the development of law. Ehrlich's contribution to law as related to society (and not as society is related to the law) greatly advanced the cause of sociology of law. However, as for the nature of law, Ehrlich's propositions seem to be somewhat vague and by no means new.

Max Weber (1864–1920), German economist and professor at Freiburg and Munich, is regarded "one of the principal founders of modern social science, in particular modern sociology."[89] Weber and Ehrlich were close contemporaries; Ehrlich was born two years before Weber and died two years after him. However, Ehrlich published his *Grundlegung* several years before Weber published his *Wirtschaft und Gesellschaft*.[90] Yet, as Georges Gurvitch noted, "Ehrlich's conceptions may be regarded as an anticipatory response to Weber's tendency to subordinate the sociology of law to dogmatic-constructive systematizations of jurisprudence."[91] Weber concentrated his philosophy on understanding legal systems, which themselves are the products and, at the same time, causes of the societies in which they are in force. To Weber law is an order guaranteed by physical or psychic coercion. His grandiose analysis of the bureaucracy that could utilize force does not describe the source of power that ultimately results in a legitimate bureaucratic "right" to coerce.

Maurice Hauriou, who with Léon Duguit and Emmanuel Levy was one of the founders of the French sociology of law,[92] and François Gény[93] saw the law as the protection of vested interests. Their legal sociology seems to show a revival of the natural-law orientation.

Three great American Supreme Court justices, Oliver Wendell Holmes, Benjamin Cardozo, and Louis Brandeis, were principal contributors in the development of the American sociology of law. Holmes brought historicism, Cardozo new realism, and Brandeis social idealism to legal sociology. Holmes[94] said experience and reality were the essence of law; Cardozo[95] was against legalistic formalism and dogmatism; Brandeis, in his experimental pragmatism, emphasized the importance of the social environment. Jerome Frank (1889–1957) probably caused uneasy feelings by his book *Law and the Modern Mind*.[96] In his psychology law and order is a father surrogate who judges a wayward child. Harold Laski (1893–1950), one of the most productive of English political theorists, strongly opposed any formalist theory. To him, the state is simply an abstraction in the name of which a government acts, and the government is made up of mortal and fallible human beings.[97] Many subjects obey passively, but only active support by the subjects is constructive; this is why the content of the law is so important. Laski, in his last writings, showed his leaning toward the philosophy of historical materialism.

Roscoe Pound (1870–1964) stands out among those who view the law as a societal phenomenon. His life was "most rewarding to the law and society."[98] His numerous works not only made him a leading advocate of sociological jurisprudence, but also a significant critic of the history of legal thinking.[99] In his "social engineering" he proposed that the duty of jurists is to ensure all social interests. The purpose of the law is to satisfy human goals and desires; the rightness of the law depends on the purpose of the law. Looking at the history, Pound saw a shift in "the basis of theories as to the end of law from wills to wants."[100] What he practiced was a predominantly utilitarian sociology of law.

From Superstitious Commands to Social Engineering

A glance through the history of legal philosophy not only affords a cursory acquaintance with a long series of superb thinking; it is also a disconcerting experience. Roscoe Pound's noble vision of the change "from wills to wants" has not been fully documented. The history of the philosophy of law, from the earliest beliefs in superhuman commands to contemporary models of "social engineering," does not reflect a consistent developmental trend in the idea of law. Both "wants" and "wills" have been represented by theories in almost all periods of time. While divine commands were often seen as concerned with human wants, ideas that have shown the glamour of a philosophy based on wants finally proved themselves as philosophies of wills. Pound's argument that psychology has played the most important part in the shift of orientation, and thus undermined the foundation of the metaphysical will,[101] calls attention only to an isolated merit. The same psychology has at the same time helped man to believe earthly "will" theories as if they were "want" philosophies; most of man's wants are infused into him by wills.

The pursuit of the nature of law, sometimes reduced to the philosophical battle between natural law and positive law, is in the final analysis a pursuit for justification of the legal command. The quest for the nature of law has failed to achieve a comforting answer, and this is a frustrating and depressing experience. To the question What is the ultimate source and nature of the responsibility-making law?, the philosophy of law offers many solutions rather than a single answer. The difficulty and the disagreement among the thinkers begins as soon as man, instead of understanding lawmaking man, leaves the orbit of visible realities to search for a power behind the power.

Since this "power behind the power" is sought for justification of the command of law, the quest for it tends to direct many thinkers to the problem of the morality of law. One's own beliefs are sometimes much too appealing for one to accept that the assumption that the moral answers are shared by all humanity at all times is simply a delusion. The pursuit of the nature of law and its morality may be seen as a pursuit of consolation. Nevertheless, it is a crucial issue to the fate of "dual responsibility."

NOTES

1. M. P. Golding (ed.), *The Nature of Law, Readings in Legal Philosophy* (New York, 1966), p. 1.
2. Gustav Radbruch, *Rechtsphilosophie* (3rd ed., Berlin, 1932), p. 6.
3. Carl Joachim Friedrich, *The Philosophy of Law in Historical Perspective* (2nd ed., Chicago and London, 1963), p. 3.
4. Herbert Lionel Adolphus Hart, *The Concept of Law* (Oxford, 1961), p. 6.
5. See *ibid.*
6. Talcott Parsons, "The Law and Social Control," in William M. Evan (ed.), *Law and Sociology, Exploratory Essays* (New York, 1962), p. 56.
7. Roscoe Pound, *An Introduction to the Philosophy of Law* (New Haven and London, 1965), p. 25.
8. Edward Westermarck, *The Origin and Development of the Moral Ideas* (2nd ed., London, 1912), Vol. II, p. 602.
9. Sir Henry Sumner Maine, *Ancient Law, Its Connection with the Early History of Society and Its Relation to Modern Ideas* (1861), with Introduction and Notes by Sir Frederick Pollock (London, 1906).
10. E. Adamson Hoebel, *The Law of Primitive Man, A Study in Comparative Legal Dynamics* (Cambridge, Mass., 1954), p. 257 and *infra.*
11. Minocher J. Sethna, *Jurisprudence* (2nd ed., Girgaon-Bombay, 1959), pp. 60–61.
12. Friedrich, *op. cit.*, p. 8.

13. Leviticus, 1: 1–2.

14. We derive most of our knowledge of the code from Plutarch (46–125 A.D.).

15. Friedrich, in *op. cit.*, p. 14, calls attention to the fact that the Platonic *polis* is often translated as "state," a term that is not quite accurate when applied to the Greek political order.

16. About 380–370 B.C., in most translations entitled *Republic*.

17. Friedrich, *op. cit.*, p. 17.

18. Leo Strauss, *Natural Right and History* (Chicago and London, 1965), p. 116.

19. Book VII, Benjamin Jowett (tr.) (Roslyn, N.Y., 1943).

20. Book V, James E. C. Welldon (tr.) (Roslyn, N.Y., 1943).

21. Their name is a reference to the *stoa* (porch) at Athens, where Zeno taught. Doctrines of the Stoics were later adopted in the Roman law.

22. Named after Epicurus (about 341–270 B.C.), who taught in Athens.

23. Dennis Lloyd, *The Idea of Law* (Baltimore, 1964), p. 77.

24. "To live honestly, not to hurt anybody, to give to everyone what is his own."

25. Lloyd, *op. cit.*, p. 79.

26. Friedrich, *op. cit.*, p. 37.

27. Friedrich, *op. cit.*, p. 43, is moving in the right direction in questioning the appropriateness of speaking of medieval governments as states, "when nothing justifies this sort of anachronism." Indeed, princes and lords ruled the communities rather than governments in the modern sense. Nevertheless, these terminological differences are open to controversy, particularly in view of some states newly developed after World War II.

28. He and others were first called "monarchomachs" by William Barclay in *De Regno et Regali Potestate adversus Buchananum Brutum, Boucherium et reliquos Monarchomachos libri sex* (Paris, 1600).

29. Friedrich, *op. cit.*, p. 64.

30. Barna Horváth, *Angol Jogelmélet* (Budapest, 1943), p. 25.

31. Friedrich, *op. cit.*, p. 65.

32. William Archibald Dunning, *A History of Political Theories from Luther to Montesquieu* (New York, 1902), pp. 210–211.

33. Horváth, *op. cit.*, p. 90.

34. Leo Strauss, *The Political Philosophy of Hobbes, Its Basis and Its Genesis* (Chicago, 1963), p. 170.

35. Horváth, *op. cit.*, p. 173.

36. W. R. Sorley, *A History of English Philosophy* (Cambridge, 1920), p. 64.

37. Wilhelm Windelband, *Die Geschichte der neueren Philosophie* (6th ed., Leipzig, 1919), I, 347.

38. Pound, *Introduction, op. cit.*, p. 7.

39. Horváth, *op. cit.*, p. 249.

40. Friedrich, *op. cit.*, p. 96.

41. For a complete list of Bentham's works see any standard textbook in the philosophy of law.

42. The problem of the changes of the law is not a major question in Austin's works; in this respect his views are not quite clear.

43. Horváth, *op. cit.*, p. 480.

44. Karl Bergbohm, *Jurisprudenz und Rechtsphilosophie* (Leipzig, 1892).

45. Rudolph Ernst Bierling, *Zur Kritik der juristischen Grundbegriffe* (2 vols., Leipzig, 1877–1883), and *Juristische Prinzipienlehre* (5 vols., Leipzig and Freiburg, 1894–1917).

46. Filmer's *Patriarcha* denied the sovereignty of the king; he did not believe in his commanding power, not even together with Parliament. However, he accepted the king's divine power as originating in the rights of the patriarchs.

47. Friedrich, *op. cit.*, p. 110.

48. Pound, *Introduction, op. cit.*, p. 116.

49. Friedrich, *op. cit.*, pp. 113–114.

50. Cohen, *op. cit.*, p. 122.

51. Gyula Moór, *Bevezetés a jogfilozófiába* (Budapest, 1922), p. 29.

52. Robert Nigel Carew Hunt, *The Theory and Practice of Communism* (Baltimore, 1963), p. 39.

53. Lloyd, *op. cit.*, pp. 251–252.

54. Freidrich, *op. cit.*, pp. 131–132.

55. Roscoe Pound, *Interpretations of Legal History* (Cambridge, 1923), pp. 53–65.

56. Henry de Bracton (d. 1268) was a judge and writer on English law. He compiled an account of the English laws and customs, the first of its kind.

57. Frederick Pollock and Frederic William Maitland, *The History of English Law* (2nd ed., Cambridge, 1898).

58. William Searle Holdsworth, *A History of English Law* (London, 1927).

59. Horváth, *op. cit.*, p. 513.

60. Sidney Hook, *Marx and the Marxists, The Ambiguous Legacy* (Princeton, 1955), pp. 12–13.

61. Harold J. Berman, *Justice in the U.S.S.R.* (New York, 1963), p. 23.

62. Imre Szabó, *Szocialista jogelmélet, népi demokratikus jog* (Budapest, 1967), pp. 150–151.

63. Berman, *op. cit.*, p. 17.

64. In Roman history frequently the word was used in a derogatory sense, as a reference to the lowest class of the community; in political economy it means indigent wage earners, laboring classes, working class.

65. Szabó, *op. cit.*, p. 31 and *infra*.

66. E. B. Paschukanis, *Obshchaia teoriia prava i marksism* (2nd ed., Moscow, 1926), Foreword; *Allgemeine Rechtslehre und Marxismus* (Berlin, 1929), p. 19.

67. A. Ia. Vyshinsky, *Voprosy teorii gosudarstva i prava* (2nd ed., Moscow, 1949), p. 73; also see his *The Law of the Soviet State* (New York, 1948).

68. S. A. Golunskii and M. S. Strogovich, *Teorija gosudarstva i prava* (Moscow, 1940).

69. M. P. Kareva and G. I. Fedjkin (eds.), *Teorija gosudarstva i prava* (Moscow, 1955).

70. D. A. Kerimov, A. J. Koroliev, and M. D. Shargorodskii, *Obschaia teorija gosudarstva i prava* (Leningrad, 1962).

71. P. S. Romashkin, M. S. Strogovich, and V. A. Tumanov, eds.: *Teorija gosudarstva i prava* (Moscow, 1962).

72. O. S. Joffe and M. D. Shargorodskii, *Voprosy teorii prava* (Moscow, 1961).

73. Hans Kelsen, *Reine Rechtslehre* (Leipzig and Vienna, 1934) ; *Der juristische und der soziologische Staatsbegriff* (Tübingen, 1922) ; *Hauptprobleme der Staatsrechtslehre entwickelt aus der Lehre vom Rechtssatze* (Tübingen, 1911) ; *Das Problem der Souveränität und die Theorie des Völkerrechts* (Tübingen, 1920) ; *Allgemeine Staatslehre* (Berlin, 1925) ; "The Pure Theory of Law: Its Methods and Fundamental Concepts," *The Law Quarterly Review,* 50 (October 1934), 474–535.

74. Lloyd, *op. cit.,* p. 193.

75. Horváth, *op. cit.,* p. 259.

76. M. Vaccaro, *Basi del diritto e dello stato* (Torino, 1893).

77. L. Petrazhitsky, *Theory of Law and State* (In Russian, St. Petersburg, 1909).

78. L. Ward, *Dynamic Sociology* (New York, 1883).

79. E. Ross, *Social Control* (New York, 1901).

80. Emile Durkheim, *De la division du travail social* (6th ed., Paris, 1932) ; *Suicide, A Study in Sociology,* John A. Spaulding and George Simpson (trs.) (New York, 1966).

81. Vilfredo Pareto, *Sociological Writings,* Derick Mirfin (tr.), edited with Introduction by S. E. Finer (New York, 1966).

82. William Graham Sumner, *Folkways* (Boston, 1906).

83. Westermarck, *op. cit.*

84. Georg Jellinek, *Allgemeine Staatslehre* (Berlin, 1900).

85. Léon Duguit, *L'État, le droit objectif et la loi positive* (Paris, 1901).

86. A. H. Post, *Bausteine für eine Rechtswissenschaft auf vergleichend ethnologischer Grundlage* (Oldenburg, 1880) ; *Die Grundlagen des Rechts, Leitfaden für den Aufbau einer allgemeinen Rechtswissenschaft auf soziologischer Basis* (Oldenburg, 1884).

87. Hermann Kantorowicz, *Rechtswissenschaft und Soziologie* (Tübingen, 1911) ; *Die Aufgabe der Soziologie* (Leipzig, 1923) ; *Aus der Vorgeschichte der Freirechtslehre* (Mannheim, 1925) ; "Some Rationalism about Realism," *Yale Law Journal,* 43, 1933–34; *Tat und Schuld* (Zurich, 1933).

88. Eugen Ehrlich, *The Fundamental Principles of the Sociology of Law* (original publ. München, 1913, trans. by W. Moll, Cambridge, 1936); "The Sociology of Law," *Harvard Law Review*, 36, 1922–23.

89. Talcott Parsons, Introduction to Max Weber, *The Sociology of Religion* (Boston, 1963), p. xix.

90. Weber, *op. cit.*

91. Georges Gurvitch, *Sociology of Law* (New York, 1942), p. 148.

92. Maurice Hauriou, *Science Sociale traditionelle* (Paris, 1896); *Principes de Droit Public* (2nd ed., Paris, 1916).

93. François Gény, *Science et technique du droit privé positif* (Paris, 1914–1922); *Méthodes d'interprétation et sources du droit positif* (Paris, 1919).

94. Oliver Wendell Holmes, *The Common Law* (Boston, 1881); *Collected Legal Papers* (New York, 1921).

95. Benjamin Nathan Cardozo, *The Nature of the Judicial Process* (New Haven, 1921); *The Growth of the Law* (New Haven, 1924); *The Paradoxes of Legal Science* (New York, 1928).

96. Jerome Frank, *Law and the Modern Mind* (New York, 1931).

97. Harold J. Laski, *Studies in the Problem of Sovereignty* (New Haven, 1917); *A Grammar of Politics* (London, 1925); *Studies in Law and Politics* (London, 1932); *The State in Theory and Practice* (London, 1936).

98. Sheldon Glueck, "Roscoe Pound and Criminal Justice," *Crime and Delinquency*, Vol. 10, No. 4, Oct. 1964, p. 352.

99. Pound, *Introduction, op. cit.*; *The Spirit of the Common Law* (Boston, 1921); *Law and Morals* (2nd ed., Chapel Hill, 1924); *Outlines of Lectures on Jurisprudence* (4th ed., Cambridge, Mass., 1928).

100. Pound, *Introduction, op. cit.*, p. 43.

101. *Ibid.*, p. 43.

III
The Morality of Criminal Law

Law and Morality

This title ventures to pose two formidable concepts in mutual relationship; neither is really well understood, and both are heavily charged with apparently insoluble problems, even if treated independently of each other. No wonder that Lon Fuller found the literature on law and morality "deficient."[1] Even a Bentham or a Jhering had to labor on these concepts for a lifetime to achieve minimal, and perhaps no, success. Herbert Hart suggested that this is a perennial issue; he listed many different types of relations between law and morality and discussed their various aspects not only under "laws and morals" but also in terms of "justice."[2] Rusztem Vámbéry asserted that a full treatment of the problem would go beyond his capability just as much as it would be beyond the patience of the reader.[3]

A return to the mythical ages of mankind may justify the claim for morality in law. The Ten Commandments is not only a body of criminal law but also an ethical code and a divine declaration. To Sir Henry Sumner Maine the origin of law was in religion,[4] while A. S. Diamond found several ancient codes free of religious dominance.[5] Who was right is not decisively relevant to the issue in question. The dispute should center on analysis of the relationship between religion and morality, which is a combination of concepts other than law and morals. Nobody can seriously doubt the alliance of religion and morality, particularly in the early stages of human history and in primitive societies, but we cannot measure the degree of their merger. Nicholas Timasheff's caution is justified: "The question of the religious roots and interconnections of primitive ethics depends very much on what religion is considered to be and on what sort of connection is asserted."[6]

In discussing gods as guardians of morality, Edward Westermarck stated, "As men are concerned about the conduct of their fellow men towards their gods, so gods are in many cases concerned about men's conduct towards one another, disapproving of vice and punishing the wicked, approving of virtue and rewarding the good"; but Westermarck knew this was not universal.[7] For example, the religious belief of the Gonds of central India was unconnected with the idea of morals.[8] The Indians in Guyana developed a code of morality, but it had little to do with their simple animistic form of religion.[9] On the other hand, the Tonga Islanders firmly believed that the gods approve of virtue and are displeased with vice.[10] The Ainu of Japan said that they cannot go contrary to the customs of their ancestors without bringing down the wrath of the gods.[11] Along with these examples Westermarck listed a number of other primitive peoples who believed in the existence of gods who are the moral lawgivers or judges; he also gave examples of deities disinterested in the moral affairs of humans.

Generally crime, vice, and sin were undistinguishable in primitive societies, and even today we turn to the superhuman for guidance when all else fails. Religion plays a major role in lawmaking if the social definition of wrongdoing in part determines the law and if, at the same time, the social definition of right and wrong is directed by theological concepts. This is why crime, vice, and sin are often seen as both merged and as functioning independently. In ancient Greece and Egypt law, morals, and religion were integrated into a single idea. In modern times man has become increasingly accustomed "to the purely secular conception of law as made by man for man and to be judged accordingly in purely human terms."[12]

Even an elementary acquaintance with criminal law makes it evident that many legal commands, past as well as present, are clearly formalized statements of religious doctrines. Homicide, theft, perjury, and other offenses violate the legal code just as much as they run counter to ethical and religious strictures. All three codes regulate human behavior. The common origin of law, morality, and religion still remains a mystery.

The connection of law with morality suggests a series of questions. How much of the criminal law was derived from ethical beliefs? Should moral factors influence the lawmaker? Can a criminal law oppose a moral command? What is a "just" law? And what is "justice"? What is the relationship between legal and moral obligations? How can one reconcile, if necessary and if possible, legal and moral responsibilities? What is or should be the role of morality in preventing crimes? All these questions are interconnected. Herbert Hart held that there are so many different relations between law and morality that "there is nothing which can be profitably singled out for study as *the* relation between them."[13]

All relations are dependent on the definition of morality. If the understanding of morality refers to some eternal and true justice created by a superhuman and immortal agency, one cannot avoid dealing with the natural law. If the question of law and morality is posed as the question of the emancipation of law, this revives the centuries-old battle of natural law versus legal positivism. Positivism does not deny the importance of morality, but it does deny that changing man-made laws necessarily be equated with moral commands. The problem with natural law is that even "eternal" and "true" justice changes, as do the theological truths from which so many of the ethical truths are derived.

The changing nature of the ethical laws does not really call for evidence. Even polar types of human behavior, such as homicide and brotherly love, incest and virginity, monogamy and free love, veracity and mendacity, peaceful living together and warring, have both been virtues at different times and in different cultures, their approbation often being attributed to divine powers. For example, one can recall the religious prostitution in Cyprus and Lydia, the homosexuality practiced within the family of Egyptian pharaohs, and the piracy and legal brigandage in the Middle Ages, which helped to maintain whole classes.[14] Approved immoralities and disapproved moralities are abundant in the history of man, and one need only cast a glance at ethical changes in our century to doubt the stability of moral truths. If modern man believes in the moral value of monogamy, this does not make polygamy in primitive societies immoral. Approval of abortion does not violate the ethical code in one culture just because in another it is defined as murder.

The evolving state of morality loosens its bonds to natural law and religion. At the same time, however, it makes its connection with law even more complicated. Law itself is a changing phenomenon, and in its relationship with ethics law is confronted with another changing phenomenon. Is the law a mirror of moral beliefs, or is morality a reflection of the law? This question of *prius* is of crucial significance. The first alternative holds "that in effect only the moral law is valid and that nothing which does not conform to the moral law itself can properly be regarded as effectively binding law."[15] The second alternative, following Hobbes and Hegel, proposes the dominance of the man-made law. A third approach would be to understand law and morality in their mutually exclusive autonomy, that is, law as not only emancipated but independent of ethics.

Emancipation of the Law

While the ethics of ancient times completely dissolved the philosophy of law in the philosophy of morals, the English and French Enlightenment made a capital impact toward emancipating law. The idea of liberating the human mind from a thousand years of intellectual tyranny, of securing the freedom and independence of man's internal world, made it necessary to distinguish between legal and ethical laws. The utopians, Dante, Machiavelli, Bodin, Grotius, Hobbes, Hume, Bentham, and Austin, to list only a few, contested the subordination of law to morality and consequently attacked the natural law. Law has no necessary relationship with morality, which is not rational and cannot be proved; laws are the commands of human beings.

Nevertheless, it appears as though the centuries-old offensive has not completely succeeded in defeating the natural law; at least this seems indicated by the sustained attacks against it even in recent times. The natural law to J. Makarewicz is the "ideal in law"; it is *selbstverständlich unveränderlich,* evidently unchangeable;[16] its unchangeable character, as Karl Gareis put it, is its *sine qua non.*[17] Herbert Hart can see little difference between the law of gravity and the Ten Commandments if the observed regularities of nature "were prescribed or decreed by a Divine Governor."[18] Morris Raphael Cohen, in discussing Raffaele Garofalo's "natural crime," remarked with justified bitterness: "Civilized Italians and Germans at the time that Garofalo wrote might have been shocked at the suggestion that their people would ever be capable of perpetrating the cruelties which Fascists and Nazis have exercised on their opponents or even on innocent children who happened to live in Ethiopian villages or to be of Jewish ancestry."[19] Indeed, Garofalo's famous belief that "pity" and "probity" are characteristics of all civilized peoples at all times was violently contorted half a century later: the "tenderness" and "honesty" of his compatriots and their allies were expressed in the torture and death of millions.

The conventional, and more flexible, distinction between positive law and natural morality suggests that morality is concerned with man's internal world, and law with external behavior. The former is controlled by feelings of remorse or guilt, the latter by threat of punishment as applied by another man. The responsibilities with which law charges human conducts are known; however, the responsibilities based on natural law or morality are nowhere catalogued. The Aristotelian *mala prohibita*, "prohibited wrongs," proscribed by man-made laws, are declared to the people by legislation; the *mala per se*, "wrongs in themselves," prohibited by their intrinsic nature, have no official bulletin board where to see them. Acts that are *mala per se* are usually vaguely defined or even undefined, and generally seem to shock the public, "but they do not give any clear criterion by which to judge what acts should thus be included and what acts should be excluded from the category of crime."[20]

Lon Fuller, who introduces himself as a natural lawyer, attempted to qualify his adherence to the unidentified moral maker and confined the relationship between law and ethics to the "internal morality of Law." He called this a "procedural version of natural law," being concerned not with the substantive aims of legal rules but with the ways in which "a system of rules for governing human conduct must be constructed and administered."[21] These natural-law conceptions do not show the stability of the moral norms, which, after all, is the original and fundamental idea of natural morality. Even the neo-Kantian Rudolf Stammler[22] has been criticized for making allowance for changes; Makarewicz called Stammler's changing content of natural law a *contradictio in adiecto*.[23]

Nevertheless, "qualified" natural law, which allows for changes in its content, may in itself indicate at least a partial emancipation of law. Karl Gareis has suggested that morals apply to human relationships only if the relationships have moral implications.[24] Stammler has identified morality with the conscience[25] and proposed the coexistence and collaboration of law and morality, in a way already known from Kant's philosophy and, even earlier, from the ideas of Christian Thomasius.[26]

To Rudolf Jhering the law is the state's means of psychic coercion[27]—the punishing power of public opinion. Gyula Moór, in a somewhat similar vein, proposed that enforcement of moral norms rests largely with the soul of the individual concerned, for they indicate the right conduct.[28] However, this again is only an attempt to emancipate law from the moral rules; the contract between external and internal coercion, as the distinction between law and morality, dissolves whenever the internal coercion validates itself by external force. Lynching, for example, is a "moral" attempt to compensate for an assumed deficiency in external coercion (the law) through an outward act based on internal judgment; at the same time, the law often uses psychic coercive devices. This approach to separating law from morality has been carried even further by a number of thinkers. Adolf Merkel found that the connecting point of law and ethics is the fact that the law expresses the common conviction of those who live in the same community.[29] As Giorgio Del Vecchio posed it, law and morals can be distinguished, but this is "not a separation, and even less an opposition."[30] However, there are common beliefs that have nothing to do with law and laws that do not meet the approval of all. Law and morality seem to be in connection as well as in conflict. In Edgar Bodenheimer's words, "It must be conceded that clashes and encounters between legal norms and moral ideals are also within the range of possibility."[31]

In almost all contemporary theories of law, the law has been dependent upon ethical systems. This is the case even in the materialistic Soviet approach; for example, the first article of the Regulations on the Soviet Comrades' Courts states that the chief

aim of the courts is to enforce "communist morality."[32] Even
Karl Janka could not deny that law and morality actually do
meet, although he attributed it to mere coincidence. To him law
and morality do not entirely cover each other; they may collide,
and thus necessarily they are independent.[33] Vámbéry ridiculed
this argument by showing that since husband and wife are of
different sexes, and since altercations take place in marriage, the
married partners are thus independent of each other.[34] The
dependence of the "independent" law on morals has been charac-
teristically defended by Georg Jellinek, who posed law as if it
were an "ethical minimum," in other words, a guarantee of the
preservation of essential moral axioms.[35]

Connection and Conflict between Law and Morality

The fact that rights and duties, or privileges and responsibilities,
as prescribed by the law and the morality have "certain striking
similarities enough to show that their common vocabulary is no
accident"[36] is a commonplace. It is also known that many laws
are ethically indifferent and may even command conduct that a
number of people may believe to be immoral. This recognition of
basic conflicts between law and morality has intensified attacks
against a morality-based natural law. A dualism of natural and
positive laws can function only with heavy logical faults and
practical difficulties. In some systems the natural law is the source
of the positive law, sometimes its controlling agent, and sometimes its supplement.[37] Rudolf Stammler's allegorical comment
that justice is empty without love and that pity is blind without
proper rules[38] reveals his failure to separate law and ethics effectively. Stammler sees hope for harmony between law and morality
if both are products of the same culture. The key of this harmony
would be an alliance of the legal and moral worlds: a just system
of law can be achieved only through morality, and the realization
of moral values is possible only with the assistance of just law.

Nevertheless, Stammler's idea of harmony seems to propose a static culture without legal and moral changes, or a changing culture where law and morality change together from one harmonious union to another. This, however, would be hardly other than a natural-law system.

The conflict in question is not so much between law and morality as between past and present. One typically lags behind the other or, perhaps, one progresses faster than the other. An example of some of the disagreements over law and morality is the famous dispute between Rudolf Jhering and Joseph Kohler about *The Merchant of Venice*.[39]

Shakespeare's immortal character, Shylock, the Jewish money-lender of Venice, has attracted widespread critical interest from a variety of angles; among them, Jhering used this Shakespearean creature for entering the problem of law and morality. Only a juristic and artistic genius such as Jhering would be able to use the magic power of justice with such an irresistible logic to prove that Portia, the "wise young judge," "a Daniel," was actually a pettifogging and shrewd advocate against the rights of the law-craving Shylock. Jhering understood Shylock, who suffered so much persecution and humiliation at the hands of the Renaissance gentlemen. Shylock was not an usurer in any criminal sense; amid the systematic massacres and immolations of the Jewish people, not to mention the extreme economic pressures on them, this was one of the few trades that the Christian world had left open to him. His moneylending was not some clandestine illegal business, but his legitimate occupation.

Shylock lent 3,000 ducats to Antonio, a merchant, on the condition that if the money was not repaid on time he would forfeit a pound of flesh. When Antonio fails to repay the loan before the agreed-upon date, Shylock insists on claiming his flesh as the contractual payment. At the ducal court, where Shylock demands the payment, Portia appears disguised as a lawyer and accepts the contract as legally binding in Venice; however, she contends that only the pound of flesh should be taken, without spilling a drop of blood, for the contract said nothing about payment of blood.

Although Shylock's contract with Antonio indeed contained a condition *contra bonos mores*, it was acceptable under Venetian law, and he should have been allowed to take the blood with the flesh. If an easement is granted to someone to secure a right of way over another's property, so Vámbéry's argument runs, he cannot be prohibited from leaving his footprints along the route.[40]

Jhering was conscious of Shylock's struggle for his rights; in Shylock the oppressed and humiliated medieval Jew was struggling for uniform application of the law. The Jew of Venice (a title given to the play in 1701), trampled under the foot of his world, had faith in the law only so long as he did not realize that the law was the vile power that had turned him into a lawless pariah and that would deprive him of his claim, property, daughter, and even of his religion, and by all this could cynically drive him to destruction. Shylock argued for the sanctity of his contract; Portia, however, told him of the "letter of the law," which would make him guilty of attempted murder if he claimed Antonio's flesh. She was merely exploiting Shylock's defenseless social position.

In this conflict of law and morality Kohler found Shylock mean and grasping. (Heinrich Heine considered him the only character in the play worthy of respect.) Kohler conceded that the contract was legally valid, but with verbose arguments, no less shrewd than those of Portia, he demonstrated that the verdict against Shylock was only a defense against the immoral use of the law. Kohler seemed to miss Jhering's analysis of the social forces that play so crucial a role in the conflict of law with moral imperatives.

The Moral Nature of the Criminal Law

While the English and French *crime* and the German *Verbrechen* mean simply a violation of law, in the Hungarian language *bün-tett* means not only a legally prohibited act but also a sinful act or an evil fault. Regardless of the term used, almost without exception criminal codes tend to punish those conducts that go against the ethical norms. The history of criminal law seems to demonstrate that the concept of crime cannot dispense with the element of immorality. To be sure, not all crimes are immoral acts, nor are all immoralities defined as crimes. This, then, should mean that immorality in itself is not the essence of crime, but it means only that the immorality of some forms of behavior is one of the most important conditions for making an act criminal. Only political crimes and petty misdemeanors appear as exceptions.

Theodor Mommsen called attention to the word *crimen* in the Roman law, which meant what was expressed by the earlier word *delictum,* "fault, sinning, an act against morality the fundamentals of which were common to all."[41] In ancient times law was not only intertwined with morality, but, by very reason of this close connection, the first law was criminal law. The biblical story of the Fall is the symbolic expression of what Sir Henry Sumner Maine proved with historic facts: that the original type of law was criminal law. How important the question of law and morality (or, better, the connection between crime and immorality) was for Mommsen can be seen from his extensive work in the field. He concluded from his analysis of the concepts of crime, punishment, and responsibility in Roman law that the law was first directed against the violators of community moral obligations.[42]

S. R. Steinmetz catalogued witchcraft, incest, treason, sacrilege, breaches of the hunting rules, poisoning, and offenses against sexual morality among the "crimes first punished by the community."[43] H. Oppenheimer revised the order of this "first" group of crimes: treason, witchcraft, sacrilege and other offenses against religion, incest and other sexual offenses, poisoning, and breaches of the rules of hunting.[44] C. S. Wake suggested that it would be a mistake "to suppose that actions which such peoples declare to be punishable as crimes are so treated because they are thought to be 'immoral,' as we understand the term."[45] However, "moral ideas also may have played a part as early as magic and religion."[46] As mentioned before, one of the earliest justifications for punishment was that the offender must be punished because he had violated the divine law.[47] Indeed, at that time violation of the religious norms also meant infringement of the moral rules, and, conversely, violation of the ethical norms meant also transgression of the laws of religion. This should clearly indicate that whenever the crime was irreligious in nature it was also immoral.

It may not be a coincidence that the emancipated new morality in France resulted in a revolution in criminal law. Diderot and d'Alembert's *Encyclopédie* (1751–1772) demanded a new respect for man and reforms in the criminal law. The repressive and cruel criminal law was attacked most forcefully by the twenty-six-year-old Italian Cesare Bonesana, Marquis of Beccaria,[48] who wrote the "French style in Italian language"[49] so impressively that Hommel said "only the angels" could speak the same. As Enrico Ferri put it, Beccaria opened a "glorious scientific cycle."[50] But the thinkers of the Enlightenment seemed aware of the fact that criminal law cannot be separated from ethics.

This new morality expressed itself in a humanitarian understanding of the crime and pity for the criminal. A characteristic distortion of this new *élan vital* is found in an ordinance of Frederick the Great, to the effect that before the offender was to be broken on the wheel, the executioner was empowered to strangle him surreptitiously.[51]

Montesquieu opposed harsh punishment because it might undermine morality and because he thought an appeal to moral sentiment would prevent crime. Voltaire saw a deterrent in the fear of shame. Beccaria and Bentham emphasized the reward of virtue. All attempted to find a legal positivism that could be contrasted to the moral negativism in criminal law. In the tumult over the emancipation of morality from religion and law from morality, the ferment of ideas brought the thinkers close to one another on perhaps only a single issue: what should be regarded as morally "wrong." The well-known accusation that the philosophers of law neglect the legal aspects of crime and that the sociologically oriented thinkers pay but little attention to its moral aspects may be true. Vámbéry is certainly correct in comparing them to two groups of wanderers who have approached a mountain from two different directions and, having seen only one side of the mountain, they nevertheless argue about its overall shape and configuration.[52]

Perhaps only anthropologists have avoided a confrontation with ethics, and probably this is why they have avoided defining crime. Raffaele Garofalo, an *"anthropologiste raisonnable,"* was one of the few who attempted a definition, through his concept of "natural crime."[53] Cesare Lombroso, however, has not found it necessary even to enter the difficulties of defining crime; thus his criminals have not been brought into contact with the problems of morality.[54] August Drähms, one of Lombroso's American adherents, accepted Lombroso's silence on the definition of crime while still aiming at a distinction between right and wrong.[55] M. A. Vaccaro perhaps preceded Garofalo, and even Durkheim, in working on the concept of public sentiment affronted by the offender's criminal action.[56]

One of the most formidable critics of the anthropological understanding of crime, Napoleone Colajanni, somewhat in the vein of Franz von Liszt, found the essence of criminal conduct in its anti-individual and antisocial motives that disrupt the peaceful conditions of social life and are contrary to the morality of a given society.[57] Enrico Ferri tended in this direction but with a number of reservations, among them that many immoral and antisocial acts are in fact not punishable.[58]

The neospiritualist Gabriel Tarde, one of the most profound minds concerned with crime (although Ferri finds he was "not a creative genius"), sees crime as related to the dominant judgment (obviously, "moral" judgment) of the social group. He rejected Garofalo's conditions of pity and probity; mass killing in a war arouses more pity than any single murder, yet the moral judgment of the social group would not regard the general who commanded the operation as a criminal.[59] As Tarde defined it, the concept of crime is dependent upon the degree of the public "alarm and indignation."[60]

Although Willem Adriaan Bonger, who committed suicide in 1940 when the German army crossed the Dutch frontier, approached the definition of crime from the standpoint of historical materialism, he gave some emphasis to the moral aspects. Crime, he said, is "an immoral act, and one of a serious character."[61] Consistent with his basic political conviction, he defined immoral acts as "those which are harmful to the interests of a group of persons united by the same interests."[62] In other words, he virtually identified immorality with antisociality. Henri Joly,[63] M. de Baets,[64] A. V. Oettingen,[65] and H. Stursberg,[66] called by Bonger "the spiritualists,"[67] and L. Proal,[68] described by Ferri as "eclectic,"[69] heavily emphasized the moral element in crime, contending that the immoral is irreligious.

Frederick H. Wines, who attempted to view crime from the penological point of view, has tried to distinguish crime from sin but admits that they are not mutually exclusive; moreover most crimes derive from the category of sins.[70] Another penologist at the end of the nineteenth century, Henry M. Boies, classed crimes according to whether they violate the natural law, the positive law, or the divine (moral) law.[71]

To bring to an end what Vámbéry called "the uncritical promiscuity of law and morality"[72] and yet maintain moral elements in the concept of criminal law was attempted with statistical methods. So-called moral statistics have often been used for an understanding of crime statistics, or vice versa. In this respect André Michel Guerry has to be mentioned, who first used the term "moral statistic" and applied cartographic methods to show the state of morals in terms of crimes.[73] Adolphe Quetelet, "the father of statistics," with his "thermic law" tried to find the relation of crimes to seasons, in other words, the seasonal variations of morals.[74] M. W. Drobisch analyzed the possible connection between the state of moral statistics and the freedom of the will.[75] Alexander von Oettingen studied the significance of moral statistics to social ethics.[76] Georg von Mayr[77] and Ferdinand Tönnies[78] quite clearly related moral statistics to criminal statistics. During the nineteenth century "the study of the 'moral health' of nations"[79] occupied many scholars, and their point of departure has become the statistical profile of crime. Even today "moral health" is sometimes measured through crime and delinquency; for example, the FBI *Uniform Crime Reports* suggest that one of the conditions that affects the amount of crime is the "mores of the population."[80] Leslie T. Wilkins, who seems to believe that the crime rate is independent of the "moral standards" of a country, disputes the use of crime as a measuring rod of morals because of the limitations of methodology and the known statistical gaps of "crimes known to the police."[81]

Many philosophers of criminal law and sociologists include moral elements in the conceptualization of crime; some believe immorality to be closely identified with crime. J. Makarewicz, in an evolutionary and comparative method, almost completely identified immoral acts with crime, and moral disapproval with punishment. He differentiated them only by the degree of reaction; only this social reaction, and, not the content of the law, he proposed, should decide whether the act is an immorality only or a crime.[82] A. Franck took a similar stand, and moreover depicted morality as the ideal for making criminal law.[83]

Those who are averse to the use of the dubious terms of morality, and are reluctant to admit that a concept of crime exclusive of ethics has to be exposed to insurmountable difficulties, have attempted to substitute a system of social responsibility for moral responsibility. Often morals and values, conscience and judgment, and concern and interest are ostensibly confused, and the role of morality is dressed up with some utilitarian and functional characteristics. This is close to the thinking of English judges in the eighteenth-century case of *R. V. Wheatley*, in which the defendant was accused of defrauding one Richard Webb by delivering to him sixteen gallons of amber and charging him for eighteen. The court refused to regard this as a criminal offense, saying, "What is it to the public whether Richard Webb has, or has not, his eighteen gallons?"[84]

Emile Durkheim,[85] in Ferri's words "the most original and the most genuine positivist" of the French sociologists, found that repressive law originates in common beliefs and sentiments and it "is, then, an index of the strength of the collective conscience."[86] In the Preface to his *Division of Labor in Society* Durkheim's interest in the moral life of society is quite pronounced, and there is little doubt about the moral or ethical nature he wanted to attribute to this "conscience." W. I. Thomas and F. Znaniecki view crime as an antagonistic action against the solidarity of the group to which the criminal himself belongs.[87] George Herbert Mead suggested that crime solidifies "upright" consciences (moral attitudes).[88] All, in fact, operate with a version of Baruch Spinoza's theme: we do not frown upon an act because it is a crime, but it is a crime because we disapprove of it.

Pitirim A. Sorokin has called attention to the "ethico-juridical heterogeneity and antagonism" of the society that guides the primitive reaction to crime.[89] Donald R. Cressey similarly suggests that immoral acts are the violations of mores and "when the mores are violated, members of the society respond with great moral indignation; punishment is likely to be quite severe."[90]

Robert K. Merton, in explaining the mechanics of deviant behavior in anomic situations, refers to "moral imperatives" and states, "Every social group invariably couples its scale of desired ends with moral or institutional regulation of permissible and required procedures for attaining these ends."[91] In any case, A. Hamon would have been less able to criticize Merton than Durkheim, when he reproached Durkheim for noticing crime only when punishment followed the act, and portrayed him with those who endeavored to find the concept of natural crime.[92] Albert K. Cohen, in his concern to create a "general theory" of deviant behavior, draws a parallel between deviance and moral weakness or moral deficiency[93] and deals with deviant actions as "determined by the ways in which people are cognitively, morally, relationally, and materially dependent upon other people."[94] Walter C. Reckless blames the "inconsistent moral front" for American crime and proposes "ethical unity" as a preventive measure.[95] Paul W. Tappan too has found that law and morality overlap and reinforce each other; to him criminal law and mores "are interdependent and mutually supportive to a large degree."[96]

Morality, Command, and Responsibility

It cannot be denied that in their understanding of crime some students of criminal law give no quarter to the functional role of morality. Some simply leave it out of their conceptualizations; others expressly object to its inclusion among the conceptual elements. The aversion to any proposed connection between criminal law and morality is perhaps attributable in part to memories of eras when religious adherence was enforced by cruel and brutal penal laws. Also, perplexity may be present in relating ethics to value systems, and hesitation in taking a stand in favor of one or another orientation. A search for a genetic understanding of crime could not avoid the dilemma of morality.

The stand for one or another ethical orientation presents a

demand against existing criminal law—except if the moral idea is already represented by the legal norm. It may be a demand for Mosaic justice, as a guide for just and equitable behavior, or for the Pauline moral law of compensation. It might be a demand for self-realization in the Aristotelian sense, or as understood in Aquinas' scholastic ethic. It may be for Immanuel Kant's deontological ethics, or for Jeremy Bentham's egoistic hedonism. The Nietzschean values and Bertrand Russell's ethical skepticism are other random examples of the great variety of ethical orientations: any moral stand may be demanded of criminal law. Actually, however, it would be a demand against criminal law if a demand were used by the criminal law against others. A moral stand guides the lawmaker to the definition and design of responsibilities.

In broad terms, the criminal law operates by charging certain behaviors with moral responsibilities. The values defended by criminal law are ultimately moral issues; they could be fully distinguished from ethical issues only if morality were returned to the province of theology. A moral system is not much different from a value system, for morality is the source of values. William Graham Sumner's "folkways"[97] are not qualitatively different from his "mores"; the difference lies only in the intensity of feelings. The fact that appropriate dress, table manners, or other folkways are not controlled by the criminal law indicates that the law may be concerned only with mores. And certainly not all mores are controlled by the commands of the criminal law; man is not made legally responsible for all violations of the morality. However, all criminal-law commands contain moral elements, even though sometimes they are almost invisible to the general public, which tends to recognize them only if an immorality arouses significant indignation.

The disorderly parking of a car may be no less immoral than a mass murder; the differential severity of the sanctions testifies only the degree of immorality as judged by the given moral or value system. Nevertheless, both fines and the death penalty are not only retortions; by taking the money or the life of the offender the criminal law also expresses a moral reproach. This moral reproach, an essential part of the responsibility-making command, is often overlooked, not only by judges, defense attorneys, public prosecutors, the general public, and the criminal himself, but also by many of those who search for the concept of crime. As birds cannot be described simply by saying that they are flying animals, and a locomotive cannot be understood just by saying that its engine has the power to pull a train, so criminal law cannot be comprehended by referring to it as if it were merely a controlling instrument of the normative system.

The moral nature of criminal law can be left unstated or even concealed; but the moral reproach as a component part of criminal law would make its moral nature difficult to deny. However, the crux of the matter is not so much the existence of morality in criminal law as its functional role in making a conduct responsible for not conforming with the morality of the command. Criminal law may be the product of a variety of social interactions, but, in its ultimate analysis, it is the "command of the sovereign," that is, the command of the social power. This social power takes a stand for a certain morality or value system and demands its acceptance as the right system. Morality is not the product of law; the law exists to enforce the morality. Parking by a hydrant is wrong, killing people is wrong, and thus laws had to be made to promote orderly parking and respect for other people's lives. Criminal law is not only a regulative tool, but primarily a teleological instrument in the service of the moral or value system designated by the social power. The members of a society are necessarily required to live in accordance with the "command of the sovereign" who threatens to hold them responsible for any deviation.

This responsibility making is not an isolated factor at any

given time. It explains crime and relates criminals to conformists in spatial, cultural, and time dimensions.[98] The history of criminal procedures reveals differing approaches to morality and, accordingly, to the definition of responsibility. No particular definition of responsibility has ever seemed right to all the members of a society. Who is responsible for what, and why? This is the question the answer to which can lead to an understanding of the moral or value system of the sovereign power. Responsibility will never be perfectly conceptualized or understood. In fact, its significance in the philosophy of crime lies in the very fact that it is relative. "Crime" does not change, but responsibility does; it changes according to the changes in the moral or value system as dictated by the sovereign.

By determining the moral or value system, the lawmaking social power helps secure and maintain group order. In this context the morality or values (and making the members of the society responsible for following them) are functional in nature; thus they cannot operate in an area of stiff formalism. For the morality-commanding law to be respected and observed, it has to operate beyond the boundaries of strict legal definitions of criminal offenses. It is a comprehensive operation that cannot avoid such questions as causality, justice in law, and free will—problems that are obstacles to a meaningful understanding and conceptualization of the dual responsibility: the responsibility with which criminal law charges certain conducts and the responsibility that refers to factors leading a person to conduct counter to the command.

The problem of free will is one of the most difficult in philosophy, yet one of the most popular. Immanuel Kant bitterly complained that a thousand years' work had been expended in vain on its solution. Nicolai Hartmann warned that we cannot even hope for a perfect answer. The debate on the controversial issue of determinism versus indeterminism is interminable. Acceptance of an unlimited application of the law of causality would be as grandiose a hypothesis as acceptance of free will as merely a metaphysical concept.

Determinism, the theory that man has no free choice and that his actions are determined by external forces, annihilates the concept of human will. In other words, determinism says that will does not motivate action but that action results automatically from outside causes. In a way, however, indeterminism leads to a similar result: a will that is not involved in any way with causal reality would be only an illusion. Johannes Buridan's donkey, also mentioned by Schopenhauer, Windelband, Gomperz, and others, clearly illustrates the complexities of the argument and can be used both to defend and to attack both views. A hungry donkey stands between two haystacks, equally fragrant, equal in size, and at equal distances away. The poor animal, having no will to decide (if the deterministic view is right), or having no motives to influence its decision (if the indeterministic view is right), eventually reaches a condition of absolute indifference and, being unable to choose one of the haystacks, dies of hunger. Incidentally, this classic story of the donkey may indicate that the validity of one's conclusion rests upon what one actually understands by the terms that are used.

Since new theories sooner or later generally prove to be merely versions of old theories, the chances are that the solution to the problem will not be easily discovered. Thus, from a practical viewpoint, useful answers contain both deterministic and indeterministic elements and differ mainly in terms of how much of each. Such a compromise may also be necessary because there is no philosophical guarantee either that adherents of the indeterministic view possess freedom of will in coming to their conclusion or that adherents of the deterministic thesis express their judgment only as mouthpieces of external forces.

The philosophy of all penal systems seems at first to be heavily indeterministic. The idea of official punishment itself indicates the lawmaker's assumption that the criminal has freedom of choice and may choose the morals or values and, accordingly, the behavior, he prefers. Criminal law assumes that man is able to form a "more or less impartial judgment of the alternative actions" and can act "in accordance with that judgment."[99] It would be senseless, so the argument runs, to offer a choice between reward and punishment if free will were not a fact. After all, criminal responsibility is based on the choice to commit a criminal act. Criminal law operates on the assumption that man is an intelligent and reasoning creature who can recognize values. In other words, only those can be punished who want a crime. At least this is the case when the penal system applies retributive punishment. Nobody can seriously dispute the point that in our penal systems, with respect to correction and rehabilitation, no rethinking has set aside the concepts of guilt, retribution, and deterrence.

The apparent freedom of will is not always as free as it appears. In reality it involves only a limited range of choices, and in these choices there is only a limited number of alternatives. Even here, biological needs may play a part in determining the action. But Kantian dualism does not fit in with any mixture of deterministic and indeterministic elements; the realistic human will can exist alone neither in the causal nature nor in the intellect. No moderate deterministic or moderate indeterministic thinking can accept the existence of man's two worlds, *mundus sensibilis* and *mundus intelligibilis*, as separate entities. Man's position in the functioning universe demands the merger of these two worlds. The culture and morality of these merged worlds mold both the causal reality and the intellect into a single unity. This culture is not some "Third Reich," as Heinrich Rickert called it;[100] it is not a self-contained third world that is linked with the other two. Furthermore, it has no connection with Hegel's strict historical and social causality, where the realities of nature, "the unsolved contradiction,"[101] cannot find their comfortable place.

The moral or value system of the culture both saturates and limits individual will. It is the actual world in which the individual lives and functions, and he learns to do so through the ordinary socializing processes. Cultural values not only are built into the person, but they also build his personality and thus limit his choices and set his alternatives. The socializing processes instill man's prejudices, likes and dislikes, beliefs and disbeliefs, affirmations and negations. Culture, through socialization, "eventually results in making the person what he is."[102] Man actively masters his culture, but only after he passively accepts it.

Except where physical necessities, which prevail throughout the material universe, rigidly dictate human action, our faculties of knowing, reasoning, and choosing are considerably arrested by indoctrination in the morality of our culture. Even certain biological phenomena can be controlled to some extent by cultural forces. The ideas of a culture and its morality are infused into a person before his faculties of knowing, reasoning, and choosing have had a chance to develop to maturity. Therefore these faculties, all related to the will, are not really free. He knows, reasons, and makes his choices, but normally what he would will to know, what he would will to reason, and what choices he would will to make are acts limited by the ideas of his culture. This is why the more a person is socialized, the more likely he is to be a conformist. Socialization and resocialization are operational concepts applied to the problem of free will.

Jean Paul Sartre's cynical remark that "I am responsible for everything, in fact, except for my very responsibility,"[103] may be recommended as a motto for those who argue against the idea of retribution in modern penal systems. The culturally imbued and limited will is, in fact, the profile of the functional responsibility. Culture and its moral or value system not only establish the direction and range of knowing, reasoning, and choosing, but also caution man to make these faculties function in the indicated direction and within the indicated range. While there are limits on the freedom of the will, it is expected that what freedom there is will be used. Man is made responsible for functioning outside (trespassing) the approved limits. At the same time, he has the responsibility for making his will function within the approved limits in order to promote his culture. Man's self-imposed limitations on his freedom of will create responsibility in him for his functional role in his world.

When man functions within his limited freedom, this is expected, and possibly rewarded; when he functions outside the limits of his freedom, this is resented, and possibly punished. This does not mean that all less adequately socialized persons, who as a result feel less restricted in their freedom of will, and whose freer wills may even choose illegitimate alternatives, are necessarily criminals. However, unlimited freedom of the will creates the possibility of full revolt against the social power that wills the society according to the culturally imbued and limited knowledge, reasons, and choices.

At the same time, man is not condemned to passivity. Inertia is not one of his characteristics, and to see him in a state of rest or to see him in motion caused only by external forces would belie his nature. Moreover, he is supposed to use his knowledge, reason, and ability to choose in order to safeguard, improve, and perpetuate his culture and morality. He is expected to be functional, and he can be made responsible for that. Man is taught to have goals and aspirations, but only for his culture and not against its values. His functional role extends as far as the limitations of his freedom of will. These limitations do not exclude his experiencing, but only arrest his evaluation of his social responsibilities. The list of active duties in his functional role is almost endless. Compared to those who criminally trespass (who go beyond the culture's limitations on their freedom of will), his functional role is to prevent a choice that would result in criminal trespassing.

A culturally imbued and limited free will based on functional responsibility testifies to the fact that we are taught only what we need to know in order to participate in our particular culture group. The power structure of this group defines the values to be learned and establishes the degree to which the will is to be imbued and limited by the culture. The operation of any power structure may well lead to the development of an opposing structure that may be capable ultimately of taking it over and changing the cultural value system. The dynamics of such a change would depend largely on the potential of those who are inadequately socialized, and who may thus use their greater freedom of will to make choices outside the culturally limited area. The change may also depend on the degree of discomfort caused by the values introduced by the new power structure; those under the original power structure may not comprehend because of the limitations it imposed on their knowledge and reasoning.

When such an upheaval is successful, a new value system and new norms may be created and old values may be rejected or reversed. In this event an extension of the socialization (or re-socialization) is unavoidable. However, so long as the existing social power prevails, the original goals and aspirations obtain, whether available or blocked; ideas and beliefs are fortified; limitations on the freedom of the will are unchanged; roles continue with the same assigned functional responsibilities. In other words, continued socialization takes place according to the cultural values of the existing power. Since man's will is not entirely free and is culturally imbued, aspirations and goals are seen as legitimate, barriers to them as justifiable, and roles as constructive.

The criminal or the delinquent, however, is roleless. He violates the norms because he has not been adequately socialized to accept the value system of the ruling social power; the freedom of his will was not adequately limited, or his knowledge, reason, and choosing were not adequately imbued with cultural values. His functional role and the applicable legal norms have not "come through" to him. As a result, fear of the law rather than respect for the harmony of the ethical and criminal codes stimulates observance of the command. His crime or delinquency is thus not necessarily an act of opposition against this norm-forming power, because he does not know and hence cannot judge these values. Rather, the law appears to him as an alien and external phenomenon with which he is unfamiliar and whose rationale is incomprehensible.

Crime or delinquency seen in terms of revolt against the social power makes sense only if the criminal or the delinquent understands the values on which the norms are based. In most instances he knows the formal norms and is aware of what can and cannot be done, but because he lacks adequate "cultural saturation" he cannot be acquainted with the values underlying the norms. He knows the formal prohibitions and rationalizes his own deviation.

The criminal and the delinquent know that murder, rape, and shoplifting are prohibited, but they do not understand why. Yet without this understanding the criminal can form only a phenomenalistic judgment whereby the world appears to operate without rhyme or reason and in an arbitrary manner that leaves him at its mercy.

The assumption that the criminal has more freedom of will, and uses illegitimate means to achieve blocked goals, does not provide a solution to the crime problem. Limitations on the freedom of will do not exclude goals and aspirations; moreover, aspiration is a functional role if it is kept within limits. All human beings have goals, not all of which can be achieved. Why have not all people, rather than only a fraction of them, turned to illegitimate alternatives?

Crime has existed since the dawn of history, and all crimes have been committed because of blocked aspirations, whether economic, intellectual, communal, or sexual. Moreover, it may be said that the whole course of personality development, from infancy to later life, has always been based primarily on learning to strive for certain cultural goals and learning to live with frustration if the goals are unattainable. This learning process and the frustrations that sometimes result are a necessary part of group membership. Even in primitive societies that practiced private vengeance or kin revenge the "offender" did not attack his victim only because of some innate drive toward violence, but because the victim had something he wanted—food, the skin of an animal, a special stone, or perhaps even the status that comes with power and success—that could not be obtained as easily in another way. In a certain sense the criminal and the delinquent have always been goal oriented. The criminal of today is not basically different from the criminal of any other period of time. Only his aspirations and the limitations on his freedom of will change from time to time and from place to place, according to the cultural and moral definitions of his era and society.

From this point of view, the status-seeking strivings of imma- ture individuals, learned from and supported by their particular culture, can be understood as a rejection of approved ways of achieving one's ambitions. Similarly, most studies today assume that the adolescent gang delinquent wants upward mobility in the normal middle-class fashion. Following their rather metaphysical view of the gang delinquent as class-conscious (with which the public generally concurs) these researchers attempt to measure delinquency and adolescence in terms of what they think they should be and not in terms of what they actually are. An example of this is the imaginary working-class boy who "standing alone to face humiliation at the hands of middle-class agents is difficult to comprehend."[104] This approach stands up only if the ambition of the criminal or delinquent to challenge the middle-class system can be interpreted as giving him the social gratification that any constructive ambition would deny him. But this would presume that his will has been culturally saturated, but not limited; in other words, that he has an accurate picture of himself, his social environment, and his society's class system. However, to make this assumption is to contradict what we know about criminals and delinquents: the ability to perceive, learn, think, and reason in a culturally approved, mature fashion cannot be effectively learned if one lives and functions in some isolated subculture where he is not imbued with the values of the dominant culture and its limitations on freedom of will cannot reach him.

Inadequate socialization can thus result in a lack of constructive ambitions or positive values, a sense of "rolelessness" may develop. Because of his inadequate socialization and faulty aspirations, the criminal or the delinquent youth cannot determine which rights and duties are his. He cannot see his functional role, and so he cannot identify the constructive roles he would otherwise play.

Given this roleless state, the criminal or delinquent, unable to recognize the positive values expected of him, cannot form the positive aspirations expected of him. If the criminal or the delinquent youth turns to destructive ambitions, this is not so much a matter of choice among alternatives as an option available to him in the absence of a positive value system.

The concept of the lower class versus the middle class and the predominant identification of the lower class with crime and delinquency make sense only if the middle class can be identified with the norm-forming social power. In no known human society are privileges and prohibitions evenly distributed, and the question of "whose ox is gored" depends for the most part on the ruling social power, as expressed by the law.

All laws are formulated on the unspoken assumption that they are just, although they may not appear so to all members of a society, particularly the disadvantaged. One can ask, "Which human interests are worthy of being satisfied and . . . what is their proper order of rank? . . . The answer to these questions is a judgment of value."[105] The law serves the value system of the existing social power structure and enacts justice as interpreted by this sytem. As Hans Kelsen notes, "Were it possible to answer the question of justice as we are able to solve problems of the technique of natural science or medicine, one would as little think of regulating the relations among men by positive law, that is by authoritative measure of coercion, as one thinks today of forceable prescribing by positive law how a steam engine should be built or a specific illness healed."[106]

Responsibility for the expected moral conduct not only raises questions about freedom of will and justice in law. If it extends to the other end of the dual responsibility, where the question is "Why does one violate the law?" it also involves the puzzle of causality as posed by the law of the particular social structure. In fact, all these ideas are interrelated. "Perhaps the most troublesome of these lay words is the term 'to cause'."[107] What the traditional concepts of objective responsibility fail to see is the location of the causal nexus in a spectrum of crime in which the functional dynamics of lawbreaking processes can be viewed throughout their development. Lombroso's *uomo delinquente* became the curiosity of wax museums, and Ferri's "new horizons" ceased being a novelty long ago. Our present static understanding of responsibility and causality is a metaphorical option and had its beginnings centuries ago.

This does not mean that the other extreme is now proposed, although the general philosophical concept of an unlimited number of causes may not be distant from the concept of limited free will. However, the *regressus in infinitum* of causes leads to conclusions that are just as absurd as those following the principle of *post hoc ergo propter hoc,* which makes justice based on it doubtful. The mother who gives birth to a murderer is one link in the chain of causes, but normally nobody would dream of charging her with a criminal contribution to the murder. At the same time, just because official statistical tables show that most juvenile delinquents come from the lower class, one cannot be suspicious of a young man simply because his father is a poverty-stricken shoeshiner. The imputation of law cannot be extended to impute the facts.

It would be absurd to contend that crimes "happen" to be committed. Crimes have causes; somebody or something is responsible for leading a man against the law. Who or what is responsible for the stand of man against the morality-expecting and responsibility-threatening law is the crucial challenge of the theories in criminology.

NOTES

1. Lon L. Fuller, *The Morality of Law* (New Haven and London, 1964), p. 3.
2. Herbert Lionel Adolphus Hart, *The Concept of Law* (Oxford, 1961), p. 151 and *infra*.
3. Rusztem Vámbéry, *Büntetöjog és ethika* (Budapest, 1907), p. 1.
4. Sir Henry Sumner Maine, *Ancient Law, Its Connection with the Early History of Society and Its Relation to Modern Ideas* (1861), with Introduction and Notes by Sir Frederick Pollock (London, 1906).
5. A. S. Diamond, *Primitive Law* (London, 1935).
6. Nicholas S. Timasheff, *An Introduction to the Sociology of Law* (Cambridge, Mass., 1930), pp. 275–276.
7. Edward Westermarck, *The Origin and Development of the Moral Ideas* (2nd ed., London, 1912), II, 663 and *infra*.
8. J. Forsyth, *The Highlands of Central India* (London, 1871), p. 145; W. Radloff, *Das Schamanenthum* (Leipzig, 1885), p. 13; cited by Westermarck, *op. cit.*, pp. 663–664.
9. E. F. Im Thurn, *Among the Indians of Guiana* (London, 1883), p. 342.
10. William Mariner, *An Account of the Natives of the Tonga Islands* (London, 1817), II, 149.
11. John Batchelor, *The Ainu of Japan* (London, 1892), p. 243 and *infra*.
12. Dennis Lloyd, *The Idea of Law* (Baltimore, 1964), p. 46.

13. Hart, *op. cit.*, p. 181.

14. Vámbéry, *op. cit.*, p. 8 and *infra*.

15. Lloyd, *op. cit.*, p. 68.

16. J. Makarewicz, *Einführung in die Philosophie des Strafrechts auf entwicklungsgeschichtlicher Grundlage* (Stuttgart, 1906; reprinted Amsterdam, 1967), p. 1 and *infra*.

17. Karl Gareis, *Rechtsenzyklopädie und Methodologie* (2nd ed., Stuttgart, 1900), p. 10 and *infra*.

18. Hart, *op. cit.*, p. 183.

19. Morris Raphael Cohen, *Reason and Law* (New York, 1961), pp. 34–35.

20. *Ibid.*, p. 29.

21. Fuller, *op. cit.*, pp. 96–97.

22. Rudolf Stammler, *Wirtschaft und Recht nach der materialistischen Geschichtsanfassung* (5th ed., Leipzig, 1924).

23. Makarewicz, *op. cit.*, p. 2.

24. Gareis, *op. cit.*, pp. 20–21.

25. Rudolf Stammler, *Die Lehre von dem richtigen Rechte* (Halle, 1902), pp. 52–92, but also earlier in his *Wirtschaft und Recht, op. cit.*, p. 547 and *infra*.

26. Christian Thomasius, *Fundamenta Iuris Naturae et Gentium* (Halle, 1705), Vol. I, Ch. I, pp. 4–6.

27. Rudolf Jhering, *Der Zweck im Recht* (Leipzig, 1877–1883), II, 10, 181.

28. Gyula Moór, *Macht, Recht, Moral* (Szeged, 1922), pp. 15–16.

29. A. Merkel, *Juristische Encyclopädie* (7th ed., Leipzig, 1922), p. 38.

30. Giorgio Del Vecchio, *Philosophy of Law*, T. O. Martin (tr.) (Washington, 1953), p. 276.

31. Edgar Bodenheimer, *Jurisprudence, The Philosophy and Method of the Law* (Cambridge, 1962), p. 251.

32. F. J. Feldbrugge, *Soviet Criminal Law*, General Part (Leyden, 1964), p. 246.

33. Karl Janka, *Der Strafrechtliche Nothstand* (Vienna, 1878), p. 139.

34. Vámbéry, *op. cit.*, p. 39.

35. Georg Jellinek, *Die Sozialethische Bedeutung von Recht, Unrecht und Strafe* (Vienna, 1878), p. 42 and *infra*.

36. Hart, *op. cit.*, p. 168.

37. Karl Bergbohm, *Jurisprudenz und Rechtsphilosophie* (Leipzig, 1892).

38. Stammler, *Die Lehre von dem richtigen Rechte, op. cit.*, p. 85.

39. Rudolf Jhering, *Kampf ums Recht* (Vienna, 1872); Josef Kohler, *Shakespeare vor dem Forum der Jurisprudenz* (Berlin, 1884); cp. also Vámbéry's impressive analysis of the dispute, *op. cit.*, pp. 59–62.

40. Vámbéry, *op. cit.*, p. 59.

41. Theodor Mommsen, *Römisches Strafrecht* (Leipzig, 1899), pp. 2–11.

42. Theodor Mommsen, *Zum ältesten Strafrecht der Kulturvölker* (Leipzig, 1905). Mommsen's questions have been answered by H. Brunner, B. Freudenthal, J. Goldziher, H. F. Hitzig, Th. Noeldeke, H. Oldenberg, G. Roethe, J. Wellhausen, and V. Willamovitz-Moellendorff.

43. S. R. Steinmetz, *Ethnologische Studien zur ersten Entwicklung der Strafe* (Leiden, 1894).

44. H. Oppenheimer, *The Rationale of Punishment* (London, 1913), p. 71.

45. C. S. Wake, *The Evolution of Morality* (London, 1878), Vol. I, pp. 293–294.

46. Maurice Parmelee, *Criminology* (New York, 1918), p. 19.

47. *Ibid.*, p. 373.

48. Cesare Bonesana, Marquis de Beccaria, *Dei delitti e delle pene* (Haarlem, 1764), *An Essay on Crime and Punishments* (trans. from the Italian with commentary by Voltaire, 5th ed., London, 1804).

49. Vámbéry, *op. cit.*, p. 100.

50. Enrico Ferri, *Criminal Sociology*, Joseph I. Kelly and John Lisle (trs.) (New York, 1967), p. 4.

51. N. Willenbücher, "Die Strafrechtsphilosophischen Anschauungen Friedrichs des Grossen," *Breslauer Abhandlungen*, 1904, Vol. 56, p. 23.

52. Vámbéry, *op. cit.*, p. 145.

53. Raffaele Garofalo, *Criminology*, Robert Wyness Millar (tr.) (Boston, 1914).

54. Cesare Lombroso, *L'Uomo delinquente* (Milan, 1876); in collaboration with G. Ferrero, *La donna delinquente, la prostituta e la donna normale* (Turin, 1893); *Delitti vecchi e delitti nuovi* (Turin, 1902).

55. August Drähms, *The Criminal: His Personnel and Environment* (New York, 1900).

56. M. A. Vaccaro, *Genesi e funzioni delle leggi penali* (Rome, 1889), pp. 154–180, 211–212.

57. Napoleone Colajanni, *Sociologia criminale* (Catania, 1889), p. 64.

58. Ferri, *op. cit.*, p. 81.

59. Gabriel Tarde, *La criminalité comparée* (Paris, 1890), p. 186; *La philosophie pénale* (Paris, 1890).

60. Gabriel Tarde, "Misère et criminalité," *Revue philosophique*, Vol. 29 (1890).

61. Willem Adriaan Bonger, *Criminality and Economic Conditions*, Henry P. Horton (tr.) (New York, 1967), p. 379.

62. *Ibid.*, p. 379.

63. Henri Joly, *Le crime* (Paris, 1888).

64. M. de Baets, *L'école d'anthropologie criminelle* (Gand, 1893); *Les influences de la misère sur la criminalité* (Gand, 1895).

65. Alexander V. Oettingen, *Die Moralstatistik in ihrer Bedeutung für eine Sozialethik* (3rd ed., Erlangen, 1882).

66. H. Stursberg, *Die Zunahme der Vergehen und Verbrechen und ihre Ursachen* (Düsseldorf, 1878).

67. Bonger, *op. cit.*, pp. xxxi, 199–209.

68. L. Proal, *Le crime et la peine* (Paris, 1892).

69. Ferri, *op. cit.*, p. 82.

70. Frederick H. Wines, *Punishment and Reformation* (New York, 1895), pp. 11–13.

71. Henry M. Boies, *The Science of Penology* (New York, 1901), pp. 31–33.

72. Vámbéry, *op. cit.*, p. 150.

73. André Michel Guerry, *Essai sur la statistique morale* (Paris,

1833); *Statistique morale de l'Angleterre comparée avec la statistique morale de la France* (Paris, 1864). It is a controversial question whether A. M. Guerry and M. de Guerry de Champneuf are the same person; probably they are not.

74. Adolphe Quetelet, *Sur l'homme et le développement de ses facultés ou essai de physique sociale* (Paris, 1835).

75. M. W. Drobisch, *Die moralische Statistik und die Willensfreiheit* (Leipzig, 1867).

76. Oettingen, *op. cit.*

77. Georg von Mayr, *Moralstatistik mit Einschluss der Kriminalstatistik* (Tübingen, 1917).

78. Ferdinand Tönnies, "Moralstatistik," in *Handwörterbuch der Staatswiss* (4th ed., Jena, 1925).

79. Thorsten Sellin and Marvin E. Wolfgang, *The Measurement of Delinquency* (New York, 1964), p. 8.

80. *Uniform Crime Reports—1966* (Washington, D.C., 1967), p. vi.

81. Leslie T. Wilkins, *Social Deviance, Social Policy, Action, and Research* (Englewood Cliffs, N.J., 1965), pp. 150–151.

82. Makarewicz, *op. cit.*

83. A. Franck, *Philosophie du droit pénal* (Paris, 1864).

84. Cited in P. J. Fitzgerald, *Criminal Law and Punishment* (Oxford, 1962), p. 3.

85. Emile Durkheim, *De la division du travail social* (Paris, 1893).

86. Talcott Parsons, *The Structure of Social Action* (New York, 1968), I, 318.

87. W. I. Thomas and F. Znaniecki, *The Polish Peasant in Europe and America* (New York, 1927), II, pp. 1753–1755.

88. George Herbert Mead, "The Psychology of Punitive Justice," *American Journal of Sociology*, 23 (1928), 557–602.

89. Pitirim A. Sorokin, *Social and Cultural Dynamics* (New York, 1937), II, 523–632.

90. Donald R. Cressey, "Crime," in Robert K. Merton and Robert A. Nisbet (eds.), *Contemporary Social Problems* (2nd ed., New York, 1966), p. 137.

91. Robert K. Merton, "Social Structure and Anomie," *American Sociological Review*, 3 (1938), 672–682.

92. A. Hamon, *De la définition du crime* (Paris, 1892), p. 3 and *infra*.

93. Albert K. Cohen, "The Sociology of the Deviant Act: Anomie Theory and Beyond," *American Sociological Review*, 1 (1965), 6–7.

94. Albert K. Cohen, *Deviance and Control* (Englewood Cliffs, N.J., 1966), p. 84.

95. Walter C. Reckless, *The Crime Problem* (4th ed., New York, 1967), pp. 775–776.

96. Paul W. Tappan, *Crime, Justice and Correction* (New York, 1960), pp. 28–31.

97. William Graham Sumner, *Folkways* (Boston, 1906).

98. Stephen Schafer, *The Victim and His Criminal: A Study in Functional Responsibility* (New York, 1968), p. 138 and *infra*.

99. Morris Ginsberg, *On Justice in Society* (Harmondsworth, Eng., 1965), p. 168.

100. Heinrich Rickert, *System der Philosophie* (Tübingen, 1921), I, 254.

101. *Unaufgelöste Widerspruch*, in Georg Wilhelm Friedrich Hegel, *Encyclopädie der philosophischen Wissenschaften* (Leipzig, 1923), p. 209.

102. Franz Alexander and Hugo Staub, *The Criminal, the Judge, and the Public*, Gregory Zilboorg (tr.) (rev. ed., Glencoe, 1956), p. 127.

103. Jean Paul Sartre, *Being and Nothingness*, Hazel E. Barnes (tr.) (New York, 1956), p. 555.

104. John I. Kitsuse and David C. Dietrick, "Delinquent Boys: A Critique," *American Sociological Review*, April 1959, p. 211.

105. Hans Kelsen, "The Metamorphoses of the Idea of Justice," in Paul Sayre (ed.), *Interpretations of Modern Legal Philosophies: Essays in Honor of Roscoe Pound* (New York, 1947), p. 392.

106. *Ibid.*, p. 397.

107. Wex S. Malone, "Nature of Proof of Cause-In-Fact," in Richard C. Donnelly, Joseph Goldstein, and Richard D. Schwartz (eds.), *Criminal Law* (New York, 1962), p. 614.

IV

From Capricious Responsibility to the Enlightenment

Fundamental Ideas of Early Responsibility

From earliest times, crime has been recognized as a violation of social imperatives. Even the most primitive groups recognized the necessity of utilizing social norms as means of societal control; the norms, however, were generally products of human experience that had been legitimized through socioreligious acceptance. Since law regulates not only what *is*, but also what *should be*, certain conducts will be defined as crime in order to protect a valuable issue in advance against a possible attack. In early times, however, the responsibility-making developed only after the crime was committed. The criminal situation was the *prius* (primary element), and the formulation of norms or responsibility-making the *posterius* (the following element). A kind of social emergency legalized the command.

Historically, there are five fundamental attitudes demonstrated by responsibility-making powers: private revenge, blood revenge, superstitious revenge, state revenge, and the mitigation of revenge. Crime has a long history, but criminal law is young and criminology even younger, and thus there is no possibility of a sensitive, well-ordered, and complete review that would really cover the history of crime from earliest times.[1] However, the general ideas can be clearly seen as they appeared in rough succession and reflected the general reaction to the crime problem.

Private Revenge

The period of private revenge mirrored the individual struggle for survival. To protect his personal security and prevent future "crimes" against him, a victim was forced to retaliate ruthlessly and to exact heavy compensation from the "offender." In this earliest period the responsibility-making social control was in the hands of the individual. His "justice" was a personal, individualistic justice. Alone, he faced attacks from outside and fought against fellow creatures who caused him harm. He had to take the law into his own hands; in effect, he made the law. He was the prosecutor and the judge. He also carried out the punishment, aimed at deterrence and retribution. His was a private revenge, and his morality of law was exclusively personal.

Attack was the best defense against attack, and the continual conflict between the "criminal" and his victim in time made the victim the criminal and the criminal the victim. The criminal-victim relationship at that time was hardly more than a mutually opposed effort to secure power.

Blood Revenge

In the age of blood revenge the locus of the response to crime shifted from the individual to the kinship group. Social control was maintained by the kindred, his blood tie. Thus, "blood feud" refers to the familial relationship and not to the sanguinary nature of the revenge. Even among highly organized hunters, such as the Cheyenne and the Comanche, tribal law prevailed. An offense against the individual was an offense against his tribe, and the punishment to be exacted against the offender was neither codified nor always standardized by offense.

A victim's debasement accrued to his entire clan, and the offender's guilt was assumed by his family. Individuals did not punish individuals; families took revenge on families. This new age marked the beginning of organized revenge; it can be viewed as the origin of "collective responsibility," which emerged again in the twentieth century and has resulted in the death of millions.

The blood revenge was still part of the struggle for survival: a safeguard for preserving all the essentials of existence, if necessary by means of unlimited aggression.[2] In addition to comparatively minor crimes occurring within the tribe or clan, the important crime type of this era was external threat by one tribe to another. Punishment for some crimes took the form of economic restitution, but usually there was aggressive retaliation. As in our modern international world, both criminal (one tribe) and victim (another tribe) wanted to weaken or exterminate each other: crime was the violation of the tribal "international law." The blood revenge tested the relationships among families.

The blood feud might have been an antecedent of the responsibility laws, but being informal and having no defined conditions it cannot be regarded as a social institution. But, as Rudolf Jhering put it, "All laws started with arbitrariness and revenge."[3] Maybe the "crime" was really an attack; but regardless of the reality, the judgment was entirely the victim's. The blood revenge had to be justified so to intensify the clan members' determination to retaliate. The blood feud did not restore any moral or legal order; its primary purpose was to secure the conditions of survival. The tribe, clan, or family could function effectively only if its strength was sufficient enough to repulse or punish any attack. Thus, blood revenge was aimed essentially at restoration of the balance of power in the world of primitive societies. At this developmental stage of history punishment was not really a response to the criminal's "product responsibility," but an expression of social defense. In other words, the attacker and his family were held responsible for endangering the existence of the attacked tribe, rather than for the "product" (the actual objective result) of the attack.

In time the blood feud and physical retribution were replaced by financial compensation. There arose the redemption of revenge (in its original German *Loskauf de Rache*), which submitted the judgment of guilt to negotiation. In most cases, agreement on the question of compensation still involved both interested political entities—the criminal's tribe, clan, or family, and that of the victim.

Superstitious Revenge

Superstitious revenge was a consolidation of religious ideas, including credulity regarding the supernatural, a misdirected reverence for spiritual forces, and an irrational fear of divine vengeance. Although this new source of "law" mitigated blood revenge, it also led to highly arbitrary and cruel punishments. The concept of crime became confused with that of sin; crime was now regarded as an act against God. Both private and blood revenge were reduced as religious institutions gained ascendancy. The practice of *asylum* (a place of refuge for criminals), *treuga dei* (a temporary peace in the name of God), and even the *lex talionis* (*talio*, a legalized retaliation) reduced the individualistic arbitrariness of previous revenges.

The capricious nature of responsibility making and the superstitious concept of crime also led to the practice of irrational revenge to placate the gods or God. Most injurious acts, because they were also offenses against a divinity, were believed capable of causing pestilence, floods, earthquakes, and other widespread devastation, and thus punishment was inflicted to appease the anticipated divine fury. Ancient demonology, mysticism, magic, and witchcraft were revived in theological terms. "Besides this qualitative equivalence between injury and retaliation, the *lex talionis* requires, in a rough way, quantitative equivalence."[4] The *talio*, the principle of "an eye for an eye, a tooth for a tooth," appealed to the morality of primitive man. Responsibility meant "The sinner must not only pay a debt to society; he must get right with God."[5] The Ten Commandments, the Indian *Manama Dharma Astra*, the Egyptian Hermes Trismegistus, and the Babylonian Code of Hammurabi, among others, carefully regulated the ruthlessness of revenge.

State Revenge

State revenge meant a monopoly on the power of retaliation by the state. The era began with the system of composition, an appeal to avoid revenge by monetary or economic compensation. Criminal law has its base in the system of composition, and the periodical tribal assemblies that met to settle the amount to be paid provide an early example of judicial proceedings. Composition was an attempt to replace feelings of personal vengeance with a more humane feeling of economic compensation to the victim.

The amount of compensation varied according to the nature of the crime and the age, rank, sex, and prestige of the injured party: "A free-born man is worth more than a slave, a grown-up more than a child, a man more than a woman, and a person of rank more than a freeman."[6] The "value" of human beings was thus based on their social position; a socially stratified composition developed. Soon after the emergence of the composition, several laws (*leges barbarorum*) elaborated an intricate system of compensation. Every kind of blow or wound given to every kind of person had its price.

Presumably *Friedlosigkeit* (outlawry) resulted from a failure to provide composition. If the wrongdoer was reluctant to pay or could not pay the necessary sum, he was declared a *friedlos* or outlaw, was ostracized, and might be killed with impunity.[7] The place of the victim on the scale of values was of great importance to the criminal; since the amount of composition was determined by his victim's rank, the criminal could tell whether or not he could pay the amount demanded. Obviously, a low assessment was in the criminal's interest. However, the criminal could be trapped by an inflated assessment, since the victim was evaluated by his own community. The criminal's risk was extreme. Loss of membership in his group meant, in effect, the loss of existence. As an outlaw he could do nothing to obtain the necessities of life; he lost the protection provided by his community and could not defend himself against the revenge of others. He could continue a meaningful and safe existence only if he paid the amount equated with the value of his victim.

The influence of state power over composition gradually increased. As a result, the criminal's position was somewhat eased. In time *Friedlosigkeit* was abandoned as a punishment for an unsatisfied composition. The community claimed a share of the victim's compensation, and as the central power in a community grew stronger its share increased.

One share of the composition was claimed by the community, overlord, or king as a commission for bringing about a reconciliation between the parties. One part of the composition went to the victim (*wergeld, busse, emenda, lendis*). The other share went to the community or the king (*Friedensgeld, fredus, gewedde*).[8] In Saxon England the *wer* (payment for homicide) and the *bot* (compensation for injury) existed alongside the *wite* (fine paid to the king or overlord). This twofold payment enabled the offender to buy back the security he had lost. The double payment clearly indicates the close connection between punishment and compensation.[9]

Before long, however, the injured person's right to restitution began to shrink, and, after the Treaty of Verdun, which divided the Frankish Empire, the fine paid to the state gradually replaced compensation to the victim. The double payment continued, but now the king or overlord took all of it. After the ancient system of law, discretionary money penalties took the place of the old *wite* and the *bot* gave way to damages, which were assessed by a tribunal.[10] As the state monopolized the institution of punishment,[11] the rights of the injured were eventually separated from the penal law: composition, as the obligation to pay damages due the victim, was placed under the civil law.

In the first decades after the Middle Ages vagabonds, adventurers, and other new types of criminals compounded the nature of the crime problem. "Criminal law" at the end of the Middle Ages was characterized by a philosophy of deterrence rather than revenge. Criminal offenses at this time were either vaguely defined or undefined. Criminal procedures were arbitrary, and barbarous punishments were frequently meted out for fictitious crimes. The public had no protection against political corruption or judicial miscarriages. Grotesque practices and bizarre punishments characterized the era. In Thüringia in 1470, for example, the oldest relative of a murdered man was commissioned to execute the convicted murderer; perhaps this was a distorted remnant of the blood revenge. In some German cities the youngest husband in the area was given a macabre honeymoon gift: the right to carry out executions. The influence of Canon Law, however, led to modification of some of these practices. Ecclesiastical courts assumed the administration of justice in all cases involving a breach of Church rules. While the ecclesiastical courts abstained from the most cruel punishments (*ecclesia non sitit sanguinem*), they reflected many of the sanguinary practices of the age.[12]

Every part of the human body was subjected to punishment. Whatever was left after mutilation of the body was destroyed by branding, stocks, pillory, or other sundry humbling or corporal measures. However, improved criminal codes began to appear after the second half of the fifteenth century, the harbingers of the

Constitutio Criminalis Carolina created by the Imperial Diet of Regensburg in 1532. This code authorized six methods of execution: burning, beheading, quartering, hanging, drowning, and burying alive. Its procedural provisions represented an effort to provide security in place of legal arbitrariness. Many of its hesitant definitions, however, prompted alternative interpretations, including those of Benedict Carpzov (1595–1666), a judge of the Leipzig witchcraft trials who sentenced 20,000 persons to death while taking pride in the fact that he had read the Bible in its entirety fifty-three times.[13]

Mitigation of Revenge

The Enlightenment reduced some of the horrors of earlier periods. As so often happens in history, minor incidents have enormous consequences, and a seemingly minor judicial error on March 9, 1762, was of central importance in mitigating the rather savage system of criminal justice. Jean Calas, a sixty-two-year-old Huguenot merchant, was accused of murdering his son, who, the prosecution claimed, had converted to the Catholic faith. In fact, the young Calas had committed suicide. Although Jean Calas repeatedly protested his innocence during two hours of legally sanctioned torture, the court sentenced him to death. He was broken on the wheel, and his family was arrested and his property confiscated by the state. When Voltaire, the most versatile philosopher of the eighteenth century, learned of this judicial murder he and his friends challenged the government, as they had in other cases, and sought a reversal of the conviction and Calas' postmortem rehabilitation. Voltaire's success in this and similar cases (Le Barre, Lally, Sirven, etc.) gave great impetus to his fight against the judicial practices of the *ancien régime*. When in 1777 the Swiss Economic Society in Bern offered a prize for the best essay on a new criminal code, Voltaire doubled the honorarium from his private funds and ⌐

contestants as a guide.

This was the age of Gaetano Filan

quieu" and eminent advocate of cri

Sonnenfels, the Austrian proponent of r

man professors Claproth and Quistorp, en

corporal punishment; the unswerving pris

gentleman, John Howard; and Jeremy Ben

ciples of morals and legislation. It was the a

the ancient understanding of responsibility.   ...d the

Encyclopedists prepared the ground for the ...er success of

Beccaria, who accomplished "the most effective work in the

reform of criminal jurisprudence."[14]

Beccaria, Bentham, and Romilly

Cesare Bonesana, Marchese de Beccaria (1738–1794), like many
progressives of his period, was raised by Jesuits, but was early
influenced by the works of Montesquieu, Hume, Bacon, Helvétius, and Rousseau.[15] A rather withdrawn person, he published
his *Essay on Crimes and Punishments* (*Trattato dei delitti e delle
pene*) anonymously, in Tuscany in 1764. The book met with total
success: "Almost at once, as if an exposed nerve had been
touched, all Europe was stirred to excitement."[16]

Beccaria proposed to reorient criminal law, then alien to the
concept of the natural rights of man, toward more humanistic
goals. His basic concern was with "usefulness"—the "necessary,"
the "just," and the "end" for which laws are instituted. In his
introductory remarks he maintains that divine and natural justice
are immutable but that the human, or political, justice is subject
to change.

To defend the accused against arbitrary administration of
justice, he proposed that judges in criminal cases should not have

interpret laws. Judges are not legislators, said
also attacked the obscurity of the laws which made
tation necessary. He opened new horizons in penal reform
offered critical propositions for a number of aspects of the
crime problem. Beccaria opposed torture and the death penalty.
Arguing for the minimal punishment necessary for the protection
of society, he stressed that the "true measure" of crime is "the
harm done to society." A believer in free will, he assumed that the
fear of strict but just punishment would restrain those who are
predisposed to crime.

Beccaria's expositions were aided by his great eloquence and
clarity in treating his subject. Although Fachineri and others
criticized him, they could not impede his success. Beccaria's work
was soon translated into many languages. Voltaire wrote a comment on his work; Catherine the Great offered him an office; the
Prince of Würtenberg addressed a document of gratitude to
him; the French courts referred to his book as if it were law
already in force. The greatest value of Beccaria's work, however,
was the foundation it laid for subsequent changes in criminal
legislation. Beccaria is regarded as the founder of the classical
school of criminology.

Jeremy Bentham proposed the law as a command and set the
basis and limit of the obedience to this command in its utility.[17]
As Harry Barnes and Negley Teeters put it, "He wrote exten-
sively on all aspects of criminal jurisprudence, penal administration, and many other types of social progress."[18] But, as Sir
Norwood East points out, "It is interesting to note that in the
index to the text of Bentham's volume on *The Theory of Legislation* reference is made to crime, offenses, and criminality, but
none to criminals or offenders."[19]

Since he believed law to be a command, Bentham saw punishment as a deterrent and preventive instrument. In his system of
hedonistic calculus he opposed "unnecessary" pain and suggested
that penal consequences should fit the crime. Bentham assumed

that man is guided by free will and can rationally consider divergent paths of behavior; Gilbert Geis thinks that "Bentham flirts continuously . . . with one of the most important tenets of criminological theory; namely, that criminal behavior is generally learned behavior."[20]

Bentham's contribution to penology was his conception of a prison called the "Panopticon" or "Inspection House."[21] He pictured a huge round glass-roofed building with cells on the outer edge where the prisoners could be easily seen and controlled from the center of the building. Bentham actually obtained a permit to build such a penitentiary in Tothill Fields and the plans were drawn up, but as Barnes and Teeters remarked, "Fortunately for penology, this monstrosity was never built."[22] The last-minute failure of the project was the fault of the government, and Bentham received compensation of £23,000. Some writers fail to understand Bentham and cannot see that "If we bear in mind the nature and importance of his work, its originality, its enormous extent, its many-sided character, its universal influence, its far-reaching practical results, and its potential virtues we are tempted to proclaim Bentham the greatest legal philosopher and reformer the world has ever seen."[23]

Sir Samuel Romilly (1757–1818), a Whig lawyer, met Bentham in Lord Shelburne's house and soon became the advocate of Bentham's reform plans in Parliament. Romilly persistently agitated for penal reform and was instrumental in securing many beneficial changes. To him crime was a social phenomenon, and he stressed the importance of improving living conditions, which he presciently suggested was an effective way to prevent crime.

From Caprice to Legality

By the era of mitigation and the appearance of men like Beccaria, Bentham, and Romilly, the capricious concept of responsibility had given way to a more regular and calculable understanding. The changing social and economic systems had prepared a fertile ground for the changing system of responsibilities.[24] It was commonly held in the eighteenth century that man possessed free will and that therefore he and no one or nothing else was responsible for his failure to obey legal proscriptions. The law represents the morality of the sovereign power; it alone defines responsibility. Without the command of law, no behavior can be regarded as crime (*nullum crimen sine lege*) and no pain or disadvantage can be inflicted as punishment. So long as human beings govern human beings, arbitrariness, prejudice, and bias cannot be fully abolished from judgment, but the glorious principles of the Enlightenment reduced them. Mysticism, magic, superstition, as well as their predecessor, the unruly revenge, were replaced by the stiff formalism and dogmatism of legality.

The eighteenth century developed the individualistic understanding of crime. Man had the right to pursue his own ends, and although he had to accept the value or moral system of his sovereign, he could nevertheless insist on acting independently and on having his individuality respected by all. Criminal justice enforced the ethical system of the lawmaking power, but within this system it accepted the challenge of individualism. Consequently, criminal acts became largely isolated from social problems. Justice started to operate based on a formalistic and rather bureaucratic legal thinking.

The lasting achievement of the individualistic criminal law is that it developed safeguards for the rights of the individual against the arbitrariness of the courts. But its statute books do not sufficiently take into account the variations in human interactions. It introduced abstraction as a dominating force, the rule of paper, and it made criminal justice merely the interpretative machinery of the printed law. The goddess Justitia too was probably impartial and knew the law very well, but her blindfold deprived her of the sight of complex interactions, group characteristics, and social problems.

Soon the question arose: Is the will really free? Is *only* the individual will responsible for nonconformity or resistance against the command? The search started for "causes" other than the will of man and for factors that contribute to the devious or deviant decision of the will. In the eighteenth-century individualistic orientation of criminal law the act was judged and the man made responsible. In the next scene in the historic drama of crime, the man is judged and the search is on for finding the responsible factor.

NOTES

1. Some instances of this history are well presented in the literature. See e.g., J. Makarewicz, *Einführung in die Philosophie des Strafrechts auf entwicklungsgeschichtlicher Grundlage* (Amsterdam, 1967) ; Edward Westermarck, *The Origin and Development of the Moral Ideas* (2nd ed., London, 1912).
2. Ferenc Mádl, *A deliktuális felelösség* (Budapest, 1964), p. 52.
3. Rudolph Jhering, *Geist des römischen Rechts* (Leipzig, 1873), I, 118.
4. Westermarck, *op. cit.*, p. 179.
5. Donald R. Taft, *Criminology* (3rd ed., New York, 1956), p. 357.
6. Harry Elmer Barnes and Negley K. Teeters, *New Horizons in Criminology* (New York, 1944), p. 401. See also Ephraim Emerton, *Introduction to the History of the Middle Ages* (Boston, 1888), pp. 87–90; Edwin H. Sutherland, *Principles of Criminology* (4th ed., Chicago, 1947), p. 345.
7. Stephen Schafer, *The Victim and His Criminal* (New York, 1968), p. 17 and *infra*.
8. Karl Binding, *Die Entstehung der öffentlichen Strafe in germanisch-deutschem Recht* (Leipzig, 1908), p. 32.
9. A. B. Schmidt, *Die Grundsätze über den Schadenersatz in den Volksrechten* (Leipzig, 1885), pp. 9–16; Binding, *op. cit.*, p. 34.

10. L. J. Hobhouse, G. C. Wheeler, and N. Ginsberg, *The Material Culture and Social Institutions of the Simpler Peoples* (London, 1915), pp. 86–119.

11. Wolfgang Starke, *Die Entschädigung des Verletzten nach deutschen Recht unter besonderer Berücksichtigung der Wiedergutmachung nach geltendem Strafrecht* (Freiburg, 1959), p. 1.

12. Rusztem Vámbéry, *Büntetöjog* (Budapest, 1913), I, 68 and *infra*; Pál Angyal, *A magyar büntetöjog tankönyve* (Budapest, 1920), I, 18 and *infra*.

13. Benedict Carpzov, *Practica nova imperialis saxonica rerum criminalium* (1635). "New edition" with "various observations" edited by Joannes Samuel Fridericus Böhmer in 1758, Frankfurt am Main.

14. Barnes and Teeters, *op. cit.*, p. 458.

15. See more about Beccaria in Elio Monachesi, "Cesare Beccaria," in Hermann Mannheim (ed.), *Pioneers in Criminology* (London, 1960), pp. 36–50; also the Introduction to an English edition of Beccaria's *On Crimes and Punishments*, Henry Paolucci (tr.) (New York, 1963), pp. ix–xxiii.

16. Paolucci, *op. cit.*, p. x.

17. See more about Bentham in Gilbert Geis, "Jeremy Bentham," in Mannheim, *op. cit.*, pp. 51–67.

18. Barnes and Teeters, *op. cit.*, p. 463.

19. Sir Norwood East, *Society and the Criminal* (Springfield, Ill., 1951), p. 98.

20. Geis, *op. cit.*, p. 57.

21. John Bowring (ed.), *The Works of Jeremy Bentham* (Edinburgh, 1843), IV, 37–248.

22. Barnes and Teeters, *op. cit.*, p. 484.

23. Coleman Phillipson, *Three Criminal Law Reformers: Beccaria, Bentham and Romilly* (New York, 1923), p. 234.

24. Georg Rusche and Otto Kirchheimer, *Punishment and the Social Structure* (New York, 1939).

V

Precursory Search
for Causes of Crime

Early Attempts to Find the Cause

Although traditionally the nineteenth-century work of Cesare Lombroso is regarded as the beginning of the scientific study of crime, the search for the causes of crime in fact started long before his anthropological study of offenders. Lombroso, as Joseph van Kan praised him, was "the great instigator of ideas in criminology,"[1] but he certainly was not the first "instigator."

When Homer in his *Iliad* depicted Thersites, a despicable and crude defamer, as one of the ugliest of the Greeks, or when Shakespeare in his *Tempest* portrayed Caliban, the Duke of Milan's brutal and deformed servant whose morality was as unpleasing as his appearance, they were merely following the monistic belief that draws a parallel between good and beautiful, and evil and ugly, a belief not uncommon to the present day. Perhaps the naïve adherents to this misbelief would have difficulty explaining how "Doctor" Mengele, one of the most merciless sadists of the Auschwitz concentration camp, was an impressively handsome man, and his no less cruel wife could have been a favorite contestant in any beauty pageant.

Man's exterior was not the only target of the early attempts to find the factors of crime. His "interior," first of all his mind, has been no less scrutinized and was related to crime even earlier than his physical appearance. While in our day many who do not agree with the social basis of crime attribute criminal behavior to mental disorders or psychic disturbances, until well into the nineteenth century the mentally unbalanced were treated as criminals. In medieval times mental disorders were attributed to demons, and the treatment for demoniacal possession was flogging, starving, burning alive, or beheading.[2] A sick mind was generally considered a result of a pact with evil forces, and so deviants and mentally disturbed people were regarded as heretics and witches. *The Witch Hammer, Malleus Maleficarum*, a manual prepared by Johann Sprenger and Heinrich Kraemer, inquisitors appointed by the Pope to German territories, stipulated the legal procedure for torturing and sentencing witches. The Inquisition was started by the Church of Rome, but Protestant churches in England and Germany soon embraced it. The victims of this style of making people responsible were innumerable. One French judge boasted that he had burned 800 women in his sixteen years on the bench; in Geneva 500 persons were burned in the year 1515; in Trèves some 7,000 people died within several years.[3]

Judging a person's qualities from his physical characteristics and pronouncing sentence on someone by estimating his mind were for a long time popular preoccupations in the search for the correct location of responsibility.

The Responsible Face and Skull

The idea of possible relationship between the shape of the human skull and the personality attracted the attention of many early thinkers, among them Aristotle, who was especially interested in the behavioral reflexes of the mind. Havelock Ellis mentions a Greek physiognomist who examined Socrates and found indications of a brutal personality and an inclination to be alcoholic.[4] Among the Roman physicians Galen placed great emphasis on the constitutional factors and their influence on behavior patterns. However, it was not until the eighteenth century that physiognomy, the study of facial features, and phrenology, the study of the external conformation of the cranium, developed as disciplines.

Perhaps J. Baptiste della Porte (1535–1615) was the founder of "human physiognomy,"[5] although his interest was not concentrated on the head. Thorsten Sellin once mentioned that della Porte may be considered the first criminologist.[6] Della Porte studied cadavers of criminals to determine relationship between body form and type of crime. For example, he recognized a thief by his small ears, bushy eyebrows, small nose, mobile eyes, sharp vision, open and large lips, and long and slender fingers. He did not hope to improve an evil man by moral suasion because he believed in the deterministic nature of man's biological makeup. In this thinking the constitution of man is responsible for leading him against the command of law.

The impact of physiognomy was made some 200 years later, when the Swiss theologian Johan Caspar Lavater (1741–1801) published his four-volume *Physiognomical Fragments*.[7] Lavater's conclusions regarding physical appearance and human conduct were based on the beard, eyes, chin, nose, and other "fragments" of the face, and they gained popular success. As George B. Vold noted, "The principal significance of physiognomy lies in the impetus it gave to the better organized and logically more impressive view that has come to be known as phrenology."[8]

The Austrian anatomist Franz Joseph Gall (1758–1828) called his study of the cranium "cranioscopy." He visited many prisons and lunatic asylums to investigate bumps and other irregularities on the skulls of the inmates. His first results were published in 1791, but his first major work on the anatomy and physiology of the brain and nervous system was published only after 1807, when he settled in Paris. After many years of struggle with his contemporaries who opposed his system, in 1825, three years before his death, he published the final version of his work in six volumes.[9]

It may be that much of Gall's impact is due to his student and one-time collaborator, Johann Gaspar Spurzheim (1776–1853), who, unlike Gall, was an easy writer and a self-confident and dynamic personality. Spurzheim, an impressive lecturer, was largely instrumental in spreading the phrenological doctrines to English and American audiences. Indeed, he died in the course of an American lecture tour.

Gall and Spurzheim's phrenology, as described by Arthur Fink,[10] was based on three propositions: the exterior of the skull conforms to the shape of the brain; the so-called mind (or brain) consists of several faculties or functions; and these faculties are related to specific areas of the brain and skull and therefore bumps on the skull are indicators of the "organs" of special faculties. "Organ" is one of Gall's favorite terms; he called his school of thought "organology." Gall found twenty-seven faculties or functions of the brain, and Spurzheim extended this list to thirty-five. Amativeness, combativeness, secretiveness, and acquisitiveness were some of the faculties that were thought to predispose to criminal conduct.

Phrenology, particularly in the second half of the nineteenth century, was taken very seriously. The reports of the Eastern Penitentiary in Philadelphia from 1855 to 1865 all contained phrenological profiles of the inmates.[11] For example, the "predominant passion" of "destructiveness" referred to the "prevalent vices" of intemperance, revenge, and anger and corresponded to the offenses of arson, attempt to poison, and manslaughter.

Gall's research prompted a considerable number of similar studies. The study of the typography of the skull and face became attractive. H. Lauvergne (1797–1859), the prison doctor of Toulon penitentiary, found that convicts often had "peculiar faces," which suggested to him brutality and "intractable instincts."[12] The physiologist N. Carus observed frequent anomalies in the cranial formation of delinquents.[13] The leading American proponent of phrenology was Charles Caldwell (1772–1853), who strongly supported Gall and Spurzheim's ideas and published the first American textbook of this discipline.[14] Caldwell thought the "will" might control the phrenological faculties. A propensity to destructiveness may result in murder; combativeness; assault; amativeness, rape, or other sex crimes; acquisitiveness, theft, or robbery; and secretiveness, treason, or fraud. Caldwell did not accept without reservation the importance of phrenological faculties in structuring human behavior; perhaps he was thinking of something similar to Walter C. Reckless' "containment,"[15] what we ordinarily call socialization. A human being living under the right social conditions could develop higher sentiments and intelligence which might inhibit the biological propensity to crime.[16] Caldwell's orientation thus differed from that of Gall and Spurzheim; he was less deterministic.

How phrenological phenomena could be responsible for violation of the changing law is not well understood (except if the configuration of the cranium could change as the law changes). Phrenology, in its nineteenth-century meaning, was not substantiated; it has been rejected, and the modern experimental science of brain pathology has advanced far from the investigation of peculiar bumps and a mysterious "intellect."

The Responsible Mind

The mind may not have been made responsible for criminal behavior earlier than the face and skull, but certainly it presents a more vivid and undoubtedly tragic history. Ignorance, superstition, and demonology, in alliance with the cruelty of man, identified mental illness with crime. Only a few ventured the risk of fighting against this darkness.

Although the Swiss physician Hohenheim (better known as Paracelsus) (c. 1490–1541) believed in astral influences (in the word "lunatic," *luna* in Latin means moon), he fought against the belief that mental disturbance was caused by possession by the devil.[17] Johann Weyer (known as Joannus Wierus) (1515–1588), shocked by the imprisonment, torture, and execution of mentally ill people, in 1563 published a book on witchcraft and showed admirable courage in suggesting that not all who were burned for their alleged affair with Satan were mentally ill.[18] Reginald Scot (1538–1599) in his book *The Discovery of Witchcraft*, published in 1584, tried to unmask superstitious practices and abuses by denying the existence of demons. However, these isolated efforts were in vain, and it took another century or two before reason and observation gained ground and mental illness and crime were viewed as separate phenomena.

"The cycle of exposé, reform, and apathy which has characterized the treatment of the mentally ill in the United States for over a hundred years finds us still with hospitals that are more like prisons than hospitals."[19] It was less than 200 years ago that, against the advice of his colleagues and public authorities, the French doctor Philippe Pinel (1745–1840), in charge of La Bicêtre mental hospital, removed the chains from the inmates. His success encouraged him to introduce the same treatment in Salpêtrière Hospital, where Jean Esquirol (1772–1840) continued his fight against cruelty and ignorance. At this time an English Quaker, William Tuke (1732–1822), opened a country house (the York Retreat) for the treatment of mental patients. Recognition was dawning that, as Enrico Ferri said, "Insanity is like any other disease and requires the care of the physician and not the whip of the galley master."[20] In the United States Benjamin Rush (1745–1813), "the father of American psychiatry," introduced similar humane treatment of mental patients at Pennsylvania Hospital in Philadelphia. His example was followed by a Massachusetts schoolteacher, Dorothea Lynde Dix (1802–1887), who 120 years ago found thousands of mental patients "bound with galling chains" and "bowed beneath fetters and iron balls." Largely through her unflagging efforts many mentally ill were removed from prisons and transferred to new specialized institutions. This, perhaps, marked the end to an era in which, as Bernaldo de Quirós says, "The insane is sane for punishment."[21]

As a natural development following the bifurcation of mental illness and criminal conduct, the medical men of this era attempted to relate crime to insanity. Pinel and Esquirol "created" a mental disorder called "monomania," a type of abnormality that expresses itself in criminal behavior. "At the beginning and in the middle of the nineteenth century we find many physicians whose contribution to the legal and criminal psychiatry had decisive significance to the development of criminology."[22] James C. Pritchard (1786–1848) identified a "new" pathology, "moral insanity," with criminal symptoms and contended that this illness deprives the patient of his moral sense. Other "pre-criminologists," as Willem Adriaan Bonger would call them, were Morel, Despine, and Broca, who in 1859 established the Société d'Anthropologie de Paris, and the Englishman Henry Maudsley.

Benoit Augustin Morel (1809–1873) claimed degeneracy as the cause of crime. His study on "physical, intellectual, and moral degeneration of the human species" found that degeneracy was a kind of retrograde natural selection. He asserted that in his "morbid anthropology" (as he called his branch of pathology) degeneracy is a deviation from the primitive or normal type. Morel said that the "strange and unknown" types of people in prisons are not so strange and unknown to those who study the morbid varieties of the human species. Prosper Despine (1812–1892) called the abnormal manifestation of intellectual and moral faculties in the insane and in the criminal "natural psychology."[23] The absence of remorse in habitual criminals is a "moral anomaly," though not incurable. Paul Broca (1824–1880), using anthropometric measurements, generally followed Morel and Despine; by his "zoological method" he studied the "natural history of man."

Henry Maudsley (1835–1918), influenced by Morel's conception of degeneracy, originally accepted that both crime and madness were products of man's degenerate qualities. Later, however, he modified his views: "To say that there is a criminal nature which is degenerate is one thing, a true thing; but to go on to say that all criminals are degenerate and bear on them the stigmata of degeneracy is another and quite false thing."[24] Maudsley's learned and far-reaching mind invited many important problems to his analysis. While he never identified crime with mental illness, he brought them close to each other; there must be some intermediate zone "between crime and insanity, near one boundary of which we meet with something of madness but more of sin, and near the other boundary of which something of sin but more of madness." He took a stand for the responsibility of epileptics. He believed in hereditary factors, although he proposed to give them individual evaluation according to the individual case. He accepted the importance of psychological causes; "At moments Maudsley's acceptance of the criminal's motivation by forces of which he was not aware seems to anticipate the Freudian concept of the Unconscious."[25] He was not sentimental toward juvenile offenders. Perhaps his most celebrated work on the crime problem was his treatise *Responsibility in Mental Disease.*[26]

Responsibility through Numbers

In the nineteenth century the face, the skull, and the mind were the main targets of search for the causes of crime, but "Meanwhile, the science of statistics was being formed."[27]

The outstanding Belgian astronomer and mathematician Adolphe Quetelet (1796–1874) leads the distinguished pioneers of social statistics. Thorsten Sellin and Marvin Wolfgang refer to him as occupying a dominant role in the development of statistics as an analytical tool;[28] Karl Christiansen suggests that Quetelet might properly be considered a sociologist and the founder of criminology.[29] Indeed, his *Sur l'homme et le développement de ses facultés ou essai de physique sociale* may be regarded as one of the most important contributions in the development of the numerical analysis and sociological understanding of crime.[30] Quetelet first investigated French homicide cases in the period from 1826 to 1831. He submitted his first results to the Royal Academy in Brussels in 1828; the first version of his book was published in 1835, its extended and revised edition in 1869.

Quetelet noted some systematic patterns of criminality; crime "is a budget that has to be paid with a frightful regularity." "What a sad condition of the human species!" he cried.[31] Actually, in vague terms Quetelet was talking about some sort of crime prediction. He blamed society for crime with a heavy emphasis. The seeds of Robert K. Merton's anomic social structure, Cloward and Ohlin's differential opportunities, Reckless' vulnerability components, and many modern theories can be recognized in Quetelet's "inclination toward crime" (*penchant au crime*) as it develops under certain social conditions. Ernst Roesner found in Quetelet's work an awareness of our most important modern criminological issues.[32]

The earliest beginnings of comparative criminal statistics may be seen in André Michel Guerry's (1802–1866) attempt to compare the moral state of England with that of France.[33] Moreau de Jonnés compared Great Britain with Ireland.[34] The International Statistical Congress in Brussels in 1853, "stirred up by Quetelet,"[35] discussed the problem of comparing crime statistics from country to country.

The Baltic theologian and moral statistician Alexander von Oettingen (1827–1905) not only was concerned with measuring social ethics, but also paid careful attention to the methods of measuring.[36] Oettingen also struggled with the still unsolved question of statistically unknown crimes.

Quetelet, Guerry, de Jonnés, and Oettingen are perhaps the

leading names, but certainly not the only ones associated with observing the responsibility for crime through numbers. The beginning of the nineteenth century produced in England sporadic statistical observations of juvenile crimes, and France began the regular annual publication of judicial statistics. The Belgian Edouard Ducpétiaux (1804–1868) studied crime and poverty in the 1845–48 crisis in Flanders. The German Georg von Mayr (1841–1925) studied "crimes known to the police" in Bavaria, and for the period 1836–61 correlated the fluctuations of the price of rye with the changing rate of certain offenses.[37] The Englishman Joseph Fletcher made an attempt to relate crimes to the price of wheat for the period 1810–47.[38] The Hungarian Béla Földes also related crime to economic conditions.[39] L. Fuld, B. Weiss, W. Starke, and E. Tarnowsky, to mention just a few more examples, presented "crime through numbers" in a similar vein. In this century most statistical efforts have aimed at the triangle of morality, crime, and economic conditions.

Increased interest in the crime problem, more extensive studies of crime, and more comprehensive searches for the responsible factors were underway by the middle of the nineteenth century.

NOTES

1. Joseph Van Kan, *Les causes économiques de la criminalité* (Paris, 1903), p. 59; also cited in Marvin E. Wolfgang, "Cesare Lombroso," in Hermann Mannheim (ed.), *Pioneers in Criminology* (London, 1960), pp. 223–224.
2. James C. Coleman, *Abnormal Psychology and Modern Life* (3rd ed., Chicago, 1964), p. 25 and *infra*.
3. W. Bromberg, *The Mind of Man: The Story of Man's Conquest of Mental Illness* (New York, 1937), p. 61.
4. Havelock Ellis, *The Criminal* (2nd ed., New York, 1900), p. 27.
5. J. Baptiste della Porte, *The Human Physiognomy* (1586).
6. Information from Leonard Savitz.
7. Johan Caspar Lavater, *Physiognomical Fragments* (Zurich,

1775) ; see an appraisal of Lavater's work in Erik Nordenshiöld, *The History of Biology* (New York, 1928).

8. George B. Vold, *Theoretical Criminology* (New York, 1958), p. 45.

9. Franz Joseph Gall, *Sur les fonctions du cerveau* (Paris, 1825).

10. Arthur E. Fink, *The Causes of Crime: Biological Theories in the United States, 1800–1915* (Philadelphia, 1938), pp. 2–19.

11. Cf. Harry Elmer Barnes and Negley K. Teeters, *New Horizons in Criminology* (New York, 1944), p. 160; Vold, *op. cit.*, p. 48.

12. H. Lauvergne, *Les forcats considérés sous le rapport physique, morale et intellectuel observés au bagne de Toulon* (Paris, 1844) ; cf. Rusztem Vámbéry, *Büntetöjog* (Budapest, 1913) p. 3.

13. N. Carus, *Grundzüge einer neuen und wissenschaftlichen Kranioscopie* (Stuttgart, 1840) ; cf. C. Bernaldo de Quirós, *Modern Theories of Criminality*, Alfonso de Salvio (tr.) (New York, 1967), pp. 3–4.

14. Charles Caldwell, *Elements of Phrenology* (New York, 1824) ; cf. Fink, *op. cit.*, pp. 1–19; Vold, *op. cit.*, pp. 45–46.

15. Walter C. Reckless, *The Crime Problem* (4th ed., New York, 1967), pp. 469–483.

16. Fink, *op. cit.*, pp. 8–9.

17. G. Zilboorg and G. W. Henry, *A History of Medical Psychology* (New York, 1941).

18. A. Castiglioni, *Adventures of the Mind* (New York, 1946).

19. Thomas J. Scheff, Introduction to *Mental Illness and Social Processes*, Thomas J. Scheff (ed.) (New York, 1967), p. 15.

20. Enrico Ferri, *Criminal Sociology*, Joseph I. Kelly and John Lisle (trs.) (New York, 1967), p. 357.

21. De Quirós, *op. cit.*, p. 5.

22. Karl O. Christiansen, "Kriminologie (Grundlagen)" in Rudolf Sieverts (ed.), *Handwörterbuch der Kriminologie* (2nd ed., Berlin, 1968), II, 191.

23. Prosper Despine, *Psychologie naturelle, essai sur les facultés intellectuelles et morales dans leur état normal et dans leurs manifestations anormales chez les aliénés et chez les criminels* (Paris, 1868).

24. Peter Scott, "Henry Maudsley," in Mannheim, *op. cit.*, pp. 147–167.

25. *Ibid.*, p. 152.

26. Henry Maudsley, *Responsibility in Mental Disease* (London, 1874) ; some of his other works: *The Physiology of Mind* (London, 1867) ; *The Pathology of Mind* (London, 1867) ; *Body and Mind* (London, 1870) ; *Natural Causes and Supernatural Seemings* (London, 1886).

27. De Quirós, *op. cit.*, p. 9.

28. Thorsten Sellin and Marvin E. Wolfgang, *The Measurement of Delinquency* (New York, 1964), p. 9.

29. Christiansen, *op. cit.*, p. 191.

30. Adolphe Quetelet, *Sur l'homme et la développement de ses facultés ou essai de physique sociale* (Paris, 1835).

31. *Ibid.*, p. 7.

32. Ernst Roesner, "Kriminalstatistik," in Alexander Elster and Heinrich Lingemann (eds.), *Handwörterbuch der Kriminologie und der anderen strafrechtlichen Hilfswissenschaften* (Berlin, 1933), II, 29.

33. André Michel Guerry, *Essai sur la statistique morale* (Paris, 1833).

34. Moreau de Jonnés, *Statistique de la Grande Bretagne et de l'Irlande* (Paris, 1838).

35. Roesner, *op. cit.*, p. 51.

36. Alexander V. Oettingen, *Die Moralstatistik in ihrer Bedeutung für eine Sozialethik* (3rd ed., Erlangen, 1882) ; see an analysis of Oettingen's approach to statistical methodology in Roesner, *op. cit.*, p. 31; and Sellin and Wolfgang, *op. cit.*, pp. 9–10.

37. Georg von Mayr, *Statistik der gerichtlichen Polizei im Königreiche Bayern und in einigen anderen Ländern* (Munich, 1867).

38. Joseph Fletcher, "Moral and Educational Statistics of England and Wales," *Journal of the Statistical Society of London*, March 1855, pp. 74–79, cited by Vold, *op. cit.*, p. 166.

39. Béla Földes, *A bünügy statisztikája* (Budapest, 1889).

VI

The Responsibility of the Criminal

The "Holy Three of Criminology"

To draw lines across a time chart is a thankless venture, for it blurs the essential continuity of human affairs. Thus it may be misleading to postulate Lombroso's work as the birth of criminology; yet calling him "the father of modern criminology" seems correct, measured by his impact and his significance. Few today can fail to appreciate that Lombroso, together with Ferri and Garofalo, the "holy three of criminology," revolutionalized the way of looking at the criminal and excited the world toward the scientific study of crime. The works of these three Italians may well last as long as criminology itself; they will live because their themes and propositions are timeless.

Their emergence symbolized clearly that the era of faith was over and the scientific age had begun. Lombroso, Ferri, and Garofalo differed in the etiologies they proposed, but the "enthusiastic physician," the "extremist sociologist," and the "sober anthropologist," as they are sometimes (but not quite rightly) called, were "all in agreement that the problem was scientific treatment of the offender rather than a discussion of penalties."[1] All three agreed in shifting the orientation from the criminal act to the criminal man. Lombroso's "atavistic" criminals, Ferri's "penal substitutes," and Garofalo's "moral sentiments," and a number of their other ideas are often disdained by modern students of criminology (most of whom have not studied them in the original or in full); but the seeds sown a century ago by the "holy three of criminology" are discernible in many modern theories.

Cesare Lombroso

Cesare Lombroso (1835–1909) is rarely discussed in a neutral tone; he is either adulated or condemned. "In the history of criminology probably no name has been eulogized or attacked so much as [his]."[2] The son of Aron and Zefira Levi, having originally Charles as his first name, Lombroso spent his childhood in Verona, then under Austrian rule. He received medical degrees from the universities of Pavia and Genoa, but much of his interest in psychology developed while studying at the University of Vienna. He was appointed to a position in forensic medicine at the University of Turin, later became professor of psychiatry and, three years prior to his death, professor of criminal anthropology. The year 1880, as Marvin Wolfgang points out, was especially significant to Lombroso,[3] and to the development of criminology in general; for this was the year when he, Ferri, and Garofalo founded the *Archivio di Psichiatria e Antropologia criminale*. His two daughters married scholarly men (Gina married G. Ferrero, Paola married Mario Carrara); as Hans Kurella, Lombroso's friend and admirer remembered, they "brought fresh worlds of ideas into contact" with their father.[4] A few months before the end of his life, Northwestern University offered Lombroso the Harris Lecturership for the academic year 1909–1910, but his advanced age prevented him from making the trip to America. After a cardiac illness ended his life so abundant in accolades and attacks, in accordance with his will his body was given to the laboratory of legal medicine at the university and his brain to the Institute of Anatomy.

In his younger years Lombroso served as an army physician, and used this opportunity to measure the physical differences among some 3,000 soldiers, particularly the patterns of their tattooing. The results stimulated Lombroso to relate psychic attitudes to physical characteristics. He was interested in the relationship between genius and insanity[5] and between genius and degeneration. He started to write on pellagra, which, he observed, retarded the development of both mental and physical faculties. These and his studies on the lesions of the central nervous system, the cranium of criminals, and the anthropometry of convicts led him to publish his major book, *L'Uomo delinquente.*[6] Perhaps influenced by the works of Morel, Darwin, and Virchow, and maybe others, here he propounded his theory of atavism. The first edition of his book contained 252 pages; its fifth and final edition, published twenty years later, 1,903 pages. Not only modifications in his thoughts but thousands of new measurements made up the additional material. It is not known why the meritorious first edition received only little attention, but the second edition did gain enthusiastic reception, setting the beginning of an ever growing reputation.

His acquaintance with the famous brigand Vilella convinced Lombroso that he was moving in the right direction toward a general understanding of "the delinquent man." Vilella was a powerful, energetic, and active man who possessed "the traditional boastfulness of the dangerous or professional criminal."[7] When Vilella died, Lombroso performed a postmortem examination. Upon opening Vilella's skull, Lombroso found an unusual depression, which he named *median occipital fossa,* and another depression, which he correlated with overdevelopment of the *vermis,* both known in the lower primates. Lombroso discussed this experience in his opening address to the Sixth International

Criminal Anthropological Congress: he said the truth had become clear—the criminal was an atavistic being, born "out of time," who shows in his person the ferocious and savage instincts of primitive man and the lower animals.

Lombroso's general theory proposed that criminals can be distinguished from noncriminals by their physical manifestation of atavistic or degenerative physical anomalies. In his concept, atavism (from the Latin *atavus*, ancestor) means a reversion to a primitive or subhuman type of man, with physically displayed inferior morphological features. The criminal is a biological throwback to an earlier stage of human evolution (here Darwin's influence can be clearly seen) who, inevitably, cannot adjust to modern civilization. This absence of adjustment to social norms leads the atavistic man to clash with his society, actually to crime. Lombroso's criminal was a "born criminal" (although he never used this term—it was Ferri's expression).

From extensive measurements of thousands of prisoners, Lombroso compiled a number of physical characteristics or malformations ("stigmata") that make the criminal a recognizable type. He stressed, however, that these characteristics only reveal the criminal, they do not *make* him a lawbreaker. Among the stigmata Lombroso catalogued, a few examples are an asymmetrical face, prognathism, or excessive jaw, eye defects, unusually large ears, prominent cheekbones, peculiarities of the palate, receding forehead, scant beard, wooly hair, long arms, abnormal dentition, twisted nose, fleshy and swollen lips, and inversion of sex organs. In addition, he included abnormalties in hearing, smell, and taste, insensitivity to pain, lack of moral sense, cynicism, vanity, cruelty, idleness, passion for gambling, special argot, extensive tattooing, and other nonphysical characteristics.

Under a barrage of criticism from his opponents, Lombroso continually sought other pathologies that might explain crime in those cases where biological atavism did not seem applicable. He found the organism of moral imbeciles similar to that of criminals, and one of his earlier studies, on a young soldier, led him to include epilepsy in the causes of crime. In the last edition of *L'Uomo delinquente* he asserted that epilepsy and moral insanity could explain nonatavistic criminal behavior.

Lombroso did not forget the group of offenders "who do not seek the occasion for the crime but are almost drawn into it, or fall into the meshes of the code for very insignificant reasons."[8] These are those who escape the irresistible pressure of atavism and epilepsy, but are still criminals; in other words, "occasional" criminals. Lombroso divided the occasional criminal type into three subgroups: "pseudocriminals," who commit offenses that do not disturb the moral sense of the society (defense of the person, honor, or family might be examples for this type); "criminaloids," the largest group of the occasional criminals, who commit offenses under pressure of the environment; "habitual" criminals, the most normal criminals, without any inborn abnormal characteristics, who violate the law due to inadequate socialization. Not classed within the occasional criminals, and also outside the epileptic and atavistic causes, are criminals "by passion"; here Lombroso was referring primarily to political criminals.

In analyzing the female criminal,[9] Lombroso found prostitution an atavistic phenomenon and a manifestation of criminality. He was aware of the statistically low participation of women in crime; but, he contended, if prostitution were included in crime statistics, the two sexes would be equally criminal.

Lombroso's orientation was primarily psychiatric and anthropological; social factors were of little importance in his schemes. As Marvin Wolfgang points out, "The emphasis is on the biological, it is true, but it would be fallacious to deny Lombroso's recognition of environmental, precipitating factors that lie outside the individual and contribute to the etiology of crime."[10] Lombroso did not fail to recognize the changing nature of law or cultural relativity; also, in the earlier editions of *L'Uomo delin-*

quente he gave heed to the influence of poverty, the effect of food prices, alcoholism, emigration, and even criminal gangs and corruption of the police.[11]

Most of the bitter attacks against Lombroso centered on his research methodology, undoubtedly the weakest point of his armory. His failure to examine critically the sources of his data, his use of "laymen's hypotheses," the absence of adequate control groups, and his crude correlation of a myriad of factors with crime are only some of the charges leveled against his research methods. Perhaps Marvin Wolfgang answers all these accusations: "We are merely trying to show that he applied a scientific approach to his data; that he obviously possessed intellectual integrity in his pursuit of understanding; that many contemporary researches use data that have little more validity than his; and that with statistical tables similar to his, conclusions purporting wide applicability have appeared in present-day research."[12]

Many contemporary students of crime nonchalantly discard Lombroso's work, some are condescending toward him, and others charge him with actually retarding the development of criminology. Robert H. Gault conceded that Lombroso's theory was a bold conception, but "He is one of a relatively few, the results of whose life work have proved that the promotion of a great idea may be of greater value than the complete proof of its validity."[13] And Thorsten Sellin rightly said that "Whether Lombroso was right or wrong is perhaps in the last analysis not so important as the unquestionable fact that his ideas proved so challenging that they gave an unprecedented impetus to the study of the offender. Any scholar who succeeds in driving hundreds of fellow students to search for the truth, and whose ideas after half a century possess vitality, merits an honorable place in the history of thought."[14]

Enrico Ferri

Enrico Ferri (1856–1929), "one of the most colorful and influential figures in the history of criminology,"[15] a disciple of Lombroso, has overshadowed his *spiritus rector* in many respects.[16] He was a brilliant criminal lawyer, a persuasive orator, a member of the Italian parliament, the editor of the socialist newspaper *Avanti,* an impressive public lecturer and polemicist, a university professor, and a highly esteemed scholar. He was the leader of the so-called positive school of criminal sciences, which attempted to explain crime "in its reality" on a scientific basis.

Ferri came from a family of low income. He began his higher education at the University of Bologna and continued it at the University of Pisa, where he studied under, and argued with, the acknowledged master of the philosophy of criminal law, Francesco Carrara (1805–1888). At the age of twenty-one Ferri published a 476-page dissertation, *The Denial of Free Will and the Theory of Imputability,*[17] and sent a copy to Lombroso, who congratulated and encouraged him but did not find him "positivist enough." After additional study in France, where he devoted much of his time to statistical studies and learning German, Ferri went to the University of Turin, where Lombroso was; here he won a docentship in criminal procedure. A deep friendship developed between Ferri and the much older Lombroso; "While Ferri owed much of his system of ideas to the stimulation of Lombroso, he also became the catalyst who synthesized the latter's concepts with those of the sociologist and had no little influence on Lombroso's thinking."[18]

Soon after, Ferri was appointed professor at the University of Bologna, only three years after he received his degree. The twenty-five-year-old professor gave his first lecture on the "new horizons" of criminal law, the title of one of his later works.[19] His book on homicide and suicide[20] was published after he changed the title of his major work from *New Horizons* to *Criminal Sociology.*

After two years in Bologna, he moved to the University of Siena, and then, in 1890, to the University of Pisa to succeed Francesco Carrara. However, he held this chair for only three years; his joining the Socialist Labor Party caused him to lose his university position. It took him more than a decade to regain a university chair, although in the meantime he used his right of lecturing as *libero docente*.[21] In 1906 he was appointed professor of criminal law at the University of Rome.

After the Fascists came to power, Ferri was invited to prepare a criminal code for the politically new Italy. He wanted to use this opportunity to translate his positivist theories into living law, largely by eliminating moral responsibility (actually the crown of his theoretical framework) and promoting his socialist orientation. Thorsten Sellin wrote, "As for Fascism, he saw something of value in it, so far as criminal justice was concerned, because it represented to him a systematic reaffirmation of the authority of the state against the excesses of individualism, which he had always criticized."[22] Whether Ferri saw Fascism only as the state intervening against excessive individualism or whether he realized, and to some extent supported, the practices of a totalitarian rule is not quite clear; a biographer of Enrico Ferri can only hope that a brilliant thinker and supreme scholar, as he was, could not agree with any misuse of ideas that are honestly meant.

The "Ferri Project of 1921" was unacceptable to the Italian government for being far too radical for the Fascist yet Catholic Italy. The rejection of his draft did not alienate Ferri from the Mussolini regime. This, however, need not justify C. Bernaldo de Quirós' cruel assumption that Enrico Ferri "at the end of his life, old and infirmed he assented to Fascism."[23]

The core of Ferri's thought involved the abolishment of moral responsibility and the replacement of it with "social accountability."[24] Ferri explained that just as cells, tissues, and organs have no independent biological existence in a body, so man has no sociological existence except as a member of a larger society.

Without society there is no law, and without law men cannot live together. The state and society have the right of self-preservation and the "natural necessity" to defend themselves. The state is unable to refrain from punishing the criminal in the defense of law and society.

As there was a pressing "need of other means of social protection than punishment," he proposed *sostituiti penali,* "penal substitutes," measures equivalent to penalties.[25] Ferri did not believe in the traditional punishments—they were of very limited use in combating crime. In view of the danger to which society is exposed by criminals,[26] Ferri reserved his penal substitutes primarily to prevention. In his system there were also repressive means, or as he called them, "eliminative means," for some crimes. "In sociological medicine," he said, "the great classes of hygienic measures (preventive means), therapeutic remedies (reparative and repressive means), and surgical operations (eliminative means) form the arsenal which enables society to face the permanent necessity of its own preservation."[27] In other words, Ferri proposed the broadest possible correctional and penal system: from social reform and socialization, through reparative measures and repressive punishment, to the death penalty, "the last and most severe" intervention, "which is the perpetual elimination of the individual whose intellectual and moral premeditated wrongs absolutely and irremediably unfit him for social life."[28]

In his "program" of a criminal sociology[29] he contends that the positive school of criminology does not mean only the anthropological study of crime, but a "complete renovation" of the scientific method in the study of "criminal social pathology." Ferri asserted that anthropology had shown that the criminal was not a normal man; the criminal represented a special class of the human race with numerous hereditary or acquired organic and psychic abnormalities. He also claimed that statistics proved that the "appearance, increase, decrease, or disappearance" of crime was dependent upon factors other than punishments. And, as one of his fundamental thoughts, he asserted that positive psychology demonstrated that the "pretended free will" is purely a subjective illusion.

Although there can be little doubt about Ferri's emphatic support of radical social reforms, he did not believe that social causes are the sole causes of crime. Nor did he concur with Napoleone Colajanni and Emile Durkheim in their doubts about the significance of individual organic factors of deviance.[30] Ferri took a multiple-cause approach to the crime problem. He saw crime as a phenomenon of complex origin with roots in both biological and physiosocial forces: "Criminal sociology is inseparable from criminal biology."[31] It is a result of this orientation that he established the "natural classification" of criminals in five fundamental categories: the insane; born, habitual, and occasional offenders; and criminals by passion.

Ferri attached great importance to crime statistics.[32] In his view criminal statistics are to criminal sociology what histology is to biology. He argued for statistical research comparing fluctuations in the crime rate with legislative changes, the number of police agents, variations in punishments, proportion of acquittals, and other aspects of lawmaking. He warned against too much caution as well as carelessness in statistical investigations and pointed out the use and abuse of statistics. Criminal statistics were extremely important for observing what he called the "law of criminal saturation" and the "law of criminal super-saturation."[33] Ferri compared man's crime with chemical substances that react to certain conditions; in a given social environment with given individual and physical conditions a given number, "no more and no less," of crimes will be committed. This is Ferri's "law of criminal saturation," actually a prediction of the crime rate. By "criminal super-saturation" he meant the functional role of some special social factors, such as the famine of

1847 or the French *coup d'état* of 1851 (Ferri's examples), which add to the regularities of crime.

Besides his theoretical formulations, Ferri also made abundant recommendations for practical reforms.[34] He analyzed the machinery of criminal justice and maintained that an equilibrium of rights and duties between the individual and society, the judicial requirement of determining the guilt of the offender, and the continuity "from the judiciary police to sentence and execution" constituted "the three general principles of the positive school." The preparation of criminal cases (he called it "judicial police"), the accusation and defense, the jury and the judge, the intelligence, independence, and power of the judges were all submitted to his critical analysis.

Detection of criminals was also part of Enrico Ferri's catalogue of practical reforms, foremost the problem of applying anthropometric techniques to the proof of identity. Ferri seemed interested in the *portrait parlé* or, as Hans Gross named it, "the speaking likeness,"[35] popularly known as *Bertillonage*. Alphonse Bertillon, director of the Bureau of Identification and from 1889 of the world-famous French Service d'Identité Judiciaire, developed a method of anthropometrical measurement of the human body, "a clear and precise method of describing a person."[36] *Bertillonage*, also its modifications by Galton and Anfosso, and as proposed by Campagnome and Ottolenghi, attracted Ferri's attention. Ferri also recommended the application of another efficient instrument of police inquiry, the sphygmograph, an early type of lie detector, originally experimented by Lombroso and Benussi.

Close to the end of his life Ferri proudly admitted that he was an idealist, for "Life without an ideal is not worth living."[37] In the very last paragraph of his *Criminal Sociology*, he wrote:

Criminal sociology as well as criminal science will finally lose its importance, for it will dig its own grave, because through the scientific and positive diagnosis of the causes of criminality, and hence through the indication of partial and general individual and social remedies to combat it in an effective manner, it will reduce the number of delinquents to an irreducible minimum, where they can enter into the future organization as a daily modification of civilized society, and where the less penal justice there shall be, the more social justice will necessarily follow.

What is the use of arguing now about the validity or feasibility of Ferri's ideals? After all, for almost a century most of his proposals have remained only that.

Raffaele Garofalo

It is by no means an indication of the order of importance that Raffaele Garofalo (1852–1934) is mentioned as the third of the three leading exponents of the positive school of criminology. Enrico Ferri described Lombroso as the anthropologist of the "new movement in criminal science" and Garofalo as the one who was "studying and developing preferentially those inductions of the new school which were more peculiarly legal."[38] Francis A. Allen suggests that the essential direction of his work was the product of his distinguished professional career.[39] Garofalo was born of Italian nobility, but of Spanish origin.[40] After receiving his law degree, he became a magistrate, a senator in the parliament, and professor of criminal law at the University of Naples. After the turn of the century the Italian Minister of Justice invited him to draft a new code of criminal procedure, but it never became a law.

Although Garofalo's work does not encompass the colorful range of topics seen in the works of Ferri, he wrote on a variety of subjects: restitution to victims of crime,[41] the "socialist superstition,"[42] the international solidarity in the combat against crime,[43] and other legal subjects. His fame, however, rests

largely on his *Criminology*,[44] based on one of his earlier monographs, published when he was only twenty-eight years old.

Garofalo agreed with Lombroso and Ferri in their attack on the
classical school of criminal law and concurred with their deterministic understanding of crime. Unconditional denial of the
freedom of will and the idea of social defense against criminality
marked the foundation of the thought of all three. To them "The
criminal is not a free moral agent but is the product of his own
traits and his circumstances."[45] Cynically called "the sober
anthropologist," Garofalo was in fact the only genuine jurist
among the three theorists, and this is why his interest in "new
horizons" led him to the judicial aspects of positivist thought.

He bitterly complained against the "naturalists" who speak of
the criminal without telling us what they mean by crime. His
criticism would be pertinent even today when some modern
criminologists and sociologists study "criminal" or "delinquent"
behavior without ever defining what this means operationally.
However, a strictly legalistic definition of criminal behavior was
not satisfactory to Garofalo; in his concept of "natural crime" he
moved toward a "sociological notion" of criminal conduct. He
admitted that "natural crime" was unconventional behavior and
that it took place independent of normal circumstances.

Garofalo's concept of natural crime is based on the fundamental moral sentiments of pity and probity. By pity he meant a
reaction of irritation against those who cause others to suffer, and
by probity the necessary respect for other people's rights. Later
he polished his concept and added the condition of causing
"injury to the society." In his rather psychological approach he
saw pity and probity as a reflection of the average moral sense of
the community.

After Garofalo found inadequacies in Lombroso's theory, and
lack of precision and exactness in Ferri's classification, he developed his next major concept, the moral or psychic anomaly of

the criminal. Since his theory of crime is based on the moral sentiments of the society, his theory of the criminal describes the offender as lacking these moralities, thus possessing a psychic or moral freedom to commit crime. The psychic abnormality of the criminal is such a crucial part of Garofalo's positivist view of crime that he made acceptance of criminal psychology a condition of his joining the "revolution" of Lombroso and Ferri.

Francis A. Allen,[46] and before him C. Bernaldo de Quirós,[47] called attention to the similarity of Garofalo's natural crime to the *ius gentium*. Although the positivists generally rejected the notion of "natural morality," Garofalo was not far from it. De Quirós said, "The old principles of morality and justice undergo so many amputations that the decalogue is reduced to only two commandments: *thou shalt not kill* (pity) and *thou shalt not steal* (probity)."[48] As a man with considerable court experience, Garofalo recognized practical needs and the difficulties of criminal reform better than the other two members of the great trio; yet, in his concept of natural crime, his noble thinking collided with the necessary practical demands of law and order.

Garofalo's sense of practical reform expressed itself in his criminal typology and in his approach to punishment. He classified criminals into four categories: murderers, violent offenders, criminals deficient in probity, and lascivious criminals. The classification was aimed at what was practical under a penal system and provided for the most appropriate measures to be used against the violators.

These measures of repression were outlined in his *Criminology*, in the chapter "The Law of Adaptation."[49] The title of this chapter reflects the influence of Darwinian biological ideas on his thinking. As nature eliminates organisms that do not adapt to the conditions of their physical environment, so the criminal should be eliminated by the society to which he cannot adapt. Garofalo recommended three means of elimination: death for those who have a moral anomaly that permanently incapacitates them from effective social life; partial elimination, including long-term or life imprisonment or expulsion to penal colonies, for those who are fit only to live in nomadic hordes or primitive tribes; and enforced reparation for natural crimes by those who demonstrate absence of altruistic sentiments. In Garofalo's examples, egoistic murderers would fall in the first category; thieves, vagabonds, habitual criminals, and, in a "relative" way, youthful offenders in the second; and those who cause damage to the victim's property or reputation in the third. Garofalo suggested that his theory of punishments, justified by the idea of social defense, can meet the sentiment of the society.

George B. Vold concluded: "In the light of these ideas about the nature of the criminal and the course of action necessary for his ultimate control, it is not surprising to find that Garofaio managed to 'adapt' himself to the Mussolini regime in Italy."[50] In this respect, Raffaele Garofalo followed Ferri's path, and one wonders what path Lombroso might have taken had he lived longer. Undoubtedly, a positivist orientation to crime and criminals that favors a strongly universalist idea of social defense can find a comfortable place among the suprauniversalist ideas of a totalitarian system.

NOTES

1. Harry Elmer Barnes and Negley K. Teeters, *New Horizons in Criminology* (New York, 1944), p. 163.
2. For an excellent study of Lombroso's life and work see Marvin E. Wolfgang, "Cesare Lombroso," in Hermann Mannheim (ed.), *Pioneers in Criminology* (London, 1960), pp. 168–227; some of the data have been taken from this source.
3. *Ibid.*, p. 172.
4. Hans Kurella, *Cesare Lombroso, A Modern Man of Science*, M. Eden Paul (tr.) (New York, 1910), p. 81.
5. Cesare Lombroso, *Genio e follia* (Milan, 1864).
6. Cesare Lombroso, *L'Uomo delinquente* (Milan, 1876).

7. Barnes and Teeters, *op. cit.*, p. 162.

8. Cesare Lombroso, *Crime: Its Causes and Remedies*, Henry P. Horton (trs.) (Boston, 1912), p. 376.

9. Cesare Lombroso with G. Ferrero, *La donna delinquente, la prostituta e la donna normale* (Turin, 1893).

10. Wolfgang, *op. cit.*, p. 207.

11. Cited by Wolfgang, *op. cit.*, p. 208.

12. *Ibid.*, pp. 205–206.

13. Robert H. Gault, *Criminology* (New York, 1932), p. 81.

14. Thorsten Sellin, "The Lombrosian Myth in Criminology," *The American Journal of Sociology*, 42 (May 1937), pp. 898–899; cited also by Wolfgang, *op. cit.*, p. 224.

15. Thorsten Sellin, "Enrico Ferri," in Mannheim, *op. cit.*, p. 277.

16. Enrico Ferri, *Criminal Sociology*, Joseph I. Kelly and John Lisle (trs.) (New York, 1967).

17. *La negazione del libero arbitrio e la teorica dell' imputabilita*, cited by Sellin, *op. cit.*, p. 280.

18. Sellin, *op. cit.*, p. 286.

19. Enrico Ferri, *I nuovi orizzonti del diritto e della procedura penale* (Turin, 1881); the revised second edition published under the title *La sociologia criminale* (Turin, 1884); in its English edition see *op. cit.*

20. Enrico Ferri, *L'omicidio-suicidio* (Rome, 1884).

21. A postdoctoral degree securing lifetime right to lecture at the university where the degree is granted; not known in the American academic system. In German *Privatdozent*, in Hungarian *magántanár*, similar to the French *professeur agrégé*. In the European systems the ordinary professorship is based on an appointment of specific duration; the *libero docente* is an earned degree, and its duration is unlimited.

22. Sellin, *op. cit.*, p. 293.

23. C. Bernaldo de Quirós, "Enrico Ferri," in *Encyclopedia of the Social Sciences* (New York, 1931), VI, 188.

24. Ferri, *Criminal Sociology, op. cit.*, pp. 352–356.

25. *Ibid.*, pp. 242–277.

26. The Soviet criminal law concept of "social danger" is perhaps

not exactly what Ferri had in mind, but the basic idea is clearly the same.

27. Ferri, *Criminal Sociology, op. cit.,* p. 414–420.
28. *Ibid.,* p. 420.
29. *Ibid.,* pp. 36–39.
30. *Ibid.,* p. 123.
31. *Ibid.,* pp. 122–124.
32. *Ibid.,* p. 168 and *infra.*
33. *Ibid.,* pp. 209–241.
34. *Ibid.,* pp. 436–554.
35. Hans Gross, *Criminal Investigation,* adapted by John Adam and J. Collyer Adam from his *System der Kriminalistik* (5th ed. edited by Richard Leofric Jackson, London, 1962), pp. 180–181.
36. Harry Söderman and John J. O'Connell, *Modern Criminal Investigation* (5th ed., revised by Charles E. O'Hara, New York, 1962), pp. 69–71.
37. Cited by Sellin, *op. cit.,* p. 299.
38. Ferri, *Criminal Sociology, op. cit.,* p. 7.
39. Francis A. Allen, "Raffaele Garofalo," in Mannheim, *op. cit.,* pp. 254–276.
40. John Lewis Gillin, *Criminology and Penology* (New York, 1926), pp. 232–235.
41. Raffaele Garofalo, *Riparazione alle vittime del delitto* (Turin, 1887).
42. Raffaele Garofalo, *La superstition socialiste* (Paris, 1895).
43. Raffaele Garofalo, *De la solidarité des nations dans la lutte contre la criminalité* (Paris, 1909).
44. Raffaele Garofalo, *Criminology,* Robert Wyness Millar (tr.) (Boston, 1914).
45. Gillin, *op. cit.,* p. 232.
46. Allen, *op. cit.,* pp. 257–258.
47. C. Bernaldo de Quirós, *Modern Theories of Criminality* (repr. New York, 1967), pp. 29–30.
48. *Ibid.,* p. 30.
49. Garofalo, *Criminology, op. cit.,* Part II, Chap. 9.
50. George B. Vold, *Theoretical Criminology* (New York, 1958), p. 39.

VII

The Responsible Criminal Type

The Use of Criminal Typologies

Cesare Lombroso, Enrico Ferri, and Raffaele Garofalo at one time or another all summarized their theories in criminal typologies. They classified criminals not only to demonstrate the applicability of their theories to the variety of criminal behaviors, but also to open the way for appropriate measures to be taken against the different criminal classes. However, it would be mistaken to think that Lombroso, Ferri, and Garofalo invented criminal typologies.[1] The classification of criminals goes back many centuries; Enrico Ferri listed in his *Criminal Sociology* a good pageful of authors who had attempted to classify lawbreakers. Criminal typology may be considered the oldest theoretical approach to the problem of crime.

Perhaps the first typology worthy of attention appeared in 1840, when H. A. Frégier distinguished between professional thieves, occasional thieves (*voleurs d'occasion*), and thieves who stole out of necessity. Frégier, basing his typology on the memoirs of Eugène François Vidocq, a criminal turned police agent, classified criminals by the degree of violence they had used.[2] M. du Camp supplemented Frégier's classification by using criminal jargon as a distinction; he placed the *basse pègre* (nonviolent thieves) in one group and the *haute pègre* (killer thieves) in the other.[3] H. Lauvergne classified murderers and rapists by whether their act was due to impulse (*entraînement*), undeveloped will (*volonté arretée*), or innate brutal instincts.[4] H. Mayhew made a distinction between criminals of casual character and those who commit crimes as an expression of their way of life.[5]

Some nineteenth-century typologies, like those of the psychiatrist A. Krauss, would fit into the extravagant classifications of modern extremist typologists and others would refer us to the primitive considerations of ancient authors. Krauss proposed three main classes and divided each class into three subclasses: "energetic" criminals, subdivided into monsters, cholerics, and passionate criminals; "evil" criminals, the demoniacs, intriguers, and crooks; and "weakling" criminals, covering mean persons, sneaks, and revelers.[6] Similar fictional divisions can be traced back to the second century A.D., when Galen distinguished among choleric, phlegmatic, sanguine, and melancholic criminals.

In recent times a rather vivid renaissance of criminal and delinquent typologies can be witnessed. Anyone studying the recent criminological literature cannot avoid noting the extent to which emphasis has shifted to the study of variations among types of criminals and delinquents.[7] Edwin H. Sutherland was perhaps not the first in the post-World War II period to claim that efforts should be directed toward explaining particular criminal behaviors, and probably not the last to urge that "Conclusions from the studies of particular areas of criminal behaviors should lead to revisions of the generalizations regarding criminal behavior as a whole."[8] Donald R. Cressey proposed that the problem of crime should be tackled by working on the causation of specific crime types.[9] Donald R. Taft proposed, "The criminologist must have homogeneous types of behavior if he is to explain them consistently."[10] George B. Vold suggested, "The problem calling for clearer thinking in the future than has been given it in the past is the systematic and realistic delineation of kinds or types of criminality actually occurring that need to be comprehended."[11]

Karl F. Schuessler and Donald R. Cressey analyzed the techniques and results of tests administered over a number of years in order to find a distinct criminal personality. They suggest that personality tests may be useful as diagnostic instruments in penal institutions rather than as a technique of criminological research. Schuessler and Cressey complained, "Most studies proceeded as if the criminal population is homogeneous, since they grouped all types of offenders together" and that "future studies of this type should at least classify individuals by type of offense in order to determine whether differences between classes of offenders exist."[12] Gordon P. Waldo and Simon Dinitz, almost two decades later, still found that "Conflict over the role of personality in criminality has not been resolved" and that personality "cannot be dismissed readily, as it is by many sociologists, and its etiologic role cannot be assumed casually, as it is by many psychiatrists and psychologists."[13] But dissent has been the rule in criminal typology. Even among the three great positivists disagreement prevailed: Ferri could not accept Lombroso's classification, and Garofalo rejected Ferri's.

Certainly no typology can be perfect. Since human behavior cannot be labeled and filed in clearly individual categories, all typologies and classifications necessarily exhibit a more or less arbitrary and heuristic character. This can be seen even more if the proposed typology appears to be forced upon the general theory (if any) or if it is not backed by a general explanation of crime, in which case the typology, by being in a vacuum, is useless except as a point of departure for other typologists. This is why so many typologies seem to be only speculative guesswork or trivial impressions supported by superficial experiences.

Criminal typology cannot be an independent venture in the understanding of crime. Ideally a typology should be derived from a single plausible hypothesis or a general theory of crime (explainability); it should be the observation of general distinguishing forms common to large numbers of crimes and criminals, which can be used as a model to which they are referable (reality); and it should be pragmatic, permitting its application to systematic grouping of types of crimes and criminals so that penological or correctional treatment can be adopted accordingly (instrumentality). A criminal typology remains a meaningless speculation if it is not linked to a theoretical model and if it has no penal or correctional application. It is not only a "criminal profile of the masses," as Ernst Seelig put it,[14] but is also a guide to correction. Modern trends lean toward "the construction of types" that "may lead to theoretical formulation."[15] To early criminologists the refinements of the statistical tour de force were not known; their theories followed their observations. They developed typologies only after they thought they understood the concept of crime, and their classifications served as a sort of test of their thinking.

Of the legions of typologies a few examples might be arranged in the following groupings:

Legal typologies, which divide criminals into existing statutory categories and refer both to crimes and criminals.

Multiple-cause typologies, which group criminals by several biological and social factors, and refer to criminals only.

Sociological typologies, which classify criminals by societal factors and refer to criminals only.

Psychological typologies, which suggest divisions of criminals along psychic or psychiatric lines and refer to criminals only.

Constitutional typologies, which classify offenders by biopsychological functions and refer to criminals only.

Normative typologies, which divide criminals according to their proclivity for a particular group of legally defined crimes and refer both to crimes and criminals.

Life-trend typologies, which deal with the overall life styles of criminals and refer both to crimes and criminals.

These are unavoidably overlapping categories, and the following examples only indicate the essential orientation of various criminal typologies in general terms.

Legal Typologies

Ever since criminal law has existed, crimes and criminals have been grouped by the "law" into different categories. Distinguishing the recidivists from the first offenders was a major step in the development of legal classes; criminals who had committed only one crime were punished more leniently than those who had committed more than one offense. The criminal codes of Saxony of 1855 and 1869, classifying criminals by motivation, ordered a somewhat uniform treatment of criminals whose crimes "developed from the same spring" and mentioned as examples crimes motivated by greediness or aimed at satisfying sexual desire.

Through the centuries the gradual evolution of criminal law and the acceptance of a few criminological ideas considerably increased the number of legal categories. Maurice Parmelee suggests that the simplest method of classifying crimes is "by means of a category of acts."[16] Another method would be grouping according to procedural specialties or according to the severity of the penalty or the purpose of punishment.

Later there developed distinctions based on the gravity of crimes: felonies, misdemeanors, and, in legal systems where a trichotomy was introduced, contraventions. Maurice Parmelee writes that at first treason was the most serious felony.[17] Originally, felonies were the offenses that "could not be compounded because of their heinousness." They were punished by death and confiscation of the criminal's property. Under the common law, felonies were murder, manslaughter, and rape, and against property arson, burglary, theft, and robbery. In time the list of felonies increased. Misdemeanors, originally called transgressions or trespasses, were crimes of lesser severity. A trichotomous classification (in French, the *crimes, délits,* and *contraventions*) was adopted in the nineteenth century by most European criminal codes, for example, in Belgium in 1867, in Germany in 1870, in Hungary in 1878.

Functional legal classifications distinguish crimes according to their orientation or object. Thus, there are ordinary, public, or political crimes. There are crimes against life, corporeal security, sexual integrity, reputation, property, and others, depending upon prevailing legislation. Briefly, there are crimes against the person and crimes against property, and public crimes and political crimes.

The English *Criminal Statistics*, which catalogues no fewer than 195 crime types, differentiates indictable from unindictable offenses. The indictable offenses are subdivided into offenses against the person, offenses against property with violence, offences against property without violence, malicious injuries to property, forgery and offenses against the currency, and "other" offenses.[18]

In the American criminal statistics, the *Uniform Crime Reports*, the "Classification of Offenses" lists twenty-nine crime types:[19]

Criminal homicide	Forgery and counterfeiting
Forcible rape	Fraud
Robbery	Embezzlement
Aggravated assault	Stolen property: buying, receiving, possessing
Burglary, breaking and entering	
Larceny, theft	Vandalism
Auto theft	Weapons: carrying, possessing, etc.
Other assaults	
Arson	Prostitution and commercial-

ized vice
Sex offenses
Narcotic drug laws
Gambling
Offenses against the family
   and children
Driving under the influence
Liquor laws

Drunkenness
Disorderly conduct
Vagrancy
All other offenses
Suspicion
Curfew and loitering laws
   (juveniles)
Runaway (juveniles)

Since criminological ideas penetrated the sphere of criminal law, special classes have developed in the legal typologies, such as the juvenile delinquent, the habitual criminal, the persistent offender, and the psychotic and psychopathic criminal. Some legal systems treat persistent offenders separately. Some give special consideration to abnormal criminals; others deal with this class only within the question of accountability. Depending on the given legislation, the lower age limit of juvenile delinquents may be fourteen years, twelve years, eight years, or none. "The distinction even within one state is often vague."[20] Legal typologies most often are only national or local classifications without any pretense of universal validity; they are technical divisions for the use of the administration of justice and are not conceived of as explanations of criminal behavior.

Raffaele Garofalo, faithful to his general juristic orientation, made efforts to develop a line that would follow the positivist thinking yet fit into his legalistic considerations.[21] He proposed four types of criminals: murderers, violent criminals, criminals without probity, and sexually perverted criminals.

He viewed murderers as "typical" criminals, that is, they lack altruism, are egoistic, and show no sentiment for justice or pity. This "typical" criminal is capable of any criminal act; he may kill, steal, or rid himself of his wife to facilitate his next marriage. Garofalo's violent criminals are of two types: the passionate and those who commit "endemic crimes," such as vendettas in Naples or political assassination of Russian nihilists. By passionate criminals Garofalo meant those fired by alcohol or extraordinary circumstances. Criminals lacking in probity engage in crimes against property. Sexually perverted criminals are cynical, lascivious criminals who commit crimes against sexual integrity or chastity.

Maurice Parmelee based his classification of criminal types on his criticism of Lombroso, Ferri, Garofalo, Havelock Ellis, and Gustav Aschaffenburg.[22] He distinguished among the feebleminded criminal, the psychopath, the professional criminal, the occasional criminal (both accidental and passionate), and the evolutive or political criminal.

Although Parmelee contended that his divisions are based on psychology, the changes in the political and economic organization of the society, and the differences in human nature, essentially they follow legal categories. His feeble-minded criminals are the "born criminals"; the psychopaths are psychotic. The professionals are largely habitual criminals. Occasional criminals include a variety of offenders, among them those who are led to crime by peculiar circumstances (accidental criminals), the nonpsychopathic passionates, and those of excitable temperament. In discussing the evolutive and political crimes,[23] Parmelee followed Enrico Ferri's[24] and J. Maxwell's[25] ideas, which contrast the involutive antisocial crimes with the evolutive social crimes.

Havelock Ellis proposed the following typology: political criminals, criminals by passion, insane criminals, instinctive criminals, occasional criminals, habitual criminals, and professional criminals.

Ellis found that the instinctive criminals are "born criminals." He regarded the habitual criminals as "usually unintelligent" persons in whom the habit dominates; his professional criminals are "usually intelligent" and guided by rational motives.[26]

A more recent classification was presented by Alfred R. Lindesmith and H. Warren Dunham.[27] They developed three basic types: the individualized criminal, the social criminal, and the habitual-situational criminal.

The individualized criminal's action stems from his basic personality. At the other end of the continuum is the social criminal, who directs his crimes against society. The continuum from the individualized to the social criminal that Lindesmith and Dunham endeavored to devise is actually only a sophisticated distribution of the values defended and classified by criminal law and refers to two highly overlapping categories.[28] The habitual-situational criminal is one who has frequent contacts with the authorities, without really being a "full-time" professional criminal—in other words, it is simply a procedural type. Also, it may be noted that, after all, every crime is an act against society even if the harm is suffered only by an individual victim. Ferri, Maxwell, and Parmelee are only examples of the many thinkers who have convincingly proved that an understanding of the individualistic, universalistic, and suprauniversalistic systems quickly clarifies this point.

More specifically legal is the typology of Nicholas Atlas, who follows the distinctions of criminal law rather expressly and bases his types on the object of the crime.[29] He listed the following five groups:

Specific crimes, that is, crimes against the regulatory functions of the state, such as treason, crimes against the safety of the sovereign, bribery and corruption, disorderly conduct, dueling, crimes against the taxes, riots, and others.

Crimes against personal reputation (libel).

Crimes against bodily security, such as assaults, homicide, rape, robbery, kidnaping, lynching, and maiming.

Crimes against property, such as burglary, forgery, fraud, larceny, coercion and extortion, and malicious mischief.

Crimes against religion and morality, such as abduction, abortion, adultery, prostitution, and incest.

Multiple-Cause Typologies

The multiple-factor approach to the crime problem attempts to reconcile biological, psychological, and sociological views. Rejecting the theory that endogenous factors are the only causes of crime, the multiple-cause typologies attempt to type criminals by using all possible factors.

Perhaps the best example of the heroic effort of reconciling the biological and sociological aspects of crime is to be found in the work of Franz von Liszt (1851–1919), who devoted so much of his life to the search for a comprehensive criminal typology and was his own courageous critic.[30] In his strenuous struggle to reach a compromise between divergent trends in criminology, he originally conceived of crime as a purely social phenomenon. Later, however, he became interested in the personality of the criminal. As early as 1882 he expressed his self-imposed responsibility for merging criminal somatology with criminal psychology and criminal sociology into a single comprehensive study of crime. A *gesamte Strafrechtswissenschaft* ("global science of criminal law") was his ultimate objective.

His first typology developed the following eight classes:

Cases in which the criminal's consciousness of having injured other people's rights is completely missing or at least obscure; here the psychic root of crime can be found in the criminal's recklessness, negligence, ignorance, or excessive eagerness to act.

Cases in which the criminal's attachment to another person by affection, devotion, love, or sympathy leads him to commit a crime in the interest of this person.

Cases in which the instinct of self-preservation leads to crime, such as crimes in emergency, crimes of economic necessity, crimes due to fear of punishment, shame, or other disadvantage.

Cases in which the crime is one of sexual concupiscence.

Cases in which crimes are committed in passion, such as grief due to real or imagined indignity, insulted personal reputation, refused love, thirst for revenge, hatred, jealousy, anger, or envy.

Cases in which crimes are motivated by a desire for glory.

Cases in which crimes are committed by "conviction," including all political crimes.

Cases in which crimes are motivated by gain or greed; here a subclass is listed referring to "businesslike" (professional) crimes motivated by an excessive desire for pleasures or by a dislike of work.

Although most of his contemporaries held his typologies in respect, Liszt himself formulated the most energetic judgment against them. In time he came to believe that many of the characteristics he listed were not of central importance. Recklessness or the deepest sympathy might be expressed without crime; despair and passion are not always connected with crime; sexual concupiscence, "conviction," desire of glory, or greed for gain may also lead to useful public acts. On the other hand, even the noblest character may commit crime. Liszt struggled to find a better typology; he made efforts toward finding a standard for measuring and defining the characteristics of crimes and criminals from the point of view of law and order. He reduced his types to the following two groups: instantaneous, or acute, criminals (*Augenblicksverbrecher*), and condition (state), or chronic, criminals (*Zustandverbrecher*).

The "instantaneous" criminals are those whose criminality is sporadic; crime is only an episode in their lives. In Liszt's typology these are the "criminals of the moment." In the "condition" criminal, violation of law is the expression of his penchant for crime.

But even this did not satisfy Liszt. He divided the *Zustandver-brecher* into the corrigible and the incorrigible. Liszt's great merit lies in his strong proposition of a "dualistic system," as he called it, the proposition of the multiple causation of crime. However, his typological efforts never fully covered his ideas.

Multiple causation was the motif of Gustav Aschaffenburg's (1866–1944) criminal typology.[31] He distinguished seven classes: criminals by chance, criminals by affection, criminals by occasion, criminals by consideration, recidivist criminals, habitual criminals, and professional criminals.

Aschaffenburg's "elective system," as Karl Birnbaum called it,[32] seems to be one more mixture of biological and sociological aspects. Liszt and Aschaffenburg were certainly not the only adherents of the multiple-factor understanding of crime, but perhaps they represent the classic attempts to devise a classification of crimes and criminals to reconcile all the angles from which the characteristics are viewed.

An example of the more recent multiple-cause typologies is the "two-candidate typologies" of Don C. Gibbons.[33] Aware that any meaningful criminal typology must have treatment implications, he presented a "typology of treatment forms" as part of his classification of criminals and delinquents. His types are called "role careers" within the definitional dimensions of offense behavior, interactional setting, self-image, and attitudes. Gibbons' "life-trend" patterns include situational aspects, psychic characteristics, psychiatric elements, and even legal definitions.

Gibbons' catalogue of types, which gives the impression of an exemplificatory list, distinguished the following nine juvenile classes: predatory gang delinquent, conflict gang delinquent, casual gang delinquent, casual nongang delinquent, automobile thief "joyrider," heroin user, overly aggressive delinquent, female delinquent, and "behavior problem" delinquent.

Gibbons also classified adult criminals, and in much the same illustrative-exemplificative manner selected the following eighteen criminal types: professional thief, professional "heavy" criminal, semiprofessional property criminal, property offender, one-time loser, automobile thief, "joyrider," naïve check forger, white-collar criminal, professional "fringe" violator, embezzler, personal offender, "psychopathic" assaulter, violent sex offender, nonviolent sex offender, nonviolent rapist, statutory rapist, and heroin addict.

The multiple-cause typology of Marshall B. Clinard and Richard Quinney[34] is based on four characteristics: the criminal career of the offender; the extent to which the behavior has group support; the correspondence between criminal behavior and legitimate behavior patterns; and societal reaction. Clinard and Quinney list the following eight criminal types:

Violent personal criminals (murder, assault, and forcible rape).

Occasional property criminals (auto theft, shoplifting, check forgery, and vandalism).

Occupational criminals (embezzlement, fraudulent sale, price fixing, false advertising, fee splitting, black marketeering, prescription violation, and antitrust violation).

Political criminals (treason, sedition, espionage, sabotage, military draft violations, war collaboration, radicalism, and the various other forms of protest that may be defined as criminal).

Public order criminals (drunkenness, vagrancy, disorderly conduct, prostitution, homosexuality, traffic violation, and drug addiction).

Conventional criminals (robbery, larceny, burglary, and gang theft).

Organized criminals (racketeering, prostitution, gambling, and narcotics).

Professional criminals (confidence games, shoplifting, pick-pocketing, forgery, and counterfeiting).

Sociological Typologies

While the legal typologies classify the juridical profiles of crime or the procedural characteristics, most other classifications type the criminals themselves. Sociological typologies attempt to identify and distinguish social forces that produce criminals. "Pure" typologies do not exist; in a literal sense all typologies are essentially multiple-cause classifications. They are divided into groups only because a dominant theoretical orientation is recognized in the makeup of the typology or in other works of its author. The architects of the multiple-cause classifications are usually oriented either to nowhere or everywhere.

It would not be wholly erroneous to consider Enrico Ferri a criminal anthropologist or to associate him with the multiple-cause understanding of crime. But his emphasis on the dominant role of social forces in crime causation also justifies his distinguished membership in the group of criminal sociologists.[35] His "natural classification of criminals"[36] at first glance resembles Lombroso's typology. Ferri proposed the following five fundamental categories of criminals: insane criminals; born criminals; habitual criminals, or criminals by acquired habit; occasional criminals, or chance criminals; and criminals by passion.

One of the major differences between Lombroso's and Ferri's typologies is Ferri's distinction between the born criminal and the insane; "the really insane" is "only an exaggeration of the born criminal type." Ferri recognized criminals "who are neither completely sane nor insane" (called by him with a Lombrosian term, *mattoide*, or "semi-insane"), a category similar to those placed by Henry Maudsley in the "intermediate zone" and who today are the psychopaths. The "born criminals" to Ferri were those who had "special marks" that revealed them biologically.

Ferri described habitual criminals by calling attention to their criminal career. Their first crime was often committed at a tender age and almost always against property. This was due to their moral weakness rather than a result of innate tendencies. Ferri explained that this moral weakness is fortified by "the impulsion of circumstances and a corrupt environment which constitute a true center of criminal infection."[37]

Ferri's occasional criminals are the "chance" criminals, led to crime by temptation. While in the born criminal a "persistent distinctive force" is discharged, the chance criminal is urged to crime "by occasion alone." Ferri listed age, sexuality, poverty, weather, moral environment, alcoholism, personal circumstances, and imitation (as suggested by Tarde) as examples of stimulants that may lead to occasional crimes.

The passionate criminals (*delinquenti per impeto di passione*) form a distinct category of the occasional criminals. They are characterized by irresistible impulses, and commit crimes against the person. They commit crimes in their youth, especially in the case of women, under the impulse of uncontrolled passion, such as anger, jealousy, or shame. Ferri remarked that they do not hesitate "to avow their misdeed" and that their excessive repentance may lead to suicide.

Ferri refused to include political criminals in his criminal types; they are not really criminals but "pseudocriminals."[38] Parmelee seems to be correct in contending that Ferri's idea fits in with his theory of evolutive crime as contrasted with atavistic crime.[39]

The "French School," first of all Adolphe Prins[40] and A. Lacassagne, whose famous aphorism was "Societies have criminals whom they deserve,"[41] relied heavily on social factors in the etiology of crime. Their three groups were: instinctive criminals, who commit crimes because of an inherited or acquired penchant; action criminals, whose crimes are not part of any personal inclination; and insane criminals, who commit crimes because they are mentally ill.

The typology of J. Maxwell[42] is similar. He distinguished two main classes and five subgroups. His main categories are habitual criminals and occasional criminals. He divided habitual criminals into two subcategories: those with an innate penchant for crime and those with an acquired penchant. His occasional criminals were divided into three subcategories, according to physiological needs, such as poverty, hunger, and sexual drives; emotional needs, such as anger, hatred, and revenge; and psychosocial needs, such as reputation, religion, superstition, and political conviction.

In the more recent literature, Paul W. Tappan classified the property offenders but paid little attention to criminals against the person.[43] In his view the latter are an "amateur" group; their crimes are often the consequence of circumstantial factors or unusual pressures, such as outbursts of passion, aggression, or pathological distortions of the sexual impulse. Property offenders reflect a more diverse etiology. Tappan designed two major classes of property criminals, with two subclasses under each:

Simple criminals:
1. Circumstantial offenders, who are led to crime by unusual circumstances beyond their power to control; they may come from the "best" or from the "worst" of homes.
2. Amateur offenders, who engage in crimes with little skill or intelligence; they may be habitual or occasional criminals; they usually come from faulty home and community circumstances.

Professional criminals:
1. Solitary offenders, who work alone and have special skill; they may come from ostensibly favorable community circumstances but commonly have experienced conflicts and frustrating circumstances in home and neighborhood that led them to an aggressive and antisocial orientation.
2. Organized offenders, who represent the peak of criminal development; they are proficient, organized in outfits with strong codes designed for self-preservation, and

usually selected from the cream of the able amateurs or
from legitimate occupations.

Tappan touched upon the classification of juvenile delinquents
on a more "multiple-cause" basis. No wonder; in the twentieth
century two world wars and their aftermaths led typologists to
focus on delinquent types rather than on adult criminals. Strong
similarities can be found among their classifications;[44] many
propose ideas only already propounded, at least essentially, in the
nineteenth century.

Frederic M. Thrasher's pioneering gang typology should be
mentioned as offering some novelty in classification.[45] Based on
his study of 1,313 gangs in Chicago, he proposed the following
four types: the diffuse gang, a rudimentary form of youth grouping, with transient solidarity and loose leadership; the solidified
gang, a result of a longer development with a high degree of
loyalty and a minimum of internal friction; the conventionalized
gang, an "athletic club" type of grouping; and the criminal gang,
which usually drifts into habitual crime.

Thrasher's typology is primarily descriptive in nature; as
James F. Short, Jr., pointed out, he "did not talk about delinquent subcultures, but his material is relevant [to it]."[46]
Thrasher's classification does not offer real insight into causal
elements, except perhaps an ecological hint to the social environment of the slum.

When such concepts as "delinquent subcultures" are used,
society is clearly being charged with responsibility for crime.
These seem to be the modern, sophisticated counterparts of
Lacassagne's "bouillon for the culture of criminality"[47] or Baer's
"corrupt atmosphere" of a given social environment,[48] for they
all view delinquent conduct as an inevitable product of societal
forces operating in the culture.

Albert K. Cohen contends that there is the possibility of two or
more types of juvenile delinquents,[49] each the result of different

kinds of causation. He proposes three types: the predominantly subcultural delinquent, the predominantly psychogenic delinquent, and the mixed-type delinquent, in whom the "psychogenic and subcultural factors blend in a single causal process."

A similar typology by Richard A. Cloward and Lloyd E. Ohlin presents not one but three delinquent subcultures.[50] They distributed their delinquent types according to the differing opportunities found at different parts (environment) of the culture (subculture). Cloward and Ohlin recognized the following three classes:

The delinquent of the criminal subculture, who follows criminal role models in a social milieu that can be characterized by close bonds between juvenile and adult offenders and between criminal and conventional elements in the area.

The delinquent of the conflict subculture, who turns to violence in search of status under conditions in which severe limitations of both conventional and criminal opportunity intensify frustrations and discontent.

The delinquent of the retreatist subculture, who represents the problem of drug use.

The subcultural sociological typologies fare no better than the other sociological classifications in being unable to discard psychological or social-psychological aspects. Perhaps only adherents of the socialist understanding of crime think they have developed "purely" sociological typologies. Since their orientation is aimed at changing the entire structure of the society, no individual types could emerge—except as they reflect remnants of the "old" way of thinking. Even Willem Adriaan Bonger, whose theory on crime is indeed far from supporting the capitalist economic system, created a classification of crime that includes personal characteristics having no relevance to the economic system of the society.[51] Bonger accepted the fact of "enormous differences" between a professional thief and an intoxicated murderer or between a rapist and a political criminal. Thus, he proposed to treat crimes in four categories, according to the motives of the offender:

Economic crimes against property, such as embezzlement or theft, economic crimes against the person, and economic crimes against the state, such as counterfeiting.

Crimes for economic or noneconomic reasons, for example, murder aiming at robbery or for revenge.

Crimes with heterogeneous motives, such as vengeance or fear of shame, for example, assaults, infanticide, and perjury.

Political crimes.

Psychological Typologies

This group of typologies stresses the mental, emotional, and psychoanalytical characteristics of the offender. Among all classifications this orientation seems to have the strongest popular appeal; hypotheses are in abundance. However, psychological typologies are not free from emphatic opposition. As early as Hugo Hoegel serious doubts were raised concerning the possibility of grouping criminals solely on the basis of psychological characteristics.[52]

An early attempt at psychological classification was Eyvind Olrik's typology, which distinguished among criminals on the basis of their will power.[53] Ottokar Tesar, who studied the psychological types of criminals in their historical concept, regarded the psychological "symptoms" as the most important classificatory factor.[54] M. Kaufmann, unable to avoid the contamination of sociological features, offered the following three types: "vagabond" criminals, for petty crimes; "energetic" criminals, for violent crimes; and "intermediate" criminals, for occasional crimes.[55]

Ferenc Finkey made considerable efforts to find a purely psychological typology, but sociological elements kept invading his thinking.[56] He distinguished among the following five groups:

Occasional or "momentary" criminals, whose crime is originated in "bad luck."

Criminals of dubious character, who are inclined to do evil.

Professional or persistent criminals, whose crime is the result of their innate or inherited inclination, their cynical character, or their antisocial tendencies.

Criminals with limited mental capacity.

Juvenile delinquents.

Finkey later expanded his list to ten:

Juvenile delinquents, whose mental processes are not fully developed.

Mentally abnormal criminals, whose crime originates in their mental illness.

"Tough" or passionate criminals, who are the most dangerous type of all criminals because they lack any human sentiment and are gratuitously cruel. (They represent the type called by Nietzsche the "perfect" criminal.)

Persistent criminals, who lack moral education and commit crimes habitually.

Swindler criminals, who cleverly commit crimes for profit.

Violent criminals, who commit crimes habitually, or at least frequently, but in any case with violence.

Emotional and fanatical criminals, including political offenders.

Criminals with antisocial tendencies, who commit crimes only occasionally.

Criminals with vaguely antisocial tendencies, whose crime is the product of the moment.

Occasional criminals, whose crimes might be excused on ethical or social grounds.

Erich Wulffen also proposed strong psychological considerations.[57] By relating criminals to crime groups he preceded certain modern formulations by half a century. However, Wulffen perhaps went too far; he subdivided criminality so minutely that his typology ultimately arrived much too close to the concepts of a legal classification. The type of the thief, the burglar, the sexual offender, the murderer, the embezzler, most of them analyzed individually, are only examples of the great variety of his classes.

A strongly expressed psychological approach is shown by Karl Birnbaum's "criminal-psychopathological" typology.[58] He contended that psychopathological investigation is not only the correct approach to criminal behavior but the only way to develop the "broadest and safest" criminal typology. He proposed two main classes, "individual" and "specific" types, with the former being divided into five subdivisions and the latter into two. His criminal-pathological typology presents the following classification:

Individual types:

1. The general organic dementias, including the arteriosclerotics and preseniles, also senile dements, congenital syphilitic types, paralitics, and postencephalitics, all with characteristics that appear in the general decline of mental conditions.

2. The schizophrenics, including the passive-asocial and active criminal personalities, the schizophrenic habitual and schizoid criminals, with characteristics that appear in their unmotivated activities.

3. The paranoics, including the degenerated and mass criminals, with characteristics that appear in their emotional delusions.

4. The epileptics, including the passive-asocial and aggressive-brutish personalities, the degenerative and traumatic

epileptics, with characteristics that appear in their tendency to social decline.

5. The alcoholics, including the episodic alcoholics, the dipsomaniacs, socially defectives, intoxicated persons, with characteristics that appear in the decline in their family, professional, and economic position.

Specific types:

1. The born feeble-minded personalities, including imbeciles and apathetic-asocials, with characteristics that appear in their retarded personality development.
2. The psychopaths, including fanatics, grumblers, sexual psychopaths, hysterics, depressives, with characteristics that appear in their different psychic conditions.

As seen from its medical nomenclature, Birnbaum's criminal typology is aimed at viewing the criminals from the angle of mental health or psychiatric diagnosis. He saw criminal behavior as a deviation from mental health; psychiatry should be functional here, rather than psychology.

More psychological was the typology of Hans W. Gruhle.[59] He distinguished five main psychological classes: criminals by inclination, criminals by weakness, criminals by passion, criminals by conviction, and criminals by necessity.

Gruhle's criminals by inclination are characterized by their antisocial way of life. They fail to accept the law and order and continually attempt to violate the law, usually with violence. According to his psychic structure, the "inclined" criminal might be an "active" (a professional criminal who earns his living by crime) or a "passive" type (who commits crimes only if he estimates the risk acceptable and worthwhile).

The criminals by weakness are not regarded by Gruhle as antisocial personalities. This type, Gruhle said, wants to avoid crime and is "happy" if there is no "need" to violate the law; but he is an "amorphous and unstable" personality: social tendencies are absent from him. The actual situation determines or motivates the behavior of this type. Some of them are mentally retarded or alcoholics. Mainly vagabonds and prostitutes belong to this group.

The criminals by passion, or "affective criminals," are dominated by their emotion, be it vindictiveness, love, irritability, jealousy, or despair.

The criminals by conviction, or "reputation," are convinced that "crime is their duty."[60] Assassins, fanatics, schizophrenics, and hysterics can be listed in this group.

The criminals of necessity, Gruhle said, in fact do not exist. As he tried to explain, a crime can never be committed only and exclusively because of need; need is only a situation that may open the way to the activation of criminal characteristics. Although Gruhle seems here to avoid acceptance of societal forces, he suggested that it is reasonable to set up this group as a separate type since criminals from the other groups may react to "necessity" in a criminal fashion. In other words, this type actually consists of all other criminal types and is meant to be a miscellaneous category.

Nor could Raymond Corsini avoid all sociological elements in his basically psychological criminal typology.[61] He mentions seven classes:

The accidental criminal, such as the reckless driver, who commits crimes "without intending to do so."

The situational criminal, who "rationalizes the rightfulness of his behavior due to the peculiar structures and press of circumstances," like the man who steals a loaf of bread to escape starvation.[62]

The irresponsible criminal, such as a child or an idiot, who is not guilty of any crime.

The neurotic criminal, who commits crime because he has a

problem to be fought, although he "does not know what he is fighting, nor even that he is fighting."

The psychopathic criminal.

The mentally unbalanced criminal, whose acts can be characterized by some "senselessness or lack of psychological necessity for the crime," such as the violent sex offenders.

The professional criminal, who makes his living on crime, such as, according to Corsini's example, Robin Hood.

To catalogue all psychological typologies is close to impossible; as Josef Kohler said, "The psyche of the criminal is an inexhaustible study of criminologists."[63] This is particularly so since the Freudian students of psychology entered the field and began to apply the rich source of psychoanalytic speculations to the problems of crime, delinquency, and deviance.

As a Freudian typology, Franz Alexander and Hugo Staub's classification should be mentioned.[64] Alexander and Staub claimed that the significance of the question "Why?" was discovered for criminology by psychoanalysis, and they formulated their typology on this ground. They delimit three general classes of criminals: the neurotic criminal, whose stand against society is a result of "intrapsychic" conflicts between social and antisocial components of his personality, a conflict that can be traced back to childhood experiences and to circumstances of later life; the normal criminal, who has identified himself with criminal prototypes; and the pathological criminal, whose criminality is conditioned by some process of organic nature.

The three categories are, in Alexander and Staub's terminology, the "chronic" criminals, as contrasted with "acute" criminals, who are normal and become criminals "under certain specific conditions." At a later stage these "acute" criminals seem to be identified with "accidental" criminals, whom Alexander and Staub divided into two subgroups: criminals whose crime results from "mistakes" and situational criminals, whose crime results from exceptional circumstances.

Another example of the psychoanalytic approaches to criminal typology, again with some sociological overtones, is David Abrahamsen's classification of acute and chronic offenders.[65]

Acute offenders, or normal criminals, "who are not really criminals," comprise situational offenders, whose antisocial feelings are provoked by particular circumstances, for example, the hungry man who passes a bakery shop and steals a loaf of bread; associational offenders, whose immediate environment mobilizes their criminal tendencies; and accidental offenders, who are "people involved in criminal acts by chance or mistake."

Abrahamsen's chronic offenders are motivated by factors other than the social circumstances; they include neurotic offenders, who commit crimes as a result of their neurotic condition—kleptomania, pyromania, dipsomania, nymphomania, dromomania, homocidal mania, and gambling are examples; offenders with neurotic character disorders and psychopathic offenders, such as the rapist, the murderer, the pathological liar and swindler, the Don Juan, the drug addict, the alcoholic, and the homosexual; psychotic and mentally defective offenders, who can be characterized by their mental illness which drives them to crime.

As these examples show, even if strictly Freudian thinking directs the construction of a criminal typology, sociological considerations necessarily emerge in the explanation of one or another type.

Constitutional Typologies

This group of typologies has in its background the hypothesis that views the criminal as a biopsychological phenomenon. The human organism and the physique of the offender are the focus of this approach.

The idea of morphological types is not a new one. As early as 1826 Léon Rostand suggested four such types: the muscular, the respiratory, the cerebral, and the digestive types, and since that time several attempts have been made in this field.[66] Perhaps Cesare Lombroso's typology should be mentioned first, although his classification may appear more biological than purely constitutional. Lombroso seemed to make a distinction between internally and externally developed types.[67]

Lombroso contended there were three endogenous (internally developed) types: the born criminal, whose criminal activities are genuine and cannot be suppressed by any external factor; the passionate criminal, who acts without deliberation and commits his crimes under the influence of his vacillating emotions (the political criminal is a special subgroup of this type); and the insane criminal, who engages in crime as a result of his mental illness.

He also proposed two exogenous (externally developed) types: the professional or habitual criminal, who acts criminally under the influence of societal factors; and the occasional or pseudo-criminal ("criminaloid"), who may have a touch of degeneracy and a weak resistance that prevent him from adhering to the law. In Lombroso's thinking, the criminaloids occupy the middle ground between the born criminal and the honest man but nevertheless represent a variety of the born criminals.

The first major constitutional typology appeared in the twentieth century, in the work of Ernst Kretschmer.[68] Following Emil Kraepelin's basic distinction between the two general mental types,[69] Kretschmer based his "body types" on medical aspects of the personality and, against the Lombrosian approach (or, perhaps, by adding to it), concluded from the entire complex structure of the human being. Despite the truth in George Vold's remark that "The concept of constitutional inferiority carries with it the special methodological pitfall that the clinical observer is likely to be prepared in advance to find the symptoms he has in mind in the offenders under observation,"[70] Kretschmer's typology gained considerable success and popularity.

Kretschmer classified the constitutional personalities into two main groups: the cycloids (the basic type of the circular insane) and the schizoids (the basic type of the schizophrenic insane). And to these he added two subdivisions: the epileptoids and the hysterics.

According to Kretschmer all these types are present in the general population, since the psychotic types are only exaggerations of healthy types. Kretschmer also distinguished the cyclothyme and schizothyme temperaments, both marked in terms of "physique and character" (the title of his book).

His cyclothyme type had a personality characterized by a lack of sophistication, informality, spontaneity, wavering of mood between gaiety and sorrow. From a physical point of view, this is the pyknic type, with a plump, rotund figure, generally soft, with little muscle, medium or short in height. Among poets these are the realists and humorists, among scholars the descriptives and empirics, among leaders the organizers and conciliators. Socially they are kindhearted, tractable, and sociable, though prone to be trivial, negligent, talkative, and sometimes rash. If criminals, they commit less serious and intellectual crimes.

Kretschmer's schizothyme type is characterized by strong reactions, hypersensitivity or strongly insensitive and apathetic responses, waywardness, and tenacity. Physically they can be asthenics or leptosomes (thin, narrowly built, lean, flat), or athletics (wide, muscular, tall, strong). Among poets these are the romantic sentimentalists, among scholars the logical systematizers and metaphysicists, among leaders the idealists and fanatics. Socially they lack involvement and tend to be introspective and egoistic. If criminals, they dominate in serious offenses, often with violence.

Kretschmer's subdivisions, the epileptoids and hysterics, cannot be clearly defined by their physical characteristics. These displastics, or mixed body types, are psychically depressed and display a tendency to explosiveness. Their criminality is rooted in their emotions and passions; if criminals, they usually commit crimes with violence. Since their sexual development is often functionally irregular, sexual crimes are not alien to them.

A series of attempts to distinguish human beings according to their biopsychological constitution has followed Kretschmer's efforts. Eduard Spranger categorized the theoretical, economical, aesthetic, religious, and social types as the "idealistic life forms."[71] Richard Müller-Freinfels recognized two constitutional types: one who lives an intellectual life (man of sensibility, man of deed, man of fantasy, man of abstraction) and one who lives an emotional life (man of sympathy, man of aggression, erotic man).[72] W. Jaensch, who proposed the B-type and T-type, built his typology on observation of juveniles and based it on the physical characteristics of two illnesses: Basedow's disease (exophthalmic goiter) and tetany. This was elaborated further by E. Jaensch into the integrated and disintegrated man.[73] Carl Jung's extrovert and introvert personality types[74] are well known in psychology and are sporadically used in studies on crime.

William H. Sheldon, probably influenced by Ernest Hooton's somatic-biological orientation, came very close to Kretschmer's thinking and developed three types of "biological delinquents":[75]

The endomorphic, with predominantly developed vegetative function, and with the characteristics of love of comfort and eating, slow action, sociability, and calm behavior.

The mesomorphic, with well developed muscles, and with the characteristics of aggression, active actions, and direct fighting behavior.

The ectomorphic, with the characteristics of introverted behavior, privacy, self-restraint, insomnia, and cool attitude toward others.

Neither Kretschmer's and Sheldon's constitutional typologies nor the other biopsychological classifications have achieved appreciable acceptance in criminology. As George Vold pointed out, "There is no present evidence at all of physical type, as such, having any consistent relation to legal and sociologically defined crime."[76]

Normative Typologies

This orientation attempts to classify criminals within a particular circle of legally defined criminal offenses according to their penchant for crime. The target of these typologies, which appear to be a mixture of legal, sociological, psychological, and constitutional considerations, is to find the normative type of criminal, in other words, to build up a system whereby the penal consequences—the actualization of responsibility—depend upon the offender's "normatively interwoven type of personality." Criminal responsibility would be decided by the deviation of his personality (and not his actions) from the command. The question whether a murderer type, a thief type, a forger type, a rapist type, or any other type of criminal does or does not exist is a constantly recurring difficulty in criminology. In normative typology recidivism, childhood experiences, pathological state of mind, body type, or any other causative factor does not influence the division of types; only the criminal's phenomenally recognized total personality is considered.

While typological classifications are generally designed for prevention or reform purposes, normative typology is designed to assign the right responsibility to the right person—that is, it is designed for sentencing purposes. For example, according to this typology capital punishment would not necessarily be inflicted on a person who actually committed a murder, but rather on an individual who, in view of his total personality, would be categorized as a murderer type, regardless of whether or not he committed a homicide. The question of guilt and responsibility hinges on the puzzle whether the person who committed a criminal offense really and correctly belongs to the hypothetical criminal type.

The origin of this typological trend is in the overly strong emphasis given to the substitution of *Tatstrafrecht* (criminal law as it relates to crime) with the *Täterstrafrecht* (criminal law as it involves the criminal). In the *Tatstrafrecht* "To establish murder or treason contains no sentence of the personality of the individual offender, and no judgment on the question as to what extent the man matches with the act."[77] Punishment is justified not because of the individual guilt, but because of the offender's "criminal being." This is why the adherents of normative criminal typologies propose atonement for "being a criminal" in addition to the traditional reprisal for the given crime and the general combat against criminality; what they propound is the extension of the traditional "double-tracked" criminology (*Zweispurigkeit*) to "treble-tracked" criminal law (*Dreispurigkeit*).

This concept contended that the *Volksanschauung* (public view) cannot be satisfied with a single "symptom" (the criminal offense) because the offender is not always what the particular crime appears to make him. From this viewpoint a single symptom (the crime alone) should not determine the direction, scope, and weight of responsibility. This typology postulates the different criminal types not only on the basis of their general criminal character, but also on the basis of their being criminals within a legally defined type—hence its name, "normative" criminal typology.

Perhaps Eric Wolf may be regarded as the pioneer of this approach.[78] He claimed that the days of "political liberalism and religious naturalism" were over and therefore "ethically indifferent positivistic individualism" should be replaced by "phenomenological personalism." Later Wolf placed his normative typology in the framework of contemporary political thought, emphasized the totalitarian idea of crime, and suggested that the

Volksanschauung operates, first of all, in cases of "disobedience and resistance" against the "national socialistic state."[79]

A further development in normative typology is shown in the work of Georg Dahm,[80] whom Hans von Hentig called the leader of the Nazi school of criminal law.[81] Dahm underlined his typology with totalitarian notions. He felt criminal personality is associated not only with crime and its legal norm but is also in opposition to the political regime; the offender has a "double criminal personal element."[82] As Dahm suggested, crime and criminal cannot be in antithesis; they represent a single type, because they are joined in an internal and "insoluble" unity. The role of *Volksanschauung* in company with legal notions, constitutional factors, and psychological elements indicates the comprehensive nature of this typological effort.

Life-Trend Typologies

Typing criminals according to their pattern of general behavior or life style is not a recent innovation. W. E. Wahlberg early made a distinction between habitual criminals (*Gewohnheitsverbrecher*) and occasional criminals (*Gelegenheitsverbrecher*), based on the criminals' way of life.[83] G. Moreau classified criminals as to whether they were professionals (whose crime was their "occupation"), habituals (whose crime reflected their "repetitive habit"), or occasional criminals (whose crime was a "casual" act under the pressure of unusual circumstances).[84]

The orientation of the "life trend" typologies seems to be similar to that of the multiple-cause classifications; however, they are in fact different, because of their deeper roots. Whereas multiple-cause typologies are based on biological, psychological, and sociological *causes* of crime, the life-trend classifications relate to the functional role of the criminal and to the positive or negative harmony of his biosociological way of life. As Ernst

Seelig put it, all components should be in a "dynamic structural coherence," without which the portrait of the criminal, as a type, may remain incomplete.[85]

This approach was attempted by Edmund Mezger in his theory of *Lebensführungsschuld* ("responsibility for life conduct"), first propounded in his paper on "crime as a whole."[86] He proposed that if the prevention of crime means penal or correctional intervention, attention must be directed to the criminal and not to the crime. Mezger believed in the existence of a criminal character, but he asserted the changing nature of this character.

Changes in character can and should be effected by the criminal himself; even if his character is crime oriented, he can do something about it. If he has chosen to do nothing to counteract his crime-oriented character, he is guilty. He himself developed his criminal character or has allowed this character to act out by his reluctance to subdue it *"His Being-so is by his own fault a Became-Being-so" (sein So-Sein ein durch eigene Schuld So-Geworden-Sein ist)*. However, Mezger conceded that if some characteristics are beyond the control of the individual, he is not to be blamed for his crime.

Thus, Mezger pays little heed to societal circumstances, and, in general, demands that the criminal himself make efforts to alter his character: the criminal's life trend is a product of his own rather than the product of society. Mezger did not utilize his *Lebensführungsschuld* hypothesis for designing a classification of criminals, but contended that this can be done by using the variety of life patterns.

Ernst Seelig based his typology on "distinctive forms of life."[87] His participation in the circle of the criminal-biological society was not without being strongly influenced by Adolph Lenz' biological viewpoint; this is why in his life-trend types the biopsychological "dispositions" of the criminal found a role to play. In this vein, Seelig argued for the following nine types:

Criminals who live on crime, whose antisocial way of life is thus seen outwardly. Examples of this type are the professional criminal, the swindler, the vagabond, the thief, and the prostitute.

Criminals who generally follow a socially approved way of life: they are often diligent workers, yet they commit crimes again and again, mainly against property. To this type belong the servant, the headwaiter, the dishonest well-bred lady who drives dangerously, the postman, and the shop assistant, all found by Seelig as having "low resistance."

Aggressive law violators with a habitual passion for assaults, such as the bully, the cut-throat, the alcoholic, and many types of murderers.

Sex criminals, including some homosexuals.

Crisis criminals, who find crime as the only solution to their conflict situations. Seelig explained that subjective features have to be considered in understanding the crisis; family conflicts and love affairs are his examples.

Emotional criminals, but, according to Seelig, only in a restricted sense. Not all criminals belong to this type, who commit crimes in moments of excitement; only those whose highly uncurbed emotion has biological roots belong here. A crime committed in a "blind rage" is an example.

Criminals with "primitive reactions," mostly imbeciles who cannot refrain from crime.

Criminals of conviction, who, in some extreme ideological thought construction, feel crime is their duty.

"Clinical-psychiatric" criminals, the mentally ill and the psychopathic. Seelig designed this type as a mixed group and classified within it the "etiological" criminals with clear exogenous or endogenous causes of crime. Here are listed the "prognostical" criminals, who are differentiated from reformables and difficults. Seelig also points here to the body-build typologies.

Life trend as a basis for a criminal typology has been used by a number of thinkers of the crime problem, including Walter C. Reckless,[88] who wrote, "The criteria of criminal careers have never been established"; therefore his "basic components" include motives, pattern of life, skills and techniques, and psychological factors.[89] Essentially, Reckless proposed the following main types:

Ordinary criminals, usually of lower-class origin, who become criminals because of neglect and unsatisfactory home life or bad associates. Reckless found them less aggressive than gangsters and racketeers.

Professional criminals, "clearly in the upper class of crime." Their crimes are directed toward economic gain; skill and accomplished technique are their important characteristics. The professional thief and the confidence man are examples.

Organized criminals, who conduct efficiently organized illegal activities. Reckless suggests that the pattern of organized crime is feudal in character. Gambling, bookmaking, and racketeering are mentioned as examples.

White-collar criminals, dishonest businessmen "who are in a position to determine the policies and activities of a business."

Ruth Shonle Cavan organized her entire text around five criminal types:[90]

Professional criminals, who are "completely incorporated into the criminal world." They are the "logical final product of the social situations that permit and encourage criminal non-conformity." They typically live solely by crime, have skill, and their lives are organized around criminality and membership in the criminal world. The professional criminal may have been a juvenile delinquent.

Organized criminals, who strive to monopolize economically

rewarding crime in a given area. They have standardized methods for the commission of crimes, organization of criminal personnel, and division of labor. Cavan proposed subdivisions of organized crime, such as the criminal gang, the criminal syndicate, the racket, and the corrupt political group.

Criminals who reside in the conventional world. These may be the casual offender, the occasional offender (whose crimes are not planned but are reactions to immediate problems), the episodic offender (who commits crimes under the stress of circumstances or temptation), and the segmented criminal (who is the Sutherlandian type of white-collar criminal).

Habitual offenders, whose crimes are in fact vices, "a debilitating habit that affects their own integrity and efficiency." These are the drunkards, drug addicts, sex offenders, gamblers, vagrants, and petty thieves.

Seriously maladjusted criminals, whose acts "cannot be attributed to motives that the normal person has experienced." Cavan named three subgroups within this type: the psychotics, the psychoneurotics, and the psychopaths.

Marshall B. Clinard attempted to group offenders along a continuum of noncareer and career types "with the criminally insane at one end and the professional criminal at the other."[91] Clinard first listed two noncareer criminal types, murderers and sex offenders, and contended that "very few persons have ever made a career" out of either. His career criminals have "a life organization built about criminal activities," which include identification and association with crime, self-conception as a criminal, and progression in seriousness of crime. Clinard mentions six career types:

Occasional property offenders, whose crimes are incidental to their normal life, and who usually commit occasional thefts of some kind.

Habitual petty offenders, one of the largest criminal groups, who engage in petty crimes, vagrancy, and disorderly conduct: they show relatively little sophistication and generally have long criminal records.

White-collar offenders, who commit crimes in the course of their business activities: businessmen, doctors, politicians, lawyers, and others who occupy high occupational status are mentioned.

Ordinary criminals, who early in life develop delinquent behavior patterns, involving primarily burglary, automobile theft, or robbery.

Organized criminals, who are members of crime syndicates or rings, including organized gambling and racketeering.

Professional offenders, who have the "most highly developed criminal careers."

Although one might disagree with Mezger's idea, which proposes to place the responsibility on the criminal and leaves little of it on the society, his *Lebensführungsschuld* concept—responsibility for life conduct—operationally covers the idea of socialization as the pivotal issue in charging responsibility for violation of the law. Based on the idea of socialization, the following life-trend typology may be proposed:

Occasional criminals, whose crime is referable to the trend of their life as an episode only. They commit crimes usually under the pressure of need, emotion, or desire.

Professional criminals, whose crime is referable to the trend of their life as a professional manifestation. Their leading motive is profit. They include:

1. Individual professional criminals, whose crime is carried out alone or, if in company of others, in an unorganized manner.

2. Members of organized crime, whose crime is carried out in the organized company of others: gangsters, whose organized professional criminality is carried out with violence;

racketeers, whose organized professional criminality is carried out by extortion or coercion; and syndicate members, whose organized professional criminality is carried out in a business-like intellectual manner.

3. White-collar criminals, whose crimes may be carried out in either individual or organized form, by using their financial or social power.

4. Sundry professional criminals, whose professional criminality can be carried out both in individual and organized form and whose crime is specialized enough to be outside other professional criminal types, such as the confidence game and black marketeering.

Habitual criminals, whose crime is referable to the trend of their life as a habit, which develops in them the potentiality of crime.

1. Alcoholics, whose crime potentiality is generated by their chronic intake of alcohol.

2. Drug addicts, whose crime potentiality is generated by their addiction.

3. Vagrants, beggars, and other wanderers, whose crime potentiality is generated by the lack of any constructive force in their way of life.

4. Prostitutes, whose crime potentiality is generated by their constant contact with immorality.

Abnormal criminals, whose crime is referable to mental disturbance or mental illness.

1. Psychotics, whose abnormal criminal potential is generated by their mental illness.

2. Psychopaths, whose abnormal criminal potential is generated by their mental disturbance.

Convictional criminals, whose crime is referable to their conviction about a political, social, religious, or other altruistic communal idea.

All these types carry three subtypes: juvenile delinquents, aged criminals, and female offenders.

All these typologies, from the legal to the life-trend classifications, are only examples of the typological efforts of some theorists. Not all theorists in criminology translated their propositions into classifications. Most attempted to understand the criminal's response to the responsibility-charging law without categorizing these responses. The biological, psychobiological, psychic, ecological, social, and economic hazards of man's responsibility for his stand against the law has usually been theorized in general terms.

NOTES

1. It can be seen often that modern proponents of criminal typologies set the beginnings of typologies at the emergence of Cesare Lombroso, at least they do not mention earlier classifications. See, e.g., Don C. Gibbons, *Changing the Lawbreaker* (Englewood Cliffs, N.J, 1965), p. 27; and Marshall B. Clinard and Richard Quinney, *Criminal Behavior Systems: A Typology* (New York, 1967), pp. 6–7.

2. H. A. Frégier, *Des classes dangereuses de la population dans les grandes villes et des moyens de les rendre meilleures* (Paris, 1840).

3. M. du Camp, "Paris, ses organes, ses fonctions et sa vie," *Revue des Deux Mondes,* 1869.

4. H. Lauvergne, *Les forcats considérés sous le rapport physique, morale et intellectuel observés au bagne de Toulon* (Paris, 1844).

5. H. Mayhew and J. Binney, *The Criminal Prisons of London* (London, 1862).

6. A. Krauss, *Psychologie des Verbrechers* (Tübingen, 1884).

7. Gibbons, *op. cit.,* p. 24.

8. Edwin H. Sutherland, *Principles of Criminology* (4th ed., New York, 1947), pp. 66–67.

9. Donald R. Cressey, "Criminological Research and the Definition

of Crime," *American Journal of Sociology*, May 1951, pp. 546–551.

10. Donald R. Taft, *Criminology* (3rd ed., New York, 1956), p. 14.

11. George B. Vold, *Theoretical Criminology* (New York, 1958), p. 314.

12. Karl F. Schuessler and Donald R. Cressey, "Personality Characteristics of Criminals," *American Journal of Sociology*, March 1950, pp. 476–484.

13. Gordon P. Waldo and Simon Dinitz, "Personality Attributes of the Criminal: An Analysis of Research Studies, 1950–65," *Journal of Research in Crime and Delinquency*, July 1967, p. 202.

14. Ernst Seelig, "Die Gliederung der Verbrecher," in Ernst Seelig and Karl Weindler (eds.), *Die Typen der Kriminellen* (Berlin, 1949), p. 1.

15. Clinard and Quinney, *op. cit.*, p. 2.

16. Maurice Parmelee, *Criminology* (New York, 1918), pp. 264–265.

17. *Ibid.*, p. 265 and *infra*.

18. *Criminal Statistics, England and Wales*, 1965 (Home Office, HMSO Cmnd. 3037), London, 1966), pp. 186–199.

19. *Uniform Crime Reports*, 1966 (F.B.I., Washington, D.C.), pp. 54–56.

20. Sutherland, *op. cit.*, p. 20.

21. Raffaele Garofalo, *Criminologia* (Naples, 1885), Part II, Chap. 1.

22. Parmelee, *op. cit.*, pp. 197–206.

23. *Ibid.*, pp. 453–468.

24. Enrico Ferri, *Criminal Sociology*, Joseph I. Kelly and John Lisle (trs.) (New York, 1967), p. 335.

25. J. Maxwell, *Le criminel et la société* (Paris, 1909); *Le concept social du crime et son évolution* (Paris, 1914), p. 52.

26. Havelock Ellis, *The Criminal* (2nd ed., New York, 1900), Chap. 1.

27. Alfred R. Lindesmith and H. Warren Dunham, "Some Principles of Criminal Typology," *Social Forces*, 19 (March 1941), pp. 307–314.

28. Marshall B. Clinard and Richard Quinney see this typological approach differently; they suggest that this is a typology "based on social behavior systems." Cf. Clinard and Quinney, *op. cit.*, pp. 7–8.

29. Nicholas Atlas, "Criminal Law and Procedure," in Vernon C. Branham and Samuel B. Kutash (eds.), *Encyclopedia of Criminology* (New York, 1949), pp. 86–95.

30. Franz von Liszt, *Strafrechtliche Aufsätze und Vorträge* (Berlin, 1905); and others. His main work is the *Lehrbuch des deutschen Strafrechts* (Berlin, 1881, published in many editions, later edited by Eberhard Schmidt).

31. Gustav Aschaffenburg, *Das Verbrechen und seine Bekämpfung* (Heidelberg, 1903).

32. Karl Birnbaum, *Kriminalpsychopathologie und Psychobiologische Verbrecherkunde* (Berlin, 1931), p. 229.

33. Gibbons, *op. cit.*, pp. 74–128.

34. Clinard and Quinney, *op. cit.*, pp. 14–19.

35. Maurice Parmelee called him a "criminal sociologist"; see Parmelee, *op. cit.*, p. 190.

36. Ferri, *op. cit.*, pp. 125–167.

37. *Ibid.*, p. 145.

38. *Ibid.*, p. 163.

39. Parmelee, *op. cit.*, pp. 191–192.

40. Adolphe Prins, *Criminalité et répression* (Brussels, 1886); *La défense sociale et les transformations du droit pénal* (Brussels, 1910).

41. A. Lacassagne, "Marche de la criminalité en France de 1825 à 1880," *Revue scientifique*, May 28, 1881, pp. 674–684; *Précis de Médecine légal* (Paris, 1906); *Peine de mort et criminalité* (Paris, 1908).

42. Maxwell, *op. cit.*

43. Paul W. Tappan, *Crime, Justice and Correction* (New York, 1960), pp. 215–234; *Juvenile Delinquency* (New York, 1949), pp. 55–164.

44. See a summary in John W. Kinch, "Continuities in the Study of

Delinquent Types," *The Journal of Criminal Law, Criminology and Police Science,* 53 (September 1962), 323–328.

45. Frederick M. Thrasher, *The Gang,* with an Introduction by James F. Short, Jr. (Chicago, 1963), pp. 47–67.

46. *Ibid.,* p. xxxi.

47. Lacassagne, "Marche de la criminalité," *op. cit.,* pp. 166–167; also cited by Willem Adriaan Bonger, *Criminality and Economic Conditions,* Henry P. Horton (tr.) (New York, 1967), p. 148.

48. A. Baer, *Der Verbrecher in anthropologischer Beziehung* (Leipzig, 1893), pp. 410–411.

49. Albert K. Cohen, *Delinquent Boys: The Culture of the Gang* (New York, 1955), p. 17.

50. Richard A. Cloward and Lloyd E. Ohlin, *Delinquency and Opportunity: A Theory of Delinquent Gangs* (Glencoe, 1960), pp. 161–186.

51. Bonger, *op. cit.,* pp. 536–537.

52. Hugo Hoegel, *Die Einteilung der Verbrecher in Klassen* (Leipzig, 1908).

53. Eyvind Olrik, "Über die Einteilung der Verbrecher," *Zeitschrift für die gesamte Strafrechtswissenschaft,* XIV, 76; *Strafgesetzgebung der Gegenwart in rechtsvergleichender Darstellung* (Berlin, 1894).

54. Ottokar Tesar, *Die symptomatische Bedeutung des verbrecherischen Verhaltens: ein Betrag zur Wertungslehre im Strafrecht* (Berlin, 1904).

55. M. Kaufmann, *Die Psychologie des Verbrechers* (Vienna, 1912).

56. Ferenc Finkey, *A magyar büntetöjog tankönyve* (Budapest, 1914); *Adatok a büntettesek jellemcsoportjainak megállapításához* (Budapest, 1933).

57. Erich Wulffen, *Psychologie des Verbrechers* (Berlin, 1908); *Gauner- und Verbrecher-Typen* (Berlin, 1910); *Der Sexualverbrecher* (Berlin, 1911).

58. Birnbaum, *op. cit.*

59. Hans W. Gruhle, "Characterologie," in Alexander Elster and Heinrich Lingemann (eds.), *Handwörterbuch der Kriminologie* (Berlin and Leipzig, 1933), pp. 203–206; "Kriminalpsychol-

ogie," in Elster and Lingemann (eds.), *Handwörterbuch, op. cit.*, pp. 911–914.

60. See Stephen Schafer, "Juvenile Delinquents in 'Convictional' Crime," *International Annals of Criminology*, I (1962), 45–51.

61. Raymond Corsini, "Criminal Psychology, Criminal Types," in Branham and Kutash, *op. cit.*, pp. 110–114.

62. See Donald R. Cressey, *Other People's Money* (Glencoe, 1953).

63. Josef Kohler, *Verbrecher-Typen* (Berlin, 1903), p. 1.

64. Franz Alexander and Hugo Staub, *The Criminal, the Judge, and the Public*, Gregory Zilboorg (tr.) (Glencoe, 1956), pp. 29–46, 119–124.

65. David Abrahamsen, *The Psychology of Crime* (New York, 1960), pp. 123–150 and *infra*.

66. Cf. Olaf Kinberg, *Basic Problems of Criminology* (Copenhagen, 1935).

67. See Lombroso's works, particularly his *L'uomo delinquente* (Milan, 1876).

68. Ernst Kretschmer, *Physique and Character*, W. J. H. Sprott (tr.) (London, 1925).

69. Emil Kraepelin, *Psychiatrie* (Leipzig, 1883).

70. Vold, *op. cit.*, p. 66.

71. Eduard Spranger, *Lebensformen, Geisteswissenschaftliche Psychologie und Ethik der Persönlichkeit* (Berlin, 1914).

72. Richard Müller-Freinfels, *Philosophie der Individualität* (Berlin, 1921).

73. About the Jaenschian typologies see the comprehensive study of E. R. Jaensch, *Zur Eidetik und Integrationspsychologie* (Leipzig, 1941).

74. Carl G. Jung, *Modern Man in Search of a Soul* (New York, 1933); *Psychology and Religion* (New Haven, 1938); and other works.

75. William H. Sheldon, *Varieties of Delinquent Youth: An Introduction to Constitutional Psychiatry* (New York, 1949); *Atlas of Man* (New York, 1954).

76. Vold, *op. cit.*, p. 74.

77. Georg Dahm, *Der Tätertyp im Strafrecht* (Leipzig, 1940), p. 8.

78. Eric Wolf, *Vom Wesen des Täters* (Berlin, 1932).

79. Eric Wolf, "Richtiges Recht im nationalsozialistischen Staat," *Freiburger Universitätsreden*, Vol. 13 (1934).

80. Dahm, *op. cit.*; "Die Erneuerung der Ehrenstrafe," *Deutsche Juristenzeitung*, 1934.

81. Hans von Hentig, "Gustav Aschaffenburg," in Hermann Mannheim (ed.), *Pioneers in Criminology* (London, 1960), p. 330.

82. Paul Bockelman, *Studien zum Täterstrafrecht* (Berlin, 1940), II, 111.

83. W. E. Wahlberg, *Das Princip der Individualisirung* (Vienna, 1869).

84. G. Moreau, *Souvenirs de la Petite et de la Grande Roquette* (Paris, 1888).

85. Seelig, *op. cit.*, p. 6.

86. Edmund Mezger, "Die Straftat als Ganzes," more elaborated in his *Deutsches Strafrecht: Ein Grundriss* (Berlin, 1938), *Kriminalpolitik und ihre Kriminologischen Grundlagen* (3rd ed., Stuttgart, 1944), *Kriminologie, Ein Studienbuch* (Berlin, 1951).

87. Seelig, *op. cit.*; see also his "Das Typenproblem in der Kriminalbiologie," *Journal für Psychologie und Neurologie*, 1931.

88. Walter C. Reckless, *The Crime Problem* (4th ed., New York, 1967), pp. 279–373.

89. *Ibid.*, pp. 280–281.

90. Ruth Shone Cavan, *Criminology* (2nd ed., New York, 1957).

91. Marshall B. Clinard, *Sociology of Deviant Behavior* (rev. ed., New York, 1963), pp. 240–291.

VIII
The Biological Responsibility Models

The Age of Criminal Biology

Neither Enrico Ferri's convincing stand for a sociological criminology nor Raffaele Garofalo's logical plea for a juristic understanding of crime could divert attention from Cesare Lombroso's massive proposition for anthropological or biological models of crime causation. Lombroso's approach not only prompted bitter attacks against his theory, but also drew passionate admirers. The last quarter of the nineteenth century and the beginning of the twentieth may perhaps be called the age of criminal biology. True, this period saw considerable development in criminal sociology and similar nonbiological orientations, as criminal biology and criminal anthropology had developed during earlier periods, but the markedly individualistic philosophies of this time were peculiarly in tune with Lombrosian thought.

The basic doctrine of criminal biology holds that a criminal is in a biologically separate category from other human beings. The criminal is, partly or totally, an abnormal organism, and this determines or at least largely motivates his criminal behavior. Thus the criminal is a biological anomaly whose criminal conduct originates in his somatic or psychic abnormalities. As Ferri phrased it, the three fundamental assumptions of criminal anthropology are "(a) the relation between the physical and moral in man; (b) the genetic relation between organs and functions; (c) the relation between the brain, the intelligence, and morality."[1] Each criminal characteristic has an anatomical, physiological, psychological, or psychiatric basis. As Ferri suggested, the criminal anthropologist studies the criminal in anatomical or physiological laboratories. The criminal's freedom of will is beaten by deterministic psychosomatic forces.

To illustrate the degree of respect in which this view was held, it may be noted that Lacassagne, perhaps the greatest rival of Lombroso, accepted an editorship of the French *Archives d'anthropologie criminelle,* and Hans Gross, who expended so much effort to oppose Lombroso's theory, edited the Austrian-German *Archiv für Kriminalanthropologie und Kriminalistik.* A number of diverse theories of atavism, degeneracy, and pathologies of various types arose at this time. Bernaldo de Quirós complained that it was almost impossible to keep the theories apart because the proposed "phenomena blend together, and touch and cross one another."[2] Certainly, grouping them under any biological or anthropological orientation is arbitrary, but it has the value of expressing the similarity of the focal concerns within each.

General Inferiority

Among those who have propounded the idea of the general inferiority of criminals, perhaps the most enthusiastic follower and friend of Lombroso's was Hans Kurella.[3] To him persistent criminality expressed itself "with an unavoidable necessity, completely irrespective of social and individual life conditions." This "necessity" could be verified by studies of the anomalies of the skull. He strongly supported the Lombrosian concept of the "born criminal." He suggested that crime is caused by the criminal's biological peculiarities, marking him as a special type of human species.

Kurella denied the role of poverty and other societal factors in crime causation; he made allowance only for passion and opportunity, and these only under unusual circumstances. The criminal nature was "a form of degeneration which is marked morphologically and biologically by atavistic peculiarities."

Willem Adriaan Bonger criticized Kurella sharply: "One does not argue with a man who gives convincing proofs that even the meaning of criminal sociology is unknown to him."[4] Bernaldo de Quirós suggested more moderately that Kurella "does not seem to have met with success."[5] Baer,[6] Näcke,[7] and Aschaffenburg,[8] among others, also analyzed Kurella's work and his atavistic view on crimes and criminals, all with negative results.

Hamilton D. Wey strongly believed in the somatic factors, recommending physical exercise to reduce criminality and overcome predisposing physical factors.[9] Still another pioneer of the somatic approach was August Drähms, who collected a vast amount of data to "prove" that man's biological makeup is responsible for his crime; like so many of his contemporaries, he unfortunately failed to use control groups.[10] Frances Kellor's results were no more convincing, although she investigated physical characteristics of white and Negro female offenders, as well as a control group of white female students.[11]

The first major criminal anthropological study after Lombroso came from Charles Buckman Goring (1870–1919), a medical officer in various English prisons. His position in the penal system offered him many research advantages not at the disposal of most of his predecessors. His study, begun on English convicts in 1901 and published in 1913,[12] examined some 3,000 recidivist offenders and a sizable control group of Oxford and Cambridge students, hospital patients, and British soldiers. A number of experts assisted Goring in his research, among them the statistician Karl Pearson. Goring is often described as antagonistic to Lombroso's idea of the born criminal, "yet Goring was quick to stress that he was not opposed so much to Lombroso's findings as to his method of arriving at them."[13]

Goring's approach covered an extensive series of measurements of bodily and psychological features. As a result of his investigation he was, as he said, "forced" to an hypothesis of "the possible existence of a character in all men which, in the absence of a better term, we call the 'criminal diathesis' . . . a constitutional proclivity," mental, moral, or physical, potent enough to determine even "the fate of imprisonment."[14] Although his examination of thirty-seven physical and six mental traits of criminality led him to refute Lombroso's criminal stigmata, he could not accept social factors as the only or even the decisive causes of crime. Goring believed a defective state of mind combining with poor physical condition determined the criminal personality.[15] He found some measures of "inferiority" in the stature and body weight of his criminal population, which he attributed to the hereditary nature of criminality.

According to Goring, the criminal was shorter and lighter in body weight than the members of his control group. However, he admitted that his violent criminals were somewhat taller and heavier than the average. Even though Goring studied only selected control groups, the symptoms of somatic inferiority he found are arguable, and the deterministic relevance of these somatic differences has not been convincingly explained,[16] Goring's work remains a remarkable product for its time.

As Goring prompted attention to the somatological orientation just before the outbreak of World War I, so before World War II a somewhat similar biologically oriented research, attempting to revive the Lombrosian thinking, was undertaken. One of Goring's fiercest critics, Ernest A. Hooton, professor of anthropology at Harvard University, published his twelve-year anthropological study, *The American Criminal*.[17] In his Introduction he charged

Goring with using unscientific methods of investigation and with bias—in general, the same criticisms later leveled at him when critics turned against his work.

Hooton selected his sample of 13,873 criminals and 3,203 controls from the states of Arizona, Colorado, Kentucky, Massachusetts, Missouri, New Mexico, North Carolina, Tennessee, Texas, and Wisconsin. Whites, Negroes, and foreign-borns were submitted to Hooton's anthropometric measurements, which resulted in an analysis of no fewer than 107 physical characteristics. In his theoretical conclusion Hooton contends that criminals are "organically inferior" and that crime is the result of "the impact of environment upon low grade human organisms"; within this context, he could hardly propose anything other than "the extirpation of the physically, mentally, and morally unfit" or their "complete segregation."[18] Low foreheads, high pinched nasal roots, compressed faces, and narrow jaws were some of the characteristics Hooton cited to support his theory of the general constitutional inferiority of criminals.

The scientific response to Hooton's work was severely unfavorable. The major criticisms were that his criminal population was not a representative sample of all criminals, that his control group was a fantastic conglomeration of noncriminal civilians (including, as it does, Nashville, Tennessee, firemen and Boston hospital outpatients) that he emphasized selected characteristics and disregarded others, that he gave no convincing evidence that the criminal's "inferiority" was inherited, and that he failed to explore other important data that were available. In their appraisal of Hooton's research, Robert K. Merton and M. F. Ashley Montagu found that his control group shows more similarity to anthropoid apes than to his criminal population.[19] George Vold rightly makes the point that had Hooton been more careful, "he might even have been forced to abandon some of his extravagant conclusions."[20]

Body Types

Another constitutional or biological orientation emerged at about this time and was popularly known as the "body type" school. Essentially, it aims at understanding man's psychological processes by an acquaintance with his somatic organism. In some ways this seems to fit more properly under the psychic approaches to the crime problem, but its emphasis is markedly on the physical peculiarities of the criminal. While the somatotype is the center of the theorizations of this school, it should not be confused with the general somatic-inferiority theories. It is not sheer physical differences that serve here as a basis for understanding crime, but the inevitable psychological concomitants of distinctive body types. Criminality is due to the inseparable connection between body build and constitutional function.

Since Léon Rostand's and Cesare Lombroso's[21] anthropological explanation of crime, several attempts have been made in this field. Perhaps Emil Kraepelin (1856–1926), who played a major role in the classification of mental diseases, can be regarded as the pioneer of this system;[22] at least both Kretschmer and Sheldon, outstanding students of body types, basically followed Kraepelin's typology.

Ernst Kretschmer classified men by specific physical characteristics and corresponded these characteristics with their temperamental differences.[23] It is difficult to judge whether Kretschmer's approach is anti-Lombrosian or an extension of it. In spite of numerous and severe criticisms raised against his assumptions and results, Kretschmer's work has been well received in many quarters; his study on biopsychological constitutional typology has achieved many editions, has been translated into several languages, and has resulted in many replications and additional research.

In all probability Kretschmer's hypothesis was derived from Kraepelin's two basic mental types, for he too classified constitutional personalities into two main groups: cycloids and schizoids, with epileptoids and hysterics forming two subdivisions. Kretschmer proposed that "abnormal persons who fluctuate between mental health and mental disorder" may be regarded as fundamental types of psychotic individuals. The "cycloid" is compared to the circular insane and the "schizoid" to the schizophrenic. Kretschmer believed these types can be found even in the general population, since psychotics are only exaggerated expressions of the basic types; thus Kretschmer also classified the cyclothyme and schizothyme temperaments as relatively healthy examples. The pyknic body type, a rotund, soft figure, represents the cyclothyme temperament; the wide, muscular, strong athletic type and the thin, lean, flat asthenic type display a schizothyme temperament.

A marked improvement on Kretschmer's theory was made by William H. Sheldon, who studied the connection between the shape of the body and delinquency tendencies.[24] He measured the somatotypes of 200 boys between the ages of fifteen and twenty-one in the Hayden Goodwill Institute in Boston. Sheldon used the term "delinquency" in a way different from the conventional legal or sociological understanding and used a special index for rating delinquency; this, however, seems closer to some psychiatric ideas than to commonly accepted sociological conceptions.

First Sheldon enumerated 650 traits of temperament in his sample. In the course of his analysis he reduced them to fifty traits that seemed to embrace all ideas of the original 650. These were then processed into a five-point rating scale, later expanded to a seven-point scale. As a result of analyzing this material, Sheldon distinguished three basic body types: the endomorphic (Kretschmer's pyknic) with viscerotonic temperament, the mesomorphic (Kretschmer's athlete) with somatotonic temperament, and the ectomorphic (Kretschmer's leptosome) with cerebrotonic temperament.

Sheldon's findings were given some support by Sheldon and Eleanor Glueck, who have repeatedly leaned toward accepting physique as an important factor in the explanation of delinquency.[25] The Gluecks seem reluctant to describe its causal nexus, but they admitted to finding an association of body type with delinquency. In addition to their own "unraveled" crime factors, they have used the bodily characteristics of their subject delinquents to gain a further understanding of delinquency. The Gluecks, as everyone else who has applied constitutional models, have failed to offer convincing evidence for the relation of physique with the legal definition and sociological notion of crime other than the correlational association.

The Sex Chromosome

The role of human sex chromosomes in the crime problem has emerged only in the last few years, as a result of recent developments in genetics. The study of chromosomes in general is of course not new, and sporadic attempts were made in the past to relate chromosome constellations to illnesses, and indirectly to asocial behavior. However, the sector of biological sciences that deals with sex chromosomes as related to crime has been established only since the late 1950s and before that we were almost totally ignorant of the contribution of genetic makeup to deviant behavior. Ferri wrote some two decades after Mendel had published his laws of genetics, but it is only in the present decade that researchers are in a position to examine large and defined groups of males and females. The study of the sex chromosome of males began in British prisons and Borstal institutions.[26]

In the normal man or woman there is one pair of sex chromosomes among the twenty-three pairs of chromosomes found in nearly every somatic cell. In the woman the two sex chromosomes are alike (both X chromosomes), but in the man they are dissimilar (one X and one Y chromosome). The Y chromosome is believed to determine maleness at conception. Therefore a normal woman has an XX chromosome pair, and a normal man an XY sex chromosome complement. A simple screening test can identify the existence of more than one X in a cell; however, a formal chromosome study is necessary on chromatin-positive males to determine the Y-position in the complement.

The clue to the important role of the Y chromosome in sex determination came from the work of Patricia A. Jacobs and J. A. Strong, who demonstrated the significance of this chromosome in sexual underdevelopment.[27] "According to the theory of the inertness of the Y chromosome in sex determination, individuals with an XXY complement should have female physical characteristics."[28] The male with XXYY chromosome constellation (the "double male") was originally described by S. Muldal and C. H. Ockey, who also showed that this male was remarkably tall with a low I.Q., sometimes bordering the imbecile level.[29] In the general population the XXYY male is extremely rare; a study in the Western General Hospital in Edinburgh found only one in over 13,000 randomly selected male births. However, M. D. Casey and his colleagues found a larger percentage of XXYY males among hard-to-manage male criminals of subnormal intelligence;[30] combining their results with another prison study, they found eight XXYY males in a group of 1,257.[31] This frequency of XXYY males is clearly greater than can be expected among the general population.

XYY chromosomes were first reported by an odd chance[32] "in an entirely symptomless man, of average intelligence, not stated to be psychologically or criminally abnormal, although it was thought worth noting that he had difficulty in satisfying various employers."[33] The incidence of the XYY sex-chromosome constitution is generally estimated in the male population at 1 in 1,500 to 1 in 2,000. This estimate, however, does not match the reported incidence of the "extra-Y syndrome" in mentally sub-normal or abnormal populations with signs of criminal inclinations found in special security institutions.

These findings led Patricia Jacobs to speculate that males with the additional Y chromosome may be predisposed to criminal behavior; therefore XYY males should occur in a disproportionately large number among criminals. Jacobs and her colleagues tested this idea; they examined 315 men and found nine with an XYY complement.[34] They also found that the average height of these XYY males was significantly greater than that of the XY males in the same institution. Casey and his collaborators confirmed these findings; in two other institutions they examined fifty men with a height of 6 feet or more and found twelve to have an XYY chromosome complement. Casey and his colleagues also found four out of fifty prisoners in Broadmoor prison and two out of twenty-four in Nottingham prison with an XYY chromosome constellation.[35] "It is becoming clear therefore that there are features about XYY males that predispose them to breaking the law, and their occurrence among the men in Nottingham prison suggests that there may be many XYY males to be found in prison populations as well as in the special and state hospitals."[36]

W. H. Price and P. P. Whatmore compared nine XYY males with eighteen randomly selected men from a group of convicted psychopaths and found three important differences. First, the average age of the XYY males at their first conviction was thirteen years as opposed to eighteen years for the control group. Second, the typical crimes of the XYY males were property crimes, while the controls' crimes were usually against the person, such as murders, assaults, and sexual offenses. Third, there was almost no history of crime in the family background of the XYY males—of thirty-one siblings only one had a criminal record; however, twelve of the sixty-three sibs of the controls had a total of 139 convictions. The XYY males were described as unstable and immature, without feeling or remorse, and showing a marked tendency to commit a succession of apparently motiveless property crimes. Price and Whatmore suggest that in view of all factors, particularly the absence of delinquencies in the family unit and their early age at first conviction, "It seems likely that the extra Y chromosome has a deleterious effect primarily on the behavior of these men, predisposing them to criminal acts."[37]

D. J. Bartlett, W. P. Hurley, C. R. Brand, and E. W. Poole made a chromosomal survey of 204 male inmates in the English prison at Grendon, a security institution for the psychiatric treatment of offenders. Their survey included details of personal and family history, criminal records, psychometric test findings, electroencephalogram (EEG) results, and blood group and Rh-factor findings. They also made buccal smear tests and took peripheral blood samples for their chromosomal analysis; even palm prints were studied. As Bartlett and his colleagues described it, the pattern of crime and previous conviction was equivocal. One XYY subject had six previous convictions and his behavior pattern began at eleven years of age; all were crimes against property, although he was a homosexual. Another XYY individual had his first conviction only at the age of thirty-four years, for a crime against property; he too was a homosexual and had attended a school for mentally handicapped children from the age of twelve to sixteen years. Both were schizoid personalities. Bartlett and his collaborators revealed five individuals of abnormal karyotype in their survey population of 204.[38]

The significance of finding individuals of abnormal karyotype in institutionalized criminal populations was perhaps answered by Price and Whatmore,[39] and Bartlett and his colleagues seemed to agree with them,[40] when they noted that the criminal behavior of such individuals had proved in the past to be resistant to conventional forms of treatment.

The 1966/1967 *Annual Report* of the British Medical Research Council suggested, "It could be that the discovery of the relatively high frequency of XYY males in certain criminal populations will help to open up the general study of the genetics of human behavior."[41] At this stage of research in human cytogenetics, it is impossible to tell what the future holds. In view of the rather narrow samples and somewhat vague sociological implications, it is premature to speculate about the likelihood of a revival of the biological criminal.

Psychosomatic Conditions

A stronger leaning toward psychic factors can be seen in another orientation, basically derived from the mechanisms of some psychosomatic or psychobiological features. Its essentials lie in the unity of the body and soul.

Louis Vervaeck, who established perhaps the first criminal-biological diagnostic clinic of the world (Service d'Anthropologie Pénitentiaire, 1907), propounded a close relationship between the physical organism and personality tendencies.[42] In his findings, the combined force of body build, morphological stigmata, irregular somatic functions, childhood diseases, alcohol, malfunction of the ductless glands, and, most important, heredity result in the development of a biologically "inferior" personality. Vervaeck conducted research in the personality peculiarities of recidivist criminals and found his hypothesis was justified in an overwhelming majority of his cases.

Adolf Lenz, an Austrian professor of criminal law who founded a criminal-biological observation institute at the University of Graz, is said to have introduced the term *Kriminalbiologie* to German literature.[43] He propounded the need for analyzing "the whole life" both physical and psychic, in order to understand the personality. He proposed that the biological and psychological parts of the personality are in a "dynamically coherent structure" and that hereditary factors and body irregularities strongly influence antisocial tendencies. He accepted the importance of the social environment, but only to a limited degree. Lenz suggested that hereditary factors predispose to crime, and if these tendencies conflict with the environment crime may result.

Karl Birnbaum, in his "criminal psychopathology and psychobiological study of criminals,"[44] went even further and proposed that the criminal should be investigated exclusively by methods of the natural sciences. In this regard he differed with Lenz, who stated that the task of modern criminal somatology is "not to forgive the criminal, but to evaluate him properly."[45] Birnbaum proposed types of criminals, whom he grouped according to their criminal-pathological characteristics and catalogued as deviants from normal health.

After World War I several crude attempts were made to examine the relationship between the glandular system and crime. Allan W. Rowe and Miriam Van Waters tested 100 inmates in the Massachusetts Correctional Institution for Women in Framingham and found no significant association between abnormal glandular functions and crime.[46] M. G. Schlapp and E. H. Smith based their "new criminology" on the assumption that about one-third of the offenders show glandular or toxic disturbances, which lead them to act as emotionally unstable individuals.[47]

Franz Exner explained crime as due to inherited predispositions that are manifested under the pressure of an unfavorable social environment.[48] His limited acceptance of societal factors caused some theorists to include him among the adherents of the multiple-cause approach; in fact, however, he always leaned toward the biological understanding of crime. While the Gluecks preferred to work with the Sheldonian mesomorphic body type, Exner used the Kretschmerian athletic type as a reference to criminals. Mental disturbances and alcoholism, if they occurred in the criminal's family with marked frequency, were listed by Exner as "outstanding" crime factors. He made efforts to prove that the frequency of crime within a family determines the likelihood of further crimes and that the frequency of arrests determines the intervals between further arrests. In other words, to Exner an understanding of the pattern of crime was central to subsequent crimes.

Erwin Frey seems to have followed Exner's orientation in predicting crime from previous crime.[49] His approach to the problem of crime is expressed in his most important work, in which he concludes that those who begin their criminality at an early age (*Frühkriminelle*) are as a result of this early history likely to be recidivists (*Rückfallsverbrecher*). In Frey's opinion early criminality and recidivists are highly correlated. At the same time he observed that recidivists are concentrated in the mentally defective and psychopathic population, usually coming from biologically "weak" families.

These may be taken as examples of the fact that recent psychobiological theories are increasingly psychologically or sociologically oriented. Their complexity places them close to the multifactor theories, and their somatic core causes them to be counted among the biological concepts. In fact, the most recent criminalbiological theories seem to have restricted their somatic basis, so that it is often conceded that a tendency to act in criminal ways can be activated by factors other than those operating in the human organism. H. Bürger-Prinz, for example, lists several sociological backgrounds that may precipitate existing "biological determination factors" and result in crime.[50] Friedrich Stumpfl has suggested that the crucial point is an awareness of this criminal-biologically relevant disposition.[51]

The Destiny of Twins

Perhaps the most sophisticated, if still not fully developed, criminal-biological theoretical approach is the study of twins. One might think that a comparison of the criminality between identical (monzygotic) twins and fraternal (dizygotic) twins would be a convincing test of the validity of the biological approaches to criminal behavior. However, as Stumpfl pointed out, this method of investigation has not yet been able to differentiate between basic natural tendencies and "social-psychiatric" factors.[52] Edwin H. Sutherland and Donald R. Cressey offer similar objections.[53]

The first major study of identical twins was made by Johannes Lange, who expressed the theme of his research in the title of his work, *Crime as Destiny*.[54] He studied thirty pairs of twins, thirteen identical and seventeen fraternal sets; one member of each of these pairs was an inmate in a Bavarian prison. He found ten pairs of identical twins where both parties were criminals (such pairs were termed "concordant"), but only two pairs of the fraternal twins were similarly concordant. Although the small sample precluded any unarguable conclusions, Lange suggested his results gave some evidence that criminality can be inherited.

Later studies, notably the work of A. M. Legras on the criminality and psychoses of twins,[55] Friedrich Stumpfl's study on the origins of crime with reference to the life career of twins,[56] and the study of Heinrich Kranz on criminal twins,[57] found little difference between the criminal behavior of identical twins and that of fraternal pairs. A. J. Rosanoff and his collaborators conducted a rather extensive twin study on the etiology of child behavior problems, juvenile delinquency, and adult criminality.[58] They found far greater concordance among identical twins than fraternal twins; however, the procedures of their study "are so inaccurate that the conclusions are worthless."[59]

The major reservations concerning the twin studies are that only a small number of twins were studied (in the mentioned works a total of 216 sets), that no simple method exists for differentiating identical from fraternal twins, and that the matter of concordance is seldom adequately dealt with. Sutherland and Cressey conclude that two positive and one negative proposition may be made about the relationship of heredity to crime. First, criminals, like all human beings, have some inherited traits;

second, some inherited characteristics may be related to criminal behavior; and third, thus far heredity has not been demonstrated to have any connection whatever with criminal behavior.[60] Indeed, like many of the other biological approaches, the twin studies show a neo-Lombrosian construct. Their validity, at least at the present state of research, is heavily clouded with doubts.

NOTES

1. Enrico Ferri, *Criminal Sociology*, Joseph I. Kelly and John Lisle (trs.) (New York, 1967), p. 57.
2. C. Bernaldo de Quirós, *Modern Theories of Criminality*, Alfonso de Salvio (tr.) (New York, 1967), p. 38.
3. Hans Kurella, *Naturgeschichte des Verbrechers: Grundzüge der Kriminellen Anthropologie und Kriminalpsychologie* (Stuttgart, 1893); *Die Grenzen der Zurechnungsfähigkeit und die Kriminalanthropologie* (Halle, 1903); *Lombroso als Mensch und Forscher* (Wiesbaden, 1913).
4. Willem Adriaan Bonger, *Criminality and Economic Conditions*, Henry P. Horton (tr.) (New York, 1967), p. 138.
5. De Quirós, *Modern Theories, op. cit.*, p. 39.
6. A. Baer, *Der Verbrecher in anthropologischer Beziehung* (Leipzig, 1893).
7. P. Näcke, *Verbrechen und Wahnsinn beim Weibe* (Leipzig, 1894).
8. Gustav Aschaffenburg, *Das Verbrechen und seine Bekämpfung* (Heidelberg, 1903).
9. Hamilton D. Wey, *Criminal Anthropology* (New York, 1890).
10. August Drähms, *The Criminal: His Personnel and Environment* (New York, 1900).
11. Frances Kellor, *Experimental Sociology* (New York, 1901).
12. Charles B. Goring, *The English Convict: A Statistical Study* (London, 1913).
13. Edwin D. Driver, "Charles Buckman Goring," in Hermann Mannheim (ed.), *Pioneers in Criminology* (London, 1960), p. 336.

14. Goring, *op. cit.*, p. 26.
15. *Ibid.*, p. 263.
16. See a summary of criticism against Goring's work in Driver, *op. cit.*, pp. 346–347.
17. Ernest A. Hooton, *Crime and the Man* (Cambridge, Mass., 1939); *The American Criminal: An Anthropological Study* (Cambridge, Mass., 1939).
18. Hooton, *The American Criminal, op. cit.*, I, 309.
19. Robert K. Merton and M. F. Ashley Montagu, "Crime and the Anthropologist," *American Anthropologist*, August 1940, pp. 384–408.
20. See a summary of criticisms against Hooton's work in George B. Vold, *Theoretical Criminology* (New York, 1958), pp. 63–65.
21. Cesare Lombroso, *L'Uomo delinquente* (Milan, 1876).
22. Emil Kraepelin, *Psychiatrie* (Leipzig, 1883).
23. Ernst Kretschmer, *Körperbau und Character* (Berlin, 1921); in English *Physique and Character*, W. J. H. Sprott (tr.) (London, 1925).
24. William H. Sheldon, *Varieties of Delinquent Youth: An Introduction to Constitutional Psychiatry* (New York, 1949); *Atlas of Man* (New York, 1954); see also his *Psychology and the Promethean Will* (New York, 1936); *Varieties of Human Physique* (New York, 1940), and *Varieties of Temperament* (New York, 1942).
25. Sheldon and Eleanor Glueck, *Unraveling Juvenile Delinquency* (New York, 1950); *Physique and Delinquency* (New York, 1956).
26. W. M. Court Brown, "Genetics and Crime: The Problem of XXY, XY/XXY, XXYY and XYY Males," unpublished paper, mimeographed (Edinburgh, 1967), p. 3; also described in "Studies on the Human Y Chromosome," *Medical Research Council Annual Report: April 1966–March 1967* (London, 1967), pp. 38–42.
27. P. A. Jacobs and J. A. Strong, "A Case of Human Intersexuality Having a Possible XXY Sex-Determining Mechanism," *Nature* (London), 1959, 183:302.
28. *Annual Report, op. cit.*, p. 38. For a biological explanation of

the variations in female criminality see Stephen Schafer, "On the Proportions of the Criminality of Women," *The Journal of Criminal Law and Criminology*, 39 (May-June 1948), 77–78.

29. S. Muldal and C. H. Ockey, "The 'Double' Male: A New Chromosome Constitution in Klinefelter's Syndrome," *Lancet*, 1960, 2:492.

30. M. D. Casey, L. J. Segall, D. R. K. Street, and C. E. Blank, "Sex Chromosome Abnormalities in Two State Hospitals for Patients Requiring Special Security," *Nature* (London), 1966, 209:641.

31. W. M. Court Brown, "Genetics and Crime: The Problem of XXY, XY/XXXY, XXYY and XYY Males," *Journal of the Royal College of Physicians*, 1967, 1:311.

32. A. A. Sandberg, G. F. Koepf, T. Ishihara, and T. S. Hauschka, "Sex Chromosomes," *Lancet*, 1961, ii:488.

33. D. J. Bartlett, W. P. Hurley, C. R. Brand, and E. W. Poole, "Chromosomes of Male Patients in a Security Prison," *Nature* (London), 1968, 219:351.

34. P. A. Jacobs, M. Brunton, M. M. Melville, R. P. Brittain, and W. F. McClemont, "Aggressive Behaviour, Mental Subnormality and the XYY Male," *Nature* (London), 1965, 208:1351. It should be noted that it is not known as yet how frequent XYY males are at birth in the general population.

35. M. D. Casey, C. E. Blank, D. R. K. Street, L. J. Segall, J. H. McDougall, P. J. McGrath, and J. L. Skinner, "YY Chromosomes and Antisocial Behaviour," *Lancet*, 1966, 2:859.

36. *Annual Report, op. cit.*, p. 41.

37. W. H. Price and P. P. Whatmore, "Behaviour Disorders and Pattern of Crime Among XYY Males Identified at a Maximum Security Hospital," *British Medical Journal*, 1967, 1:533; cf. *Annual Report, op. cit.*, p. 40 and *infra*.

38. Bartlett, Hurley, Brand, and Poole, *op. cit.*, pp. 351–354.

39. Price and Whatmore, *op. cit.*

40. Bartlett, Hurley, Brand, and Poole, *op. cit.*, p. 354.

41. *Annual Report, op. cit.*, p. 41. Moor suggests that we are still far from that, although the hope is not utopian; see Lise Moor, "Aberrations chromosomiques portant sur les gonosomes et

comportement antisocial, état actuel de nos connaissances,"
Annales Internationales de Criminologie, 1967, Vol. 6–2, p. 472.

42. Louis Vervaeck, *Syllabus du cours d'anthropologie criminelle donné à la prison de Forest* (Brussels, 1926).

43. Adolf Lenz, *Grundriss der Kriminalbiologie* (Berlin and Vienna, 1927); "Der Kriminalbiologische Untersuchungsbogen des Grazer Institutes und der Wiener Polizeidirection," *Mitteilungen der Kriminalbiologischen Gesellschaft*, 1929, Vol. II; *Mörder, Die Untersuchung der Persönlichkeit als Beitrag zur Kriminalbiologischen Kasuistik und Methodik* (Graz, 1931); "Die Bedeutung der Kriminalbiologie," *Archiv für Kriminalbiologie*, 1931, 88: 222–226.

44. Karl Birnbaum, *Kriminal-psychopathologie und Psychobiologische Verbrecherkinde* (Berlin, 1931).

45. Lenz, *Mitteilungen, op. cit.*, p. 139.

46. Allan W. Rowe and Miriam Van Waters, "Physical Associations with Behavior Problems," *Endocrinology*, 1935, 19:129–143.

47. M. G. Schlapp and E. H. Smith, *The New Criminology* (New York, 1928).

48. Franz Exner, *Kriminologie* (Berlin, 1949).

49. Erwin Frey, *Der frühkriminelle Rückfallsverbrecher* (Basel, 1959).

50. H. Bürger-Prinz, *Motiv und Motivation* (Berlin, 1950).

51. Friedrich Stumpfl, "Kriminalbiologie," in Rudolph Sieverts, *Handwörterbuch der Kriminologie* (2nd ed., Berlin, 1967/1968), I, 506.

52. *Ibid.*

53. Edwin H. Sutherland and Donald R. Cressey, *Principles of Criminology* (7th ed., Philadelphia, 1966), pp. 127–128.

54. Johannes Lange, *Verbrechen als Schicksal* (Leipzig, 1919); the English translation, prepared by Charlotte Haldane under the title *Crime and Destiny* (New York, 1930) deprived the original title of its expressive flavor—the correct translation of the title should be "crime *as* destiny."

55. A. M. Legras, *Psychose en Criminaliteit bei Tweelingen* (Utrecht, 1932).

56. Friedrich Stumpfl, *Die Ursprünge des Verbrechens, dargestellt am Lebenslauf vom Zwillingen* (Leipzig, 1936).

57. Heinrich Kranz, *Lebensschicksale Krimineller Zwillinge* (Berlin, 1936).

58. A. J. Rosanoff, Leva M. Handy, and Isabel A. Rosanoff, "Etiology of Child Behavior Difficulties, Juvenile Delinquency, and Adult Criminality," *Psychiatric Monographs* (Department of Institutions, California), 1941, No. 1.

59. Sutherland and Cressey, *op. cit.*, p. 127.

60. *Ibid.*, p. 128.

IX
The
Psychological Responsibilities

The Invisible Mind

The psychological and psychiatric approaches to crime are not clearly distinct from those of a biological orientation. However, the somatic approaches stress the physical characteristics of the criminal and regard the psychic components as only supplementary, whereas the psychological and psychiatric orientations seek answers to the crime problem in mental processes regardless of any physical stigmata or disorder.

In this group of theories a person's psyche, or mind, is made responsible for leading him to respond negatively to the responsibility-charging legal command. From hereditary mental degeneration, through mental illness and psychopathic disorders, to psychoanalytically revealed emotional disturbances, a wide range of deviations from the psychic normal has been offered as explanations of criminal behavior. The human mind, this invisible part of the human organism, something that cannot be investigated by anatomical dissection or observed by X-rays, has an almost magical appeal to many who want a convenient answer to the problem of crime. The invisibility of the mind perplexes many laymen and even professionals; many of them, having more regard for medical psychiatry, are inclined to view speculative psychology as "a mixture of black magic and quackery." In discussing the uses and abuses of psychology, H. J. Eysenck pointed out that psychology is "a science in its early, formative period, not sufficiently advanced to answer all the vital questions which are often asked of it, but already in a position to offer solutions to some of our problems."[1]

The stream of thought that understands crime and the criminal in terms of one or another kind of mental abnormality began to develop after demonology gave way to more scientific practices, and by the end of the nineteenth century psychiatry and psychology were making rapid strides in understanding mental factors. This development furnished criminological explanations and theories in such abundance that it is difficult, because of their heavily overlapping aspects, to catalogue them into self-contained groups. Generally, carried to their ultimate conclusion, the psychological and psychiatric theories assume that mentally inadequate persons represent criminal potentials, or better, that the origin of criminality can be traced to mental inadequacies.

Mental Degeneration

Among the psychiatric and psychological explanations of crime perhaps mental degeneration was the earliest. Investigators of the causes of criminality became interested in the person who, as Vaschide y Vurpas described him, "finds himself in comparison with his most recent ancestors constitutionally weakened in his psycho-physical resistance, and realizes only in an incomplete measure the biological conditions for the hereditary struggle for existence. This weakness, which manifests itself by permanent stigmata, is essentially progressive except in the case of uneven regeneration, and causes with more or less rapidity the extinction of the species."[2]

The pioneering work of Benoit Augustin Morel and his "morbid anthropology" have already been mentioned. Likewise Henry

Maudsley, who referred crime to man's degenerate qualities. Among the many others Charles Féré, who discussed criminality and degeneracy,[3] and A. Corre, who proposed a similar approach in his "criminal ethnography,"[4] should be mentioned. Marandon de Montyel presented a contribution to the clinical study of the relationship between degeneracy and criminality.[5]

Mental degeneracy as a hereditary factor is understood as a kind of reversion to a lower type. Numerous "family trees" are constructed as evidence of the correlation between degenerate families and antisocial conduct. Prosper Despine described the Chrétien family, in which several generations were associated with crime. P. Aubry presented the Kéromgal family in order to prove that murder is contagious.[6] Poelman's "Zero family," the offspring of a drunken woman, portrayed 102 beggars, 107 illegitimate children, 54 almshouse paupers, 181 prostitutes, 7 murderers, and 76 other serious criminals in the course of six generations, costing the public 1,206,000 dollars.[7] McCulloch's "Tribe of Ishmael," Blackmar's "Smoky Pilgrims," Davenport's "Nam family," and Kite's "Pineys" are only examples of other grisly family trees, where crime and deviance among the members were explained by hereditary mental degeneration, based on a methodologically dubious collection of data.

The "family tree" understanding of crime and criminals became widely known through a spectacular conglomerate of deviants, the Juke family, presented by Richard Dugdale and later by Arthur A. Estabrook.[8] Dugdale traced back this family of degenerates to a man named Max, who was a descendant of Dutch settlers in New York and was born some time in the first half of the eighteenth century. Two of his sons married into "the Juke family of girls." There were six sisters, probably all illegitimate; one of them, Ada Juke, was known as "the mother of criminals." From her, in a seventy-five-year history of this family, Dugdale traced about 1,200 descendants. Among them he found 280 paupers, 60 habitual thieves and 140 other criminals, 300 prematurely born infants, 7 murderers, 50 common prostitutes, 440 with venereal disease, and a number of other deviants. They cost the public some 1,308,000 dollars, "without reckoning the cash paid for whiskey" and other unmeasurable damages. Estabrook continued Dugdale's analysis and traced the Jukes up to 1915, totaling the known members to 2,094. Estabrook found an additional 170 adult paupers, 118 criminals, 378 prostitutes, 86 brothel keepers, and a number of other deviants.

Another impressive study of this type came from Henry Herbert Goddard, who gave an account of the Kallikak family.[9] This study revealed the story of a feeble-minded girl during the Revolutionary War and the fate of her descendants. A Martin Kallikak had an affair with this girl that resulted in an illegitimate son, who in time had 480 descendants. After the war Kallikak returned home and married a Quaker girl of good family; 496 descendants were traced to this union. In this legitimate line only one was found mentally abnormal, two were alcoholics, and none were criminal. However, in the illegitimate, feeble-minded line 143 were feeble-minded, 36 illegitimate, 33 sexual immorals or prostitutes, 24 alcoholics, 8 brothel keepers, 3 epileptics, 3 criminals, and a number of other abnormals or deviants.

These studies, however, with their rather deficient research methods, are no more authoritative than the numerous writers from Aeschylus to Ibsen who presented descriptions of similar "hereditary degenerations." Even in the Roman mythology Vulcan's deformity is explained by the fact that Jupiter was drunk in course of his begetting. It should be made clear that these studies concentrate on the hereditary nature of mental degeneration, and they should not be confused with the "family centered" theories, which analyze the influence of family systems and family circumstances on crime and delinquency by emphasizing social factors.

Psychoses and Other Mental Defects

Another understanding of mental abnormality as an explanation of man's criminal behavior, crime as a pathognomonic phenomenon, has gained a popularity among lay observers as well as professional investigators. While for a long time the mentally ill were treated as criminals, the reverse has also been true. This orientation regards criminals as mental abnormals. The adherents of the explanation of crime in terms of psychotic disorders generally do not view crime as a discharge of pathological proclivities. Delusions and hallucinations, departures from reality, disorganization and lessening of inner controls, and other symptoms of a severe psychotic personality abundantly suggest that psychotics and other mental defectives are certainly capable of criminal behavior. Their largely unpredictable conduct, caused by their illness or defect, may result in crime at any given time. However, theorists of this approach to crime perceive criminality, in general, as a product of mental abnormality.

Among them Henry Maudsley should be mentioned again, who leaned to the belief that crime is a substitute for mental illness and vice versa.[10] To Maudsley, crime is an outlet for pathological urges; criminals would go mad if they were not criminals, and "they do not go mad because they are criminals." His entire approach to crime and criminals is medical in nature.

Isaac Ray (1807–1881) initially supported phrenological theories; later, however, he became one of the most influential contributors to psychiatry and psychiatric jurisprudence.[11] At the beginning of his career he translated two volumes of Gall's phrenological work, but most of his life was devoted to the problems of psychiatry and law. In *Medical Jurisprudence of Insanity* he suggested that there is "an immense mass of cases" at our disposal "where people are irresistibly impelled to the commission of criminal acts while fully conscious of their nature and consequences."[12] He contended that the administration of justice will often be "imperfect until the light of medical science is freely admitted and used."[13]

More forcefully, Auguste Forel propounded the closest relationship between crime and mental disorder.[14] His understanding of "constitutional mental anomalies" was wholly based on psychiatry.

Gustav Aschaffenburg was perhaps the most moderate among those who held that psychoses and other mental defects are responsible for crime.[15] Although his focus was on the psychiatric aspects of crime, he made generous allowance for social and psychological factors, so much so that he might be comfortably listed among those who attempted to offer a multiple-cause theory. In his respected journal, *Monatschrift für Kriminalpsychologie und Strafrechtsreform* ("Monthly for Criminal Psychology and the Reform of Criminal Law"), which he edited for over three decades (1904–1935), Aschaffenburg never failed to leave ample room for the sociological study of crime and delinquency. Although his psychiatric understanding of crime cannot be doubted, his self-restrained attitude qualified him as one of the leading members of the impartial European criminologists.

Aschaffenburg's "elective" criminal typology clearly reveals his acceptance of aspects of crime other than psychiatric factors. His diversified approach to criminality seems to hint at the futility of attempting the solution of the crime problem purely with a psychiatric model. Aschaffenburg saw criminology as a gentlemen's game; Hans von Hentig described him in his moving necrology as "a social being *par excellence*." Aschaffenburg published his major work, *Das Verbrechen und seine Bekämpfung,* in 1903 and was probably close to preparing a new edition, but the political changes in Germany prevented him from doing so. After this, Hentig wrote, "He came to the hospitable shores of the United States broken in heart and broken in health. His hope to find a publisher came to naught. He who had played a prominent part at all international meetings in Rome, in Prague, in

London, died in oblivion. . . . He died from an overdose of disappointment."[16]

In addition to these examples of those who related crime to mental abnormality in general, numerous others claim to have found the origin of crime in one or another specific abnormality or functional defect of the psyche.[17] A. Marro attributes the final cause of crime to defects of the central nervous system,[18] P. Kovalevsky to injuries of the inhibitory centers.[19] F. Galton found the criminal with normal intellectual faculties, but with deeply perturbed affective aptitude.[20] G. Jelgersma proposed a criminal neurosis, a somewhat Lombrosian idea, and titled it "the born wrongdoers,"[21] while M. Benedikt interpreted crime in terms of neurasthenia.[22]

The understanding of crime as a purely pathognomonic phenomenon, as an expression of a psychotic state of mind or a symptom of some mental defect, has increasingly been refuted. As Seymour Halleck put it, "For every zealot who heralds psychiatric concepts and treatment as the only answer to the crime problem, there is a critic who believes that psychiatric contributions to criminology are unscientific and misleading."[23] Indeed, the solely psychiatric view of crime causation seems to have lost its viability, and now the psychiatric search for the causes of crime embodies psychological points of view.

Mental Testing

One of the psychiatric-psychological features used in criminology is mental testing, that is, the use of systematic devices to measure intelligence and mental ability.[24] The first widely accepted device came from Alfred Binet, who, in collaboration with Théodore Simon, constructed his first test scale in 1905 (since that time several times revised), known originally as the Binet-Simon Intelligence Scale. At the center of this system lies the "intelligence quotient" (I.Q.), which is the ratio of the mental age of the subject multiplied by 100 and divided by the chronological age. This testing method is intended to show whether the tested person's innate ability has advanced to the level that is expected at his chronological age and, if not, how far it lags behind.

Before World War I scattered experiments were made to assess the I.Q. of certain prison populations.[25] These, and the psychological examinations conducted by the United States Army in World War I, produced controversial results. Since then a multitude of studies have been undertaken to prove the usefulness of mental testing devices.[26] Many believe in the Rorschach Test, known as the "ink blot" test, designed by Hermann Rorschach in 1911. This test uses a number of ink blot formations; the diagnosed individual is asked to describe what he sees in the ink blots, and his responses are then recorded, interpreted, and scored by a trained analyzer. A similar projective test is the Holtzman Inkblot Technique, which uses a considerable variety of ink blots in alternate sets of forty-five cards each. Another widely used test is the Minnesota Multiphasic Personality Inventory (MMPI), in which the examined individual is supposed to agree or disagree with a large number of simple statements by referring to the social, ethical, and health categories to which he thinks he belongs. The Thematic Apperception Test (TAT), the Make A Picture Story (MAPS) test, and the Kahn Test of Symbol Arrangement are a few examples of other psychological devices measuring intelligence, character, and mental abilities.

Numerous experiments seem to prove that these mental tests offer no insight into the crime problem beyond that which can be gained through other sources. In the past it was a popular opinion that most prisoners are mentally defective or subnormal in intelligence and that mentally defective or subintelligent persons are particularly prone to criminality. However, Sutherland and Cressey are correct in stating, "Inferior mentality is neither the specific cause nor the outstanding factor in crime and delinquency."[27] No significant relationship has been found between low intelligence and crime or delinquency, and it is well established that only a fractional proportion of those with a low I.Q. will violate the criminal code. In fact, many criminals and delinquents display high intelligence.

Psychological Disorders

All psychiatric and psychological approaches to the problem of crime have gained popularity at one time or another, but the most popular is the orientation that employs psychiatrically molded general psychology, that is, analytic psychology or dynamic psychiatry. Hugo Hoegel doubted the validity of theories in this group of thinkers and investigators;[28] others too are reluctant to accept the exclusive responsibility of the invisible and intangible psyche. However, the often metaphysical conceptualization of these theories is generally well received. This orientation is not an invention of our times; its widespread practice since the 1930s indicates a renaissance of an old way of thinking. Krauss's extravagant speculations on criminal types,[29] Tesar's "symptomatic" criminal psychology,[30] Lacassagne's psychological medicine,[31] Prins's social defense,[32] Maxwell's social psychology,[33] Wulffen's criminal typology,[34] and Gruhle's "psychical combinations"[35] are some examples of the psychological orientation of the past.

Enormous impetus was given to this already extensive trend by Sigmund Freud's (1856–1939) epoch-making contributions to psychology that opened the way to the understanding of psychodynamics.[36] As Lombroso modified his basic hypothesis several times, so Freud approached the human mind with varying assumptions. He paid increasing attention to societal factors, and perhaps, had he lived longer, he might have become one of the greatest sociologists. However, his followers usually draw upon his earliest doctrines and modify them away from sociological aspects toward a stronger psychological emphasis. Freud himself dealt little with the crime problem; it has been his followers who have applied psychodynamic or psychoanalytic explanations for an answer to crime and delinquency.

Many believe that Freud's "discovery" of the unconscious part of the psyche and his interpretation of the functioning of the human mind, coupled with his explanation of the dynamics of personality development, are central to any understanding of criminal and delinquent behavior. Freud divided the psyche into three parts: the id, which represents the inborn biological and instinctual drives, and the superego and the ego, which emerge as the child grows and develops. Early childhood experiences and sexual factors play an important role in the formation of the ego and superego and in the process of personality development. There are certain desires and conflicts that are not acceptable, and the ego by its defense mechanisms represses them into the unconscious. However, these conflicts and other complexes may re-emerge from the unconscious in another guise, for example, they may express themselves in the form of crime.

In other words, in the Freudian formulation, crime and delinquency are substitute expressions of repressed personality experiences. Stealing may be committed "as an attempt to obtain objects to substitute in a symbol for the longed-for penis in the case of the little girl, or the more potent father's penis in the case of the little boy."[37] Or the criminal, "who is acting from a guilty conscience," attempts "by a more or less trivial delinquency to express his crime, and in this way he appeases his unconscious guilt and makes a bargain."[38]

In Freudian therapeutic strategy (psychoanalysis) the unconscious material can be uncovered, and discharged, by the "free association" of the "patient" with his repressed complexes; this is supposed to re-educate and restructure his personality. The therapist helps this uncovering and interpretative process, but he can gain insight and help his patient only if he himself is free from repressed materials; if he is not, the therapist may misinterpret the patient's repressions or even transmit his own complexes to the patient. This is why therapists are supposed to be analyzed before they begin practice. Whether Freud analyzed himself, or how he could avoid transmitting his repressed material to his patients, is not clearly answered in the ordinarily accessible literature.

Freud's doctrines gained rapid popularity, and his adherents are usually firmly convinced of the validity of their hypothesis. As Gregory Zilboorg put it, "The psychoanalytically oriented penologists have for some time been thinking of the future penal institution as a special kind of hospital, where the delinquent, the minor and major criminal might be cared for and studied and re-educated in accordance with modern principles."[39]

Some of Freud's collaborators and disciples found themselves in disagreement with certain aspects of the original system and went their separate ways.

Carl G. Jung (1875–1961), an early associate of Freud, founded "analytic psychology," which deviated from the Freudian emphasis on sexual factors. He focused on the "collective unconscious" (actually, a sociological experience expressed in psychological terms), by which he explained certain cultural aspects of society. Also, he distinguished between introverted and extroverted personalities and stressed their importance in the adjustment processes.

Alfred Adler (1870–1937), the founder of "individual psychology" and another close collaborator of Freud, emphasized the human desire to belong to a group and to have status within it. Many modern gang theorists (Albert K. Cohen, James F. Short, Jr., Richard A. Cloward and Lloyd E. Ohlin, and Walter B. Miller among others) depict the status-seeking American juvenile delinquents in Adlerian terms. In Adler's thinking, in the drive to achieve status, a "will to power" or an "inferiority complex" may develop, and this may explain behavior.

Otto Rank (1884–1939), a member of the original Freudian

circle, emphasized the birth trauma and stressed the importance of the will. Guilt arises in conflict situations if the will cannot make the right decision.

Karen Horney (1885–1952) emphasized cultural and interpersonal experiences. Her seminal idea of anxiety as a product of feelings of helplessness in a basically hostile world reflects the constrictions of a culture on all its members. Somewhat similar was the direction of Harry Stack Sullivan (1892–1949), who explained human behavior in terms of man's efforts to satisfy his biological needs by culturally approved means.

Among the markedly psychological studies the work of August Aichorn, a psychologist (and not psychiatrist), should be mentioned; he described and explained "wayward youth" and believed that "right" parental affection could adjust a juvenile to the community. His destructive delinquent boys were unable to follow authoritative guidance, and they were indifferent to other people's feelings or property. Aichorn proposed to prove to these boys that there are adults in our society who really care about them.[40]

Kate Friedlander, in a somewhat Lombrosian vein, suggested that delinquents do not differ from nondelinquents in qualitative terms. She proposed that unfavorable factors in the social environment may precipitate antisocial conduct, but only in persons with an antisocial character. These individuals are easily frustrated and irritated, and they respond to uncomfortable situations with hostility.[41]

Another Freudian, Kurt R. Eissler, arrived somewhat closer to the sociological views. Delinquency is an abnormal aggressive behavior, which may be extroverted ("alloplastic") or introverted ("autoplastic"). But, in Eissler's "searchlights on delinquency," both forms of aggression represent abnormal reactions to the value system of the society.[42]

The assumption that delinquency can be traced to early emotional disturbances is the subject of an impressive study by

William Healy and Augusta F. Bronner, who attempted to throw "new light on delinquency" by being concerned with both theory and treatment.[43] Healy, a psychiatrist and an American pioneer of the multiple-cause orientation, and Bronner, a psychologist, formed a clinical team and took a dynamic psychiatric view of delinquency. They studied only those delinquents who had a nondelinquent sibling of the same sex and within two years of the same age. They excluded from their sample subintelligents, those who had difficulties with the English language, and those who refused clinical treatment.

In the course of their three-year study, Healy and Bronner compared 105 delinquents with their 105 nondelinquent siblings and centered their attention on the nature of the parent-child relationship. They found significant emotional disturbances in 91 percent of the delinquent cases, as compared to 13 percent of the nondelinquents. Sutherland and Cressey questioned the validity of these results, charging that the investigators showed a predisposition toward interpreting delinquency in terms of emotional disturbance, that emotional disturbance was not demonstrated to be the cause of delinquent behavior, and that the delinquency-producing emotional disturbance was not adequately investigated.[44]

This criticism is probably true, in general terms. It is not easy to investigate and measure emotion, a complex state of feelings that involves so much conscious experience with often contradictory covert and overt responses. Nevertheless, adherents of the psychoanalytical approach to crime and delinquency seem convinced that no other approach can reveal the full truth about the criminal. Alexander and Staub admit that "a psychoanalytical investigation of a specific criminal case presents certain specific difficulties" because "the criminal, when facing the representatives of the law, feels differently" and that "neither acquittal nor the verdict of guilty creates any favorable conditions which make the criminal accessible to psychoanalysis,"[45] but their general confirmation of the psychoanalytical theories leaves little allowance for other viewpoints. They wrote, "Psychoanalysis was the first branch of human knowledge which undertook to investigate the psychology of the real individual, i.e., of the deeper motive powers of human actions."[46] Accordingly, only psychoanalysis can answer the "paradoxical situation" where "a criminal act may be committed out of unconscious, unsocial motives."[47]

In his "formula of criminal behavior," David Abrahamsen clearly represents the dynamic psychiatric understanding of crime, yet he seems to give some way to the "total situation." In his view there are three circumstances in which a person may behave contrary to the criminal law: when existing antisocial inclinations are exposed to criminal influences; when there is a strong unconscious desire for punishment, developed through past experiences, and the criminal obtains this punishment by committing a crime; and when emotional weakness and insecurity are expressed in the form of aggression. Abrahamsen's belief in the existence of "antisocial inclinations" takes into account the role of social forces that mobilize "criminalistic tendencies."[48] This function of social factors prompted him to suggest that there is an interplay of multiple-cause elements in the etiology of criminal behavior,[49] and this brought him near (but only near, not to) the multifactor understanding of crime.

NOTES

1. H. J. Eysenck, *Uses and Abuses of Psychology* (Harmondsworth, 1953), p. 18.
2. Vaschide y Vurpas, "Qu'est ce qu'un dégénéré?" *Archives d'anthropologie criminelle*, 1902, XVII, cited by de Quirós, *Modern Theories of Criminality* (New York, 1967), pp. 45–46.
3. Charles Féré, *Dégénérescence et criminalité* (Paris, 1888).
4. A. Corre, *Les criminels* (Paris, 1889); *L'ethnographie criminelle* (Paris, 1895).

5. Marandon de Montyel, "Contribution a l'étude clinique des rapports de la criminalité et de la dégénérescence," *Archives d'anthropologie criminelle,* 1892, cited by de Quirós, *op. cit.,* p. 46.

6. P. Aubry, *La contagion du meurtre* (Paris, 1894).

7. Cf. C. B. Davenport, "Hereditary Crime," *American Journal of Sociology,* XIII (November 1907), p. 402.

8. Richard Louis Dugdale, *The Jukes, A Study in Crime, Pauperism, Disease, and Heredity* (New York, 1895) ; Arthur H. Estabrook, *The Jukes in 1915* (New York, 1916).

9. Henry Herbert Goddard, *The Kallikak Family, A Study in the Heredity of Feeble-mindedness* (New York, 1913).

10. Henry Maudsley, *Body and Mind* (London, 1870).

11. Isaac Ray, *A Treatise on the Medical Jurisprudence of Insanity* (3rd ed., 1855) ; *Contributions to Mental Pathology* (Boston, 1873) ; for more about Isaac Ray see Winfred Overholser, "Isaac Ray," in Hermann Mannheim (ed.), *Pioneers in Criminology* (London, 1960), pp. 113–134.

12. Isaac Ray, *A Treatise on the Medical Jurisprudence of Insanity* (3rd ed., 1855), p. 263.

13. Overholser, *op. cit.,* p. 132.

14. Auguste Forel and Albert Mahiam, *Crime et anomalies mentales constitutionelles, la plouie sociale des déséquilibrés à responsabilité diminuée* (Geneva, 1902).

15. Gustav Aschaffenburg, *Das Verbrechen und seine Bekämpfung* (Heidelberg, 1903) ; for more about Aschaffenburg see Hans von Hentig, "Gustav Aschaffenburg," in Mannheim, *op. cit.*

16. Hentig, "Aschaffenburg," *op. cit.,* pp. 327, 334.

17. See de Quirós, *op. cit.,* pp. 48–55.

18. A. Marro, *I caratteri dei delinquenti* (Turin, 1887) ; *La Puberta studiata nell'uomo e nella donna* (Turin, 1898).

19. P. Kovalevsky, *La psychologie criminelle* (Paris, 1903).

20. F. Galton, *Inquiries into Human Faculty and Its Development* (London, 1883) ; *Hereditary Genius* (London, 1892).

21. G. Jelgersma, "De geboren misdadiger," *Tijdschrift v. Strafrecht,* 1891.

22. M. Benedikt, "Biologie und Kriminalistik," *Zeitschrift für d. ges. Strafrechtswissenschaft*, VIII; *Anatomical Studies upon Brains of Criminals* (New York, 1881).

23. Seymour L. Halleck, *Psychiatry and the Dilemmas of Crime, A Study of Causes, Punishment and Treatment* (New York, 1967), p. xii.

24. For a historical account of mental testing, see Otto Klineberg, "Mental Tests," in *Encyclopedia of the Social Sciences* (New York, 1933); or Vold, *op. cit.*, pp. 79–89.

25. Henry H. Goddard, *Feeblemindedness, Its Causes and Consequences* (New York, 1914).

26. See, among others, Carl Murchison, *Criminal Intelligence* (Worcester, 1926); Edwin H. Sutherland, "Mental Deficiency and Crime," in Kimball Young (ed.), *Social Attitudes* (New York, 1931), pp. 357–375; L. D. Zeleny, "Feeble-mindedness and Criminal Conduct," *American Journal of Sociology*, 38 (January 1933), 564–578; Simon H. Tulchin, *Intelligence and Crime* (Chicago, 1939); Harry M. Shulman, "Intelligence and Delinquency," *The Journal of Criminal Law, Criminology and Police Science*, 41 (March-April, 1951), 763–781; Mary Woodward, "The Role of Law Intelligence in Delinquency," *British Journal of Delinquency*, 5 (April 1955), 281–303.

27. Edwin H. Sutherland and Donald R. Cressey, *Principles of Criminology* (7th ed., Philadelphia, 1966), p. 164.

28. Hugo Hoegel, *Die Einteilung der Verbrecher in Klassen* (Leipzig, 1908).

29. A. Krauss, *Psychologie des Verbrechers* (Tübingen, 1884).

30. Ottokar Tesar, *Die symptomatische Bedeutung des verbrecherischen Verhaltens: ein Betrag zur Wertungslehre im Strafrecht* (Berlin, 1904).

31. A. Lacassagne, "Marche de la criminalité en France de 1825 à 1880," *Revue scientifique*, May 28, 1881, pp. 674–684.

32. Adolphe Prins, *Criminalité et répression* (Brussels, 1886).

33. J. Maxwell, *Le criminel et la société* (Paris, 1909).

34. Erich Wulffen, *Psychologie des Verbrechers* (Berlin, 1908).

35. Hans W. Gruhle, "Kriminalpsychologie," in Alexander Elster and

Heinrich Lingemann (eds.), *Handwörterbuch der Kriminologie* (Berlin and Leipzig, 1933), pp. 911–914.

36. Among the numerous well-known works of Sigmund Freud, see *A General Introduction to Psychoanalysis* (New York, 1920); *Das Ich und das Es* (Vienna, 1923); *Hemmung, Sympton und Angst* (Vienna, 1926); *An Outline of Psychoanalysis* (New York, 1949).

37. Margaret W. Gerard, "Emotional Disorders of Childhood," in Franz Alexander and Helen Ross (eds.), *Dynamic Psychiatry* (Chicago, 1952), p. 198.

38. Franz Alexander and Louis B. Shapiro, "Neuroses, Behavior Disorders, and Perversions," in Alexander and Ross, *op. cit.*, p. 133.

39. Gregory Zilboorg, "Psychoanalysis and Criminology," in Branham and Kutash (eds.), *Encyclopedia of Criminology*, p. 405.

40. August Aichorn, *Wayward Youth* (New York, 1935).

41. Kate Friedlander, *The Psychoanalytical Approach to Juvenile Delinquency* (New York, 1947).

42. Kurt R. Eissler, *Searchlights on Delinquency* (New York, 1949).

43. William Healy and Augusta F. Bronner, *New Light on Delinquency and Its Treatment* (New Haven, 1936).

44. Sutherland and Cressey, *op. cit.*, p. 174.

45. Franz Alexander and Hugo Staub, *The Criminal, the Judge, and the Public*, Gregory Zilboorg (tr.) (Glencoe, 1956), pp. 135–136.

46. *Ibid.*, p. 22.

47. *Ibid.*, pp. 24–25.

48. David Abrahamsen, *The Psychology of Crime* (New York, 1960), pp. 33–41.

49. *Ibid.*, p. 29.

X

The Responsibility of Multiple Factors

From the Monofactor to the Multifactor Orientation

The chronological history of criminological theories may be used to support an argument for placing the multiple-cause theories after the biological and psychological orientations. This is not to claim novelty for the multifactor understanding of crime or to place the birth of this orientation at a set time. When Enrico Ferri published his *Criminal Sociology* he estimated there were many hundreds of adherents of the multifactor approach to the crime problem (he called them "eclectics"),[1] and perhaps he himself was an eclectic in the literal sense of the term. The historical periods, when the various theoretical trends appeared, heavily overlap. Nevertheless, it is generally recognized that acceptance of the multiple-cause theories of crime gained impetus only after the first biological and psychological explanations had mastered the field.

Another argument for locating here the orientation of the multifactor is that the theorists of criminal biology, criminal anthropology, and criminal psychology seem more cognizant of the role of social factors than sociologists usually are of biological, anthropological, and psychological phenomena. It is only when dealing with delinquency (and not adult crime) that the sociologically oriented investigators utilize psychological constructs.

The variety of propositions in the sphere of criminal biology and criminal psychology made known a mass of factors that may be responsible for leading man against the legal norms. Although Lombroso changed his views at least four times, Ferri vacillated from one extreme to another, and Freud reinterpreted himself several times, the history of criminology can boast theorists who steadfastly held to their original ideas. Divergent opinions, mainly in the infancy period of criminology, led to much rancor and argument among the theorists whose approach to the problem of crime was mutually antagonistic.

These ardent debates brought into existence the third great stream of thought in criminology, the compromissary orientation, better known as the multifactor approach or by its former name, the multiple-cause theory. The discrepancies among the monofactor theories led to the multifactor understanding of crime. This bio-socio-psychological approach to crime and criminals endeavors to reconcile the disparate orientations and holds to the basic assumption that not a single cause but many factors lead man to criminal activity.

The International Association of Penal Law

The pioneers, albeit neglected pioneers, of the multifactor orientation were the Dutch G. A. Van Hamel (1842–1917), the Belgian Adolphe Prins (1845–1919), and the German Franz von Liszt (1851–1919). Although not the first adherents of this understanding of crime, in 1888 they gave impetus to the cause of the multifactor theories by establishing the International Association of Penal Law. Van Hamel, Prins, and Liszt made great efforts to gather the best thinkers of criminal law and criminology so that both conservative and modern trends would be represented. The importance of sociological factors was stressed along with the psychological and psychiatric causes, and it was emphasized that in the search for the origin of crime both the criminal and his social environment must be thoroughly investigated.

Perhaps the best illustration of this orientation is the work of Liszt, who devoted so much of his life to it. At the beginning Liszt described the criminal as the sociological phenomenon; later, however, he turned his interest to the personality of the offender. Liszt attempted to unite all the orientations in one great comprehensive study of crime and criminals, "the global science of criminal law" or (*Gesamte Strafrechtswissenschaft*), which included not only the various understandings of crime causation, but also penology, criminal politics, and criminal statistics. Because he incorporated both biological and sociological factors, he may truly be regarded as the founder of this dualistic system of criminology. Van Hamel and Prins offered similar theoretical propositions; with Liszt, they contended that crime was a "social-pathological phenomenon."[2]

Ferri thought well of the "logical tendencies" of Van Hamel, but described Prins's and Liszt's ideas as "hopeless" and "sterile."[3] Ferri's revolutionary mind could never appreciate the proposed compromise. He found Liszt "undecided between the old and the new ideas . . . in the hazy zone of eclecticism."[4]

From the "Individual Delinquent" to the "Containment"

Van Hamel, Prins, and Liszt succeeded in stimulating a great many followers. The immense knowledge accumulated by a century of criminological thinking may mislead the onlooker to think that the contemporary criminologist is therefore well informed. However, criminology is still faced with a mass of problems. The pressure of unanswered issues and the riddle of responsibility almost inevitably force the majority of thinkers to bow to the multifactor orientation. Some cannot think of any other solution, others want to avoid extravagant novelties, a few desire to safe-guard objectivity, still others really believe in the multifactor approach as the only way to understand why man violates the law.

One of the American pioneers of the multiple-cause under-standing was William Healy, whose work rather clearly indicates that the multifactor orientations aim at finding the individual crime factors in the individual cases.[5] "Persons who study indi-vidual cases by means of this approach are convinced that one crime is caused by one combination of circumstances of 'factors,' another crime is caused by another combination of circumstances of 'factors.' "[6] Healy analyzed over 800 delinquency cases brought before a juvenile court in a five-year period. He found no fewer than 138 distinct delinquency factors, mainly "mental abnormalities and peculiarities" and "defective home condi-tions." Healy classified his factors into fifteen major classes.

A decade later the English Cyril Burt applied a similar multi-factor individual approach in his study *The Young Delinquent*.[7] In his sample, somewhat smaller than Healy's, he identified 170 relevant factors and classified them into nine major categories.

A recent example of a multiple-cause understanding of crime and delinquency is Walter C. Reckless' "containment theory,"[8] also known as the "Halt" theory.[9] Reckless proposes a combina-tion of "internal and external containments, probably with greater weight assigned to the internal." It somewhat resembles the Freudian concept of the psyche, by placing in the center of the theory the "self-concept" (not really different from Freud's "ego"), which can be evaluated as either "good" or "bad" and which is supposed to be a "normal product" of man "within the normal range of childhood, adolescent, and adult development." Reckless suggests that his is the best general theory to explain "the largest amount" of criminal and delinquent behavior. How-ever, he warns that the self-concept notion does not apply to compulsive acting-out neurotics, psychopaths, those with extreme character disorders, emotional disturbances, or pathogenic damages or who commit "crimes of the moment," or "when a total group, family, tribe, or village is devoted to a life of parasitic activities."

According to this containment theory, behavior, deviant or conforming, is the result of a struggle between "social pressures," "social pulls of the milieu," and "inner pushes of the individual" —all seen in a vertical arrangement. The "social pressures" are exemplified by poverty, unemployment, economic insecurity, family conflicts, minority group status, lack of opportunities, and class and social inequalities. "Social pulls" are exemplified by individual prestige, bad companions, delinquent or criminal subculture, deviant groups, mass media, propaganda, suggestions, and so on. The "inner pushes" refer to restlessness or discontent, marked inner tensions, hostility, aggressiveness, aggrandizement and need for immediate gratification, extreme suggestibility, rebellion against authority, sibling rivalry, hypersensitivity, feelings of inadequacy and inferiority, guilt reactions, mental conflicts, anxieties, compulsions, phobias, organic impairments (brain damage, epilepsy, etc.), and others.

These merely exemplified, but undefined, pressures, pulls, and pushes struggle with one another, and the "structure of containment" may serve as a "buffer." This buffer (this is the "Halt") is made up of several components, again only exemplified by the "moral front": institutional reinforcement, reasonable norms and expectations, acceptance, fostering a sense of belonging and identity, etc., and qualities in the individual himself, such as self-control, ego strength, well-developed superego, and high resistance to diversions. Reckless concludes that it depends upon this "buffer" whether or not the individual develops into a delinquent or criminal.

In elaborating on his containment theory, Reckless placed it "somewhere" between the push, pull, and pressure theories. Any precise placement might be controversial. The containment theory displays a rather heavy involvement in a number of different directions.

Orientation or Theory

Sutherland and Cressey call attention to the fact that adherents of the multifactor orientation "sometimes take pride in their position, pointing to the narrow particularistic explanations of other schools and to their own broadmindedness in including all types of factors."[10] But this pride is not fully justified. The multiple-cause theory is not a theory in the true sense of the term; at best, it is an omnibus theory, since it accepts all other theories.

Albert K. Cohen, in one of the most penetrating critiques of the multifactor theories, does not deny the value of this approach.[11] He finds their careful enumeration of factors and their "statistical summarization" an important phase of research. Nevertheless, Cohen propounds three main observations against the multifactor theories. First, he suggests that a multiplicity of factors should not be confused with a multiplicity of variables; even a single theory may use many variables. Second, referring to the "assumption of intrinsic pathogenic qualities," he suggests that associated factors should not be confused with causes; each factor may have crime-producing potential, but one factor alone may not be strong enough to produce criminality. And third, Cohen points to the fallacy that "evil causes evil," an assumption of most multifactor approaches; it is not necessarily true that evil consequences (crime) spring from evil precedents.

Because so many divergent factors are already known in criminology, and so many divergent factors are used by most theories, it has become difficult to determine which theories really reflect and which do not reflect the multifactor orientation.

NOTES

1. Enrico Ferri, *Criminal Sociology*, Joseph I. Kelly and John Lisle (trs.) (New York, 1967), pp. 21–22, 33, 364–405.

2. Franz von Liszt, *Das Verbrechen als Sozialpathologische Erscheinung* (Dresden, 1899).

3. Ferri, *Criminal Sociology, op. cit.*, p. 33.

4. *Ibid.*, pp. 394–395.

5. William Healy, *The Individual Delinquent* (Boston, 1915).

6. Edwin H. Sutherland and Donald R. Cressey, *Principles of Criminology* (7th ed., Philadelphia, 1966), pp. 61–62.

7. Cyril Burt, *The Young Delinquent* (London, 1925).

8. Walter C. Reckless, *The Crime Problem* (4th ed., New York, 1967), pp. 469–483.

9. Walter C. Reckless, "Halttheorie," *Monatschrift für Kriminologie und Strafrechtsreform*, 44 (June 1961), 1–14.

10. Sutherland and Cressey, *op. cit.*, p. 63.

11. Albert K. Cohen, "Multiple Factor Approaches," in Marvin E. Wolfgang, Leonard Savitz, and Norman Johnston (eds.), *The Sociology of Crime and Delinquency* (New York, 1962), pp. 77–80.

XI

The Responsibility of the Surroundings

Criminal Ecology

Ecology is a branch of biology dealing with the relationship of organisms to their environment. Ecologists study the habits and modes of life of living organisms as related to their surroundings. "Human ecology" deals with the environmental relationships between human beings and social space. Delinquency and crime are among the many issues studied in the ecological mirror. While criminal biology and criminal anthropology are closely related to psychology and psychiatry, the ecological understanding is strongly linked with sociology.

Like so many "new" ideas in modern criminology, interest in criminal ecology can be traced back to the early nineteenth century, when efforts were made to make man's surroundings responsible for his crime and to connect crime and delinquency with the social distribution of people and the physical characteristics of their surroundings. Enrico Ferri, in an early edition of *Criminal Sociology*, called attention to the generating force of "a particular physical and social environment."[1] Vold refers to Gabriel Tarde,[2] whose "law of imitation" would be the original theoretical background for criminal ecology.[3] This might be true in view of Tarde's reference to "learned behavior," which is a theoretical assistance to the ecological consideration of crime.

The cartographic method as it relates crime to the physical environment can be traced back to Guerry in the first half of the nineteenth century.[4] Mayhew investigated crime in England and Wales, and found its rate was above average in industrial centers and below average on the border of the counties.[5] Quetelet,[6] Lacassagne,[7] Oettingen,[8] and others paid similar attention to environmental factors. Georg von Mayr emphasized that in studying criminality, which he called "an important social-pathological product," the "condition of accumulation of the population must have a special importance."[9] The attention of the early contributors to criminal ecology was largely directed to the comparative study of rural and urban crime patterns. Gustav Aschaffenburg,[10] H. H. Burchardt,[11] and Hellmuth von Weber[12] are a few Europeans who used ecological techniques to assess rural-urban variations in crime. One might even list among the ecological approaches Enrico Ferri's[13] and William Douglas Morrison's[14] "cosmic" consideration of crime, Meyer's "tellurionic" interpretation,[15] and Gaedeken's speculation about the "physico-chemical influence of meteorologic agents" on crime.[16] Modern criminal ecology attempts to introduce ecological determinism in its search for spatial influences on social life and deviant behavior.

Delinquent Areas

Sophonisba Breckenridge and Edith Abbott made pioneering efforts to examine "delinquent neighborhoods" in Chicago.[17] Their attention was directed to such environmental-geographical factors as rivers, canals, large lodging houses, and railroad tracks, which seemed to be related to delinquency. Robert Park, Ernest Burgess, and Roderick McKenzie took a similar approach in their experimental sociological study by dividing the Chicago area into a series of concentric zones.[18] At the core of the city they found the main area of business (central city). Around this core moving toward the city periphery were the zones of light manufacturing (zone of transition), then workingmen's homes, businessmen's housing, industrial development, apartment houses, and finally suburbs. Although their approach has since been criticized, they detected distinguishing social characteristics in each zone, and through their findings they stimulated other ecological studies, mainly in Chicago, but also in other cities throughout the world.

Clifford R. Shaw concentrated on the problem of delinquency and introduced the concept of "delinquency areas."[19] As he marked the residences of "official" delinquents on the map of Chicago, Shaw arrived at a number of ecological conclusions. He revealed that the delinquency rate systematically declined the farther the zone was from the center of the city, a tendency he explained in terms of physical deterioration of the interior zones, with their variety of social pathologies including crime, mental illness, suicide, and poverty. Delinquency rates, Shaw discovered, appeared virtually constant in the "delinquency areas" over a considerable period of time despite the changing ethnic composition of the area population.

Henry D. McKay subsequently joined Clifford Shaw in further ecological investigations in Birmingham, Cleveland, Denver, Philadelphia, Richmond, and Seattle, where they found delinquency characteristics similar to those in the original Chicago project.[20] At a later date, with much the same results, they restudied Chicago in order to establish adequate ecological control regarding delinquency rates "in relation to differential characteristics of local communities in American cities."[21]

Calvin Schmid's research in the Minneapolis–St. Paul area also confirmed the higher delinquency rates in the central districts of the city and decreasing rates toward the periphery.[22] Stuart Lottier's Detroit findings supported Schmid's conclusions,[23] but

Bernard Lander disagreed with "ecological determinism" and rejected the so-called zonal hypothesis of juvenile delinquency.[24] On the basis of his research in Baltimore, he believed that the high level of delinquency in certain areas of the city was due to social disorganization and a general anomic situation rather than to ecological factors. High delinquency rates were found to be clustered with a low percentage of homeowners and, in a curvilinear fashion, with the percentage of nonwhites in the area. Roland Chilton made an attempt to reconcile the findings of earlier delinquency-area studies.[25] His results do not support Lander's conclusion; Chilton related delinquency to certain economic variables in the area.

A critique of the ecological studies came from the Englishman Terence Morris, who himself studied an English town and surveyed and analyzed most of the American and British efforts in this field.[26] He and other critics questioned the methods generally used in these analyses. Nevertheless, although the ecological theorists have failed to account for unofficial delinquency, have not always distinguished court statistics from police statistics, have not classified delinquency according to social stratification, and have not clearly distinguished sociocultural borders from political boundaries, they still offer many important insights into the problem of crime and delinquency.

The responsibility of man's surroundings for crime seems to have a permanent appeal to the investigators of the crime problem. Even if this is not the prime target of a research study, man's physical world is often treated in the analysis. Marvin E. Wolfgang in his search for homicide patterns extended his attention to temporal and spatial aspects.[27] Hans von Hentig saw "the criminal man as a puppet of time and space."[28] Stephen Schafer attempted to find significance of time and spatial features in criminal-victim relationships.[29] In his study on the natural environment, Wolf Middendorf discussed the climate and weather, the rhythm of the seasons and "nature as the place of the act."[30]

Many old beliefs concerning the influence of physical surroundings are no longer valid: man has become the master of many physical forces. Ecological factors are not the only causes of crime, but human efforts could neutralize most of them.

NOTES

1. Enrico Ferri, *Criminal Sociology* (New York, 1897), p. 55.
2. Gabriel Tarde, *La Philosophie Pénale* (Paris, 1890).
3. George B. Vold, *Theoretical Criminology* (New York, 1958), p. 188.
4. André Michel Guerry, *Essai sur la statistique morale* (Paris, 1833).
5. H. Mayhew and J. Binney, *The Criminal Prisons of London* (London, 1862).
6. Adolphe Quetelet, *Sur l'homme et la développement de ses facultés ou essai de physique sociale* (Paris, 1835).
7. A. Lacassagne, "Marche de la criminalité en France de 1825 à 1880," *Revue scientifique*, May 28, 1881.
8. Alexander V. Oettingen, *Die Moralstatistik in ihrer Bedeutung für eine Sozialethik* (3rd ed., Erlangen, 1882).
9. Georg von Mayr, *Moralstatistik mit Einschluss der Kriminalstatistik* (Tübingen, 1917).
10. Gustav Aschaffenburg, *Das Verbrechen und seine Bekämpfung* (Heidelberg, 1903).
11. H. H. Burchardt, *Kriminalität in Stadt und Land* (Berlin, 1936).
12. Hellmuth von Weber, "Kriminalsoziologie," in Rudolph Sieverts, ed., *Handwörterbuch der Kriminologie* (2nd ed., Berlin, 1967/1968), pp. 71–74.
13. Enrico Ferri, "Variations thermométriques et criminalité," *Archives d'Anthropologie Criminelle et des Sciences Pénales*, 1886.
14. William Douglas Morrison, *Crime and Its Causes* (London, 1891).

15. A. Meyer, *Die Verbrechen in ihrem Zusammenhang mit dem wirtschaftlichen und sozialen Verhältnissen in Kanton Zürich, Abhängigkeit von tellurischen Faktoren* (Jena, 1895).

16. P. Gaedeken, "Contribution statistique à la réaction de l'organisme sous l'influence physico-chimique des agents météorologiques," *Archives d'Anthropologie Criminelle et de Médecine Légale,* 24 (1909), 173–187.

17. Sophonisba P. Breckenridge and Edith Abbott, *The Delinquent Child and the Home* (New York, 1912).

18. Robert E. Park, Ernest W. Burgess, and Roderick D. McKenzie, *The City, The Ecological Approach to the Study of the Human Community* (Chicago, 1925).

19. Clifford R. Shaw, *Delinquency Areas* (Chicago, 1929).

20. Clifford R. Shaw and Henry D. McKay, *Social Factors in Juvenile Delinquency,* National Commission of Law Observance and Enforcement, Report on the Causes of Crime, Vol. 2., No. 13 (Washington, D.C., 1931).

21. Clifford R. Shaw and Henry D. McKay, *Juvenile Delinquency and Urban Areas, A Study of Rates of Delinquents in Relation To Different Characteristics of Local Communities in American Cities* (Chicago, 1942).

22. Calvin F. Schmid, *Social Saga of Two Cities, An Ecological and Statistical Study of the Social Trends in Minneapolis and St. Paul* (Minneapolis, 1937).

23. Stuart Lottier, "Distribution of Criminal Offenses in Metropolitan Regions," *The Journal of Criminal Law, Criminology and Police Science,* 29 (1939).

24. Bernard Lander, *Toward an Understanding of Juvenile Delinquency* (New York, 1954).

25. Roland J. Chilton, "Continuity in Delinquency Area Research: A Comparison of Studies for Baltimore, Detroit, and Indianapolis," *American Sociological Review,* 29 (February 1964), 71–83.

26. Terence Morris, *The Criminal Area* (London, 1958).

27. Marvin E. Wolfgang, *Patterns in Criminal Homicide* (Philadelphia, 1958).

28. Hans von Hentig, *Das Verbrechen, I. Der Kriminelle Mensch im Kräftespiel von Zeit und Raum* (Berlin, 1961).

29. Stephen Schafer, *The Victim and His Criminal* (New York, 1968).

30. Wolf Middendorff, "Natürliche Umwelt," in Rudolph Sieverts (ed.), *Handwörterbuch der Kriminologie* (2nd ed., Berlin, 1968), II, 240–254.

XII

The Responsibility of the Society

The Criminal as a Product of His Society

The sociologically oriented approaches to the problem of crime assume that the criminal is not an isolated individual; he is a product of his society. Rather than seeking the causes of crime in the individual himself, as hypothesized by biological and psychological theorists, the sociologist comprehends the criminal as a member of his social group, viewing him as a phenomenon whose criminal conduct originates in the abnormalities of his social existence or in society's behavior toward him. Therefore the criminal, socially different from those whose social behavior is "proved" normal by their conformity to the law, is a variation of the socialized human group. His criminality is a form of antisociality. Because the criminal is by definition socially distinct from the conventional members of the society, he is unaffected by threat of the traditional retributive punishment. Any solution to the crime problem, it is argued, can be found only in an analysis of the criminal's relationship to his social environment.

Although the sociological explanations have often been criticized, they are far and away the most influential at the present time. Even the most extreme adherents of the somatic or psychic approaches are unable to ignore the impact of social factors in the etiology of crime and delinquency. The sociological orientation, however, is not monolithic, but seen with numerous and distinct emphases. As phrenology led to the concept of moral insanity, which then became the constitutional inferior, and recently appeared as the psychopath or sociopath, so the modern sociological understanding of crime is the product of development.

Simple references to poverty, food prices, immigration, class stratification, slums, prostitution, alcoholism, and other economic and social problems developed into thinking in terms of culture conflict, subcultures, opportunity structure, anomie, differential association, and other sophisticated theoretical constructions. Several of them show only testing or broadening of old theories. For example, Leon Radzinowicz suggested that recent studies of delinquent gangs, by social scientists, were made "in a comparatively restricted field."[1] Pitirim A. Sorokin contended, "The main body of current research represents mainly a reiteration, variation, refinement and verification of the methods and theories developed by sociologists of the preceding period," and "few of these improvements represent anything revolutionary or basically new."[2]

Many of the sociological theories of crime and delinquency overlap. They draw from one another, from different sectors of the social sciences, and even reach for assistance from other disciplines. Since they use a multifactor theoretical construction, it is extremely difficult, if not impossible, to catalogue these theories according to orientation. Some may be considered "offensive" in nature. They "attack" the criminal, whose "free will" reacts to social injustice and provokes him to attack the society in the form of crime. Or they are offensive against the wrongs of the society and "attack" the society as a whole. Other theories seem to be "defensive"; they view crime and delinquency as products of a disorganized society or social pressures. They emphasize the need for social defense against criminality because criminal conduct is learned or acquired by the criminal in his social context. Some lean in the direction of social psychology, focusing on crime as a product of socialization processes; others refer to cultural differences or to value and norm conflicts; and still others explain crime in terms of the imperfect or divided structure of society.

The Offensive Understanding of Crime

This approach assumes that man freely decides whether or not to engage in crime. The criminal, who made a negative choice, is ultimately responsible for his own criminal conduct. His inadequately socialized will, free of the restrictions an adequate socialization would have imposed on him, is responsible for leading him against the criminal law.

Since the criminal believes that his aspirations cannot be satisfactorily realized, he eventually comes to see his society as either unnecessarily constraining or as partially or wholly unjust. In order to attain his aspirations, he attacks society by violating those legal norms that stand in his path. If he is hungry, he steals bread; if he wishes to live luxuriously, he robs a bank; if he dislikes his work, he forges a check so to live at another's expense. If he hates someone, he kills him. The decision is his alone.

Cesare Beccaria is the classic representative of this understanding of crime. His formalistic, retributive approach has dominated criminal practice for 150 years. Most legalists, courts, and penal systems continue to operate on this principle, although they often deny it, and, actually, occasional reforms have broken the rigidity of this approach.

The wrongs of society, and the pressure they exert on the law violator (another dimension of the offensive understanding of crime), alleviates the responsibility of the criminal for his crime since he cannot escape the criminogenic strains and tensions of society. Society is charged with the responsibility of socializing the individual will, and its failure leads to man's criminal decision. Criminal conduct is therefore merely a personal response to pressure and stress. Society and not the criminal, proponents of this theoretical position assume, is the guilty party.

Léonce Manouvrier, an anthropologist and a prominent member of the French environmental school, whose work was praised by Bonger as one of the best on crime,[3] suggested that the criminal is merely an expression of the social milieu, and only perfection of social laws can diminish the volume of crime.[4] "Everybody is guilty in crime," Adolphe Quetelet accused, "except the criminal"; it is the society that prepares the crime, he said, and the criminal is only an instrument on which the society plays.[5] Another member of the French school, J. A. E. Lacassagne, author of the famous dictum "Societies have the criminals they deserve," also blamed society as a whole for the emergence of the criminal man. "The social environment," he proposed, "is the bouillon for culturing criminals, and the microbe, that is, the criminal, is an element of importance only if the medium was found where it can grow."[6] Lacassagne, who preceded Walter Miller's "generating milieu,"[7] Albert Cohen's "delinquent subculture,"[8] and other modern environmentalist hypotheses by some eighty years, impressed even the formidable Franz von Liszt, whose memorable efforts attempted to bring together the diversified theoretical trends. Liszt too suggested that crime is a "necessary, unavoidable result of the given conditions."[9]

Leon Radzinowicz suggested that those "criminologists who were not Marxists began to speak their language."[10] However, while the "offensive theory of pressured criminality" postulated a strong environmental influence in crime causation, it was not the language of the socialist theory of crime. The Marxist theory holds the economic structure solely responsible for criminal conduct, and the "offensive" theorists relate crime to inappropriate social values and demand a change in the value system without proposing economic structural changes. While this school of thought gained great popularity among those who believed in social determinism, perhaps it achieved its greatest triumph when its adherents, led by Manouvrier, pressed Lombroso to recognize the role of sociological factors.

Crime as Socially Acquired Behavior

In the "defensive" approaches to the crime problem the criminal's personal responsibility is not denied, but the interrelation between criminal and his environment remains the essential theoretical element. One defensive theory admits some aspects of social psychology. Crime is explained as a socially acquired conduct; it is learned through interpersonal relationships, or it may be the product of imperfect, misdirected, or undirected socialization. This hypothesis suggests that "persons acquire patterns of criminal behavior in the same way that they acquire patterns of lawful behavior."[11]

It may be argued that Benoit Augustin Morel was first to propose that crime was learned, and called attention to the "moral contagion" that results from publication of crimes in newspaper.[12] Paul Aubry, in his study on "the contagion of murder," held that contagion is a symptom of Morel's "morbid psychology," the main factors of which are "suggestion" and "imitation."[13] Maladjustment, or the lack of adaptation by the individual to his society, is the keynote in the works of M. A. Vaccaro, who saw crime as a rebellion by the criminal against the lawmaker's command.[14] These early "imitation" and "socialization" theories foreshadowed the contemporary biological and anthropological approaches to crime. They did not deny the role of factors such as heredity, disturbed nervous system, or anatomical peculiarities; however, they viewed biological or physical factors as only a force preparing the ground for more decisive social causes.

Although he was not the first to propose a learning theory, Gabriel Tarde (1843–1904) is generally credited with formulating criminal patterns as a product of interaction with others.[15] He was a philosopher, a sociologist, a psychologist, a practical lawyer, and a statistician—but always and in all capacities keenly interested in the crime problem.[16] His emphasis on the social origins of crime had a lasting impact on criminological thought in both Europe and America. A formidable critic of Lombroso, he denied the significance of physical anomalies but did not reject the role of all biological factors in human behavior. In his comparative survey of several criminological studies (Benedikt, Ferri, Lacassagne, Marro, Virgilio, and others) he refuted the existence of the born criminal[17] but did make allowance for Lombroso's epileptic character of prisoners. Nevertheless, both towering issues of his philosophy, the moral responsibility and the laws of imitation, clearly indicate that in Tarde's thinking crime is a social product and represents a socially acquired conduct.

The individual's personal identity or self-concept and the common core of customs, interests, and education are the basic pillars in Tarde's moral-responsibility concept. It complements his basic theory of the "laws of imitation," which proposed three types of imitation or repetitive behavior patterns. First, men imitate the fashions and customs of others, and the more contact among people the more imitation takes place. Second, a superior is often imitated by his inferior; Tarde listed a few crimes that were originally known only to the higher classes but in course of history spread to lower social levels. And third, if two mutually exclusive fashions or customs conflict, the newer one will be more imitated.

Tarde's emphasis on the social texture of crime is considered "a cornerstone of present American criminological theories."[18] He never makes clear why the first crime, which set the imitative patterns in motion, was committed or why the majority of a society remains law-abiding and only a minority imitates the criminal. Nevertheless, Tarde's original and independent thinking has stimulated several contemporary theorists to offer similar or refined propositions. "It is a tribute to Tarde's originality and foresight that seventy years ago he expounded the ideas on crime causation that are the working hypotheses of American criminologists today."[19]

Perhaps the most outstanding adherent of Tarde's theories was Edwin H. Sutherland, who not only developed his theory of "differential association," but heavily leaned on Tarde in his penetrating analysis of "the professional thief."[20] The first formal statement of his theory of differential association appeared in the third edition of his *Principles of Criminology* in 1939.[21] Sutherland pointed out that his theory was already stated in the previous editions of his book, but only "in scattered passages and was not developed."[22] He made it clear that even in its formal presentation "obviously this theory is not the last work on the subject; in fact, it is stated thus openly in the expectation that it will be criticized and will thus lead to the development of a more satisfactory theory of criminal behavior."[23]

Sutherland offered his tentative theory in the form of seven propositions.[24] First, the processes of systematic criminal behavior are fundamentally the same as the processes of lawful behavior; they differ only in the standards by which they are judged. Second, criminal behavior is determined in a process of association with criminals, just as lawful behavior is determined in a process of association with law-abiding people. Third, differential association is the causal process in the development of crime. Fourth, frequency and consistency of contacts with criminal patterns determine the chance of criminal behavior. Fifth, individual differences in personal characteristics or in social situations cause crime only as they affect the "differential association." Sixth, cultural conflict is the underlying cause of differential association. Seventh, social disorganization is the basic cause of systematic criminal behavior.

Sutherland soon recognized some weak points in his theory and corrected them in the fourth edition of his book, published in 1947. The content of what is learned from criminal behavior patterns differs from what is learned from anticriminal behavior patterns; this is why Sutherland called this process "differential association." People become criminal not only because of contacts with criminal behavior patterns but also because of their isolation from anticriminal patterns. Resembling Tarde's first law of imitation, Sutherland's differential association refers to a ratio of associations with both criminal and anticriminal behavior patterns. Moreover, explained Cressey, the association need not be with criminals, since a noncriminal may present criminal patterns and a criminal can show noncriminal behavior.

Sutherland's theory has been frequently criticized on several grounds. Leon Radzinowicz does not hold the hypothesis in high regard: "It was only because of Sutherland's high standing and solid reputation that this thesis evoked as much interest as it did."[25] Nigel Walker similarly commented that the differential-association theory simply illustrates the fate of so many criminological hypotheses, "which begin with the observation of the obvious, generalize it into a principle, and are eventually reduced again to a statement of the limited truths from which they originated."[26]

Crime as socially acquired behavior may be seen also in the theories of Edmund Mezger's *Lebensführungsschuld*, idea of "responsibility for the life conduct," which refers in part to the expected socialization of the criminal[27] and Ernst Seelig's *Lebensformen*, which implies "forms of life" amenable to socialization processes. In these two examples the socialization or learning of anticriminal behavior is proposed on a social base, but it should come from "within" the criminal. It could be argued that Sutherland's "white collar criminal" belongs to this category.

Donald R. Cressey's concept of "rationalization"[28] contends that the verbalizations applied by the criminal to his own conduct are rationalizations that are learned through his contact with criminal behavior patterns. Another theory, which recognizes "justifications for deviance that are seen as valid by the delinquent but not by the legal system or society at large" is that of Gresham M. Sykes and David Matza,[29] who discussed the "techniques of neutralization" exercised by the smaller social groups to which the delinquent belongs.

An example of another focus among the theories that explain crime as an acquired conduct is Eric Wolf's[30] and George Dahm's[31] assumption of the existence of "normative personalities." These hypotheses are based on the idea of "phenomenological personalism"; the criminal is viewed as an "existential being" whose attachment to a normative crime type is the result of his social circumstances. The possibility of biological causes, however, is not discarded in these theories, and social factors are vaguely indicated.

Responsibility of the Culture and Its Norms

Another trend of the defensive-type sociological theories of crime holds the culture, its values and norms, and their conflict responsible for leading man against the criminal law. While the offensive approaches seem to propose cultural change, the defensive theories seem to aim at cultural correction. In this vein Adolphe Prins, before he joined Liszt and van Hamel, recognized "a sort of degeneration of the social organism."[32] Donald R. Taft's "theory of crime in American culture"[33] suggests that crime must be prevalent in a society characterized by "dynamic quality, complexity, materialism, growing impersonality, individualism, insistence upon the importance of status, restricted group loyalties, survivals of frontier traditions, race discrimination, lack of scientific orientation in the social field, tolerance of political corruption, general faith in law, disrespect for some law, and acceptance of quasi-criminal exploitation," and, he adds, the list could be extended. Taft proposed that in such a culture there will be many conflicts, often taking the form of crime. His theory is clearly an accusation: crime is a product of the culture. This orientation encompasses the whole culture of the society, rather than the interaction of the individual with other individuals or with his social group.

Emile Durkheim contended that the existence of criminality in culture is normal.[34] More than that, he proposed that crime is necessary; it is a fundamental condition of social life, and it is useful because without it the normal evolution of morality and law would be aborted. For progress to take place, Durkheim argued, individual originality should be able to express itself, including the originality of the criminal. In this light, the role of crime in a culture thus acquires a quite different interpretation from those that identify crime with evil, want to diminish or abolish it, and to this end propose massive programs of social change.

Culture is viewed through its conduct norms by Thorsten Sellin, who understands crime in terms of their conflict.[35] Culture conflicts are inevitable, Sellin suggests, when "the norms of one cultural or subcultural area migrate to or come in contact with those of another." This occurs when cultural codes clash on the border of contiguous culture areas, when the law of one group is extended over the territory of another, or when members of one culture migrate to another. The culture conflict (to which Tarde's concept of moral responsibility might be one possible answer) in Sellin's assumption is apt to result in violation of norms "merely because persons who have absorbed the norms of one cultural group or area migrate to another" and "such conflict will continue so long as the acculturation process has not been completed."

In this branch of the "defensive" sociological theories of crime some social-psychological aspects appear, but crime is viewed in the context of the whole culture or subculture.

Crime as a Product of Structural Disturbances

American criminology after World War II is perhaps best characterized by rejection of the "piece by piece" analysis of the causes of crime, focusing instead on the structural disturbances of inbalances of the society as the comprehensive cause of all the causes. Indeed, it would be arrogant nonsense to say that any of the other orientations—biological, psychological, or sociological—provided us with a final answer. In the last quarter-century hypotheses citing the imperfect social structure attempted to fathom the problem of crime through the smokescreen created by a legion of explanations that claim the solution but do not solve the problem. Not the anomalies of the physical organism or heredity, not degeneration or unconscious experiences, and not slums, poverty, broken homes, or other individual factors are emphasized in these theories. The assumptions about the processes of learning criminal behavior or about culture conflicts and maybe some others are sometimes called on to support the structure-centered theories, but all social or social-psychological factors are at best only ancillary to the focal issue of structural disturbances. Inadequate socialization is not emphasized as a major factor of crime, although even a perfectly structured society would have crime, unless its members were perfectly socialized to the conditions of this perfect social structure. In this respect structure-centered theories, in the end analysis, seem to be close to proposing natural laws.

While these theories generally contending inconsistencies in the social structure and uneven distribution of values, means, goals, and rewards, they do not typically recommend any radical change in the basic value system and in the economic or social construction of the society. Ideologically, this is one of the critical points where they differ from the change-demanding and often socialist-type theories: they do not spell out desired structural reforms and the ways of achieving them; they suggest structural corrections rather than changes.

The responsibility of disturbances in the social structure for generating crime is an idea that has been propagated for a long time, in fact centuries before our modern structure-centered theories emerged. Cesare Beccaria in his *Essay on Crimes and Punishments* in 1762 reported differential treatment of social classes; even executions were different: disgracing hanging for members of the lower classes and honoring beheading for the higher classes. Friedrich Engels in his *Condition of the Working-Class* in England in 1845 wrote that the social order made the workers' family life almost impossible, and thus children could be nothing but unhappy and tend toward crime. Enrico Ferri in his *Criminal Sociology* in 1884 recalled "a fact too often forgotten by legislators, criminalists, and superficial observers," that is, the "three sociological strata of delinquents." Ferri here called attention to the lower class, the members of which "are deprived of education and always held by material and moral wretchedness in the primitive condition of a savage fight for existence"—and from where the greater part of criminals is recruited.[36]

The central thrust to these theories has come from Emile Durkheim (1858–1917), the great French student of social organization who introduced the concept of anomie. He touched upon this concept in his *Division of Labor*[37] and later elaborated on it in *Suicide*.[38] As used by Durkheim, anomie means a lack of rules, absence of norms, lawlessness, or weakened norms that may lead to deviant behavior; anomic situations develop in societies that cannot or do not provide clear norms to guide aspirations and behavior. Norms provide security for the members of the society while they necessarily limit the success of aspirations. If the social constraints on the individual break down, individual security is not only shaken, but the limits of individuality become less certain. When the balance between cultural aspirations and social opportunities is lost, antisocial or deviant behavior may develop.

Durkheim's theory does not offer a convincing explanation for all crimes, delinquencies, and deviant behaviors, among others failing to explain why some individuals in anomic situations do not become criminals while others do. Robert K. Merton, using basically Durkheim's idea of anomie, relates crime and deviance to the unequal achievement of success by all men.[39] In his thinking, some social structures exert pressure on certain people to engage in nonconformist rather than conforming conduct. Merton differentiates two elements important for the purpose of analyzing "social structure and anomie": man's cultural aspirations and the institutional norms or acceptable modes of achieving these goals. An effective equilibrium, Merton argues, is maintained "as long as satisfactions accrue to individuals who conform to both constraints," that is, satisfaction from achieving goals and satisfaction with the institutionally set modes of striving toward these ends.

Merton believes that American society places great emphasis on individual success, while at the same time it excludes part of the society from achieving this success. Deviant behavior is not generated simply by the lack of opportunities. As Merton put it:

A comparatively rigidified class structure, a feudalistic or caste order, may limit such opportunities far beyond the point which obtains in our society today. It is only when a system of cultural values extols, virtually above all else, certain common symbols of success for the population at large while its social structure rigorously restricts or completely eliminates access to approved modes of acquiring these symbols for a considerable part of the same population, that antisocial behavior ensues on a considerable scale.

Members of the society who find themselves in this anomic trap are pressured to reach for deviant or criminal modes of action.

Donald Cressey pointed out that this theory explains the over-representation of lower-class members (Cressey used the term "working class") in the American criminal population, and also the overrepresentation of young males, Negroes, native white Americans, and urban dwellers.[40]

Albert K. Cohen found Merton's anomie highly plausible as regards adult professional crime and property delinquency of older and semiprofessional juveniles, but it fails to account for the existence and nature of the delinquent subculture as he described it.[41] Nevertheless, Cohen too places the deviants of his subculture in the lower class, stating that statistical studies tend to confirm the popular impression that "gang delinquency is primarily a working-class phenomenon." His "nonutilitarian," "malicious," and "negativistic" juvenile crimes occur only in one segment of the general culture (the "delinquent subculture"), the lower-class area. Cohen assumes that the lower-class boy (he often calls him "working-class boy") with low status as measured by middle-class terms has a major problem of adjustment to his status frustration. One possible response to this frustration is "the creation and maintenance" of the delinquent subculture, which offers status value and an outlet for aggression (this throws some light on delinquency against property).

Richard A. Cloward and Lloyd E. Ohlin have drawn from Emile Durkheim's rich intellectual inventory, but they also used Robert K. Merton's assumption of a disorganized American society, Clifford R. Shaw and Henry D. McKay's ecological findings, and Edwin H. Sutherland's hypothesis of differential association to build their own theory on features of the social structure that regulate the selection and evolution of deviant solutions.[42] They called their hypothesis "the theory of differential opportunity systems." Cloward and Ohlin claim the "lower-class areas of large urban centers" are the locale of adolescent male delinquent subcultures. They postulate three delinquent subcultures: the "criminal subculture," where the delinquent is "devoted to theft, extortion, and other illegal means of securing income"; the "conflict subculture," where violence predominates as a way of winning status; and the "retreatist subculture," where the consumption of drugs is stressed.

In Cloward and Ohlin's thinking, the social structure is responsible not only for the status frustration of the lower-class adolescent male, but also for available alternative solutions—opportunities. The opportunities available determine which of the three delinquent subcultures will prevail in a given social setting. Cloward and Ohlin too assume that the lower-class adolescent male is in an anomic situation that pressures him, depending on the opportunities, into one or another available subculture. And they too assume that this is an important feature of American life.

Walter C. Reckless' concept of the "categoric risk" belongs to the structure-centered school.[43] By "the analysis of the population characteristics of the arrested doers of criminal deeds," he found varying chances or risks that particular groups or categories of individuals have of being arrested or being admitted to a penal institution. Although Reckless submitted to his analysis the risk of sex, the risk of age, and the risk of nativity, he also called attention to the risk of race and to the risk of social class affiliation.

As mentioned, the term "anomie" first appeared in Durkheim's work in 1893, but almost half a century was needed before it was revived and applied to the understanding of crime in terms of social structural disturbances and another two decades before it became one of the most popular explanations in criminology. Although the pattern and quality of crime, and the patterns of the social structure, have changed since Durkheim observed anomic situations, and are likely to become increasingly divergent in our rapidly changing society and power structures, there is continuing interest in the anomie concept as a medium of understanding the criminal and the delinquent.

It is frequently maintained that the greater the discrepancy between culturally prescribed aspirations and available opportunities, the greater the crime probability. Although in recent times the anomie concept, and its social structural aspects, has been the most provocative contribution to the never-ending search for the answer to crime and delinquency, it offers little systematic or operational methods for solution. Thus, the anomie explanation of crime is deficient, and in the future criminology will inevitably face some difficulties if it remains a devoted believer in the anomie concept in the face of swift social changes.

Most analyses of anomic situations restrict themselves to the allegedly disorganized American culture, as if anomie were the only explanation of the American crime rate or delinquent subcultures, and thereby may lead to misinterpretations and hinder the analysis of criminal and delinquent behavior. Some studies avoid overt expression of the Mertonian variation of Durkheim's idea of suicide as their point of departure, but nevertheless continue their hypotheses in terms of striving for goals, blocked aspirations, lower-class deviance, and choices of illegitimate means for achieving goals. They seem to feel that American delinquency and crime can be explained simply by the fact that not all our success values and aspirations are attainable, being blocked in large part by such handicaps as class barriers. This understanding has been advanced as if success goals, aspirations, and barriers to their achievement for a considerable part of the population were exclusively American phenomena. It is as though in one form or another these theorists were looking for some "American" symptoms of the universal crime problem. In these studies the "dissociation between culturally defined aspirations and socially structured means"[44] is an exclusive feature of the American society and necessarily characteristic of its disorganized structure.

Opportunities or lack of same for achieving goals are present in all societies, regardless of how they are structured. Wealth, income, job, status, prestige, and the like are goals sought not only by America's affluent if disorganized society, but also by other peoples, both now and in other ages. If this were not true, the picture of crime as a world problem would appear quite differently and we would see radical differences in the nature of crime throughout the variety of cultures. If, for example, the major fact in the explanation of gang behavior is that a significant number of lower-class members "aspire beyond their means,"[45] it could be demonstrated that the same situation exists in other societies but does not result in gang delinquency.

Contrasted with the allegedly disorganized American social structure, the Soviet Union may be regarded as an overorganized society. Yet aspirations, goals, barriers, and illegitimate alternatives are not unknown there. Achievement, upward striving, encouragement of competition, and equal rights for all are not only part of the Soviet culture, as they are of American society, but are officially stressed. The "Stakhanovite" movement[46] encouraged individuals to produce more than their quotas so to reap both financial rewards and greater status. In addition, various "socialist competitions," both in physical and intellectual work, emphasize achievement and make substantial awards of money and decorations. Even the entire range of Party positions, from top to bottom, are sought amid fierce competition, partly because of the higher status and better living conditions that come with them. As W. W. Rostow noted, the Soviet regime has developed the incentive for competition by a "rising scale of real income for those who work harder or who are prepared to accept more responsible tasks" as well as an "elaborate graduation of awards and prizes to supplement material incentives with the almost universal desire of men for communal approval. In general the regime does not frustrate those ambitious to acquire prestige."[47] The status symbols in Soviet society might be different from those in American society, but the people do not aspire any less for them than Americans do for theirs.

This is not to say that opportunities are not limited in Soviet society. Although propaganda and highly organized, pervasive social control try to develop restraints so that the people will accept the available rewards, dissatisfaction cannot be avoided in those cases where individuals or social groups cannot achieve desired goals. "It appears to be the case that important conflicts exist between the aspirations and expectations which are generated by life in Soviet Russia and the realities which are confronted."[48] If in America the encouragement to compete is not balanced with unlimited opportunities for success, this is no less so in Soviet territories, where the goals are apparently equally uncoordinated with opportunities. The basic distinctions between the two societies seem to consist of a greater amount of state compulsion under the Soviet system, different definitions of aspirations, and in the composition of the privileged and unprivileged groups. But problems arising from social stratification seem inevitable once societies have evolved beyond the simplest level.

NOTES

1. Leon Radzinowicz, *Ideology and Crime* (New York, 1966), p. 97.
2. Pitirim A. Sorokin, "Sociology of Yesterday, Today and Tomorrow," *American Sociological Review*, 30 (December 1965), 834.
3. Willem Adriaan Bonger, *Criminality and Economic Conditions*, Henry P. Horton (tr.) (New York, 1967), p. 175.
4. Léonce Manouvrier, "La genèse normal du crime," *Bulletins de la Société d'Anthropologie de Paris*, IV (1893), 405–458.
5. Adolphe Quetelet, *Sur l'homme et le développement de ses facultés ou essai de physique sociale* (Paris, 1835), pp. 95–97.
6. *Le milieu social est le bouillon de culture de la criminalité; le microbe, c'est le criminel, un élément qui n'a d'importance que le jour où il trouve le bouillon qui le fait fermenter.*

Les sociétés ont les criminels qu'elles méritent. J. A. E. Lacassagne made these statements in the course of a discussion at the first international anthropological congress in 1885 in Rome; see *Actes du Premier Congrès International d'Anthropologie Criminelle, Biologie et Sociologie, Rome, 1885* (1886–1887), pp. 165–167.

7. Walter B. Miller, "Lower Class Culture as a Generating Milieu of Gang Delinquency," *Journal of Social Issues,* 14 (1958), 5–19.

8. Albert K. Cohen, *Delinquent Boys: The Culture of the Gang* (New York, 1955), pp. 24–32.

9. *Die notwendige, unvermeidliche Wirkung der gegebenen Bedingungen.* Franz von Liszt, "Die deterministischen Gegner der Zweckstrafe," a paper of 1893 reprinted in his *Strafrechtliche Aufsätze und Vorträge* (Berlin, 1905).

10. Radzinowicz, *op. cit.,* p. 45.

11. Donald R. Cressey, "Crime," in Robert K. Merton and Robert A. Nisbet (eds.), *Contemporary Social Problems* (2nd ed., New York, 1966), p. 173.

12. Benoit Augustin Morel, *De la contagion morale; du danger que présente pour la moralité et securité publique la relation des crimes donnée par les journaux* (Marseille, 1870), cited by de Quirós, *Modern Theories of Criminality* (New York, 1967), pp. 59–60.

13. P. Aubry, *La contagion du meurtre* (Paris, 1894).

14. M. A. Vaccaro, *Genesi e funzioni delle leggi penali* (Rome, 1889).

15. Gabriel Tarde, *La Philosophie Pénale* (Paris, 1890).

16. For more about Tarde see Margaret S. Wilson Vine, "Gabriel Tarde," in Hermann Mannheim (ed.), *Pioneers in Criminology* (London, 1960), pp. 228–240.

17. Gabriel Tarde, *La criminalité comparée* (Paris, 1890).

18. Wilson Vine, *op. cit.,* p. 228.

19. *Ibid.,* p. 230.

20. Edwin H. Sutherland, *Principles of Criminology* (4th ed., New York, 1947).

21. Donald R. Cressey, "The Theory of Differential Association: An Introduction," *Social Problems*, 8 (Summer 1960), 3.

22. Edwin H. Sutherland, *op. cit.*, p. v.

23. *Ibid.*, p. v.

24. *Ibid.*, pp. 4–9.

25. Radzinowicz, *op. cit.*, p. 82.

26. Nigel Walker, *Crime and Punishment in Britain* (London, 1965), p. 95.

27. Edmund Mezger, *Strafrecht* (Munich, 1948).

28. Donald R. Cressey, *Other People's Money: A Study in the Social Psychology of Embezzlement* (Glencoe, 1953).

29. Gresham M. Sykes and David Matza, "Techniques of Neutralization: A Theory of Delinquency," *American Sociological Review*, 22 (December 1957), 664–670.

30. Eric Wolf, *Vom Wesen des Täters* (Berlin, 1932).

31. Georg Dahm, *Der Tätertyp im Strafrecht* (Leipzig, 1940).

32. Adolphe Prins, *Criminalité et répression* (Brussels, 1886), p. 13.

33. Donald R. Taft and Ralph W. England, Jr., *Criminology* (4th ed., New York, 1964), pp. 275–279.

34. Emile Durkheim, *Rules of Sociological Method* (Glencoe, 1950), pp. 65–73.

35. Thorsten Sellin, *Culture Conflict and Crime*, Social Science Research Council, Bulletin 41 (New York, 1938).

36. Enrico Ferri, *Criminal Sociology*, Joseph I. Kelly and John Lisle (trs.) (New York, 1967), pp. 226–228.

37. Emile Durkheim, *De la division du travail social* (Paris, 1863).

38. Emile Durkheim, *Le suicide* (Paris, 1897).

39. Robert K. Merton, "Social Structure and Anomie," *American Sociological Review*, 3 (1938), 672–682; also "Social Problems and Sociological Theory," in Merton and Nisbet, *op. cit.*, pp. 775–823; and *Social Theory and Social Structure* (New York, 1957).

40. Cressey, "Crime," *op. cit.*, p. 180.

41. Cohen, *op. cit.*

42. Richard A. Cloward and Lloyd E. Ohlin, *Delinquency and Opportunity: A Theory of Delinquent Gangs* (Glencoe, 1960).

43. Walter C. Reckless, *The Crime Problem* (4th ed., New York, 1967), pp. 97–98.

44. Merton, "Social Structure and Anomie," *op. cit.*

45. Cloward and Ohlin, *op. cit.*, p. 88.

46. In 1935 Alexei Stakhanov cut a record amount of coal and in a few hours earned more than the coal miners' average monthly wage.

47. W. W. Rostow, *The Dynamics of Soviet Society* (New York, 1960), pp. 164–165.

48. *Ibid.*, p. 189.

XIII

The Responsibility of Economic Conditions

The Responsibility of Poverty

The disadvantages of poverty as they hinder an immense number of people from conforming to social norms is clearly a matter of vital importance to society, and criminology cannot afford to ignore the struggle against want and misery or fail to see poverty's responsibility for crime. Not only is there an obvious need to prevent or reduce the distress that crime causes to its victims, but also, and perhaps chiefly, there is an imperative need to prevent or reduce the suffering and distress that are causes of crime. Even before criminology was born, poverty was considered at least partly responsible for leading the sufferer of economic misery against the command of criminal law. "The poor" are a social category; "no one is socially poor until he has been assisted," contended George Simmel, who gathered all the assisted poor into one social group.[1]

Crime and delinquency, of course, are not confined to the poor. Nevertheless, the statistical correlation between poverty and crime has been proved beyond doubt. A century ago the French attorney-statistician A. Corne described poverty as the milieu most conducive to crime. He bitterly claimed that poverty was an endemic misery utterly without hope for any happiness, a condition that could not be conquered. It results in living from one day to the next, accepting hunger and illness as part of the human condition, a decay of body and soul. Corne asks sarcastically, How can all these degradations engender courage and energy to resist crime?[2] The labeling process of bygone centuries left a mark on the poor that has never completely disappeared. People still speak of the "poor but honest," and what this phrase expresses is the way man in the past looked upon his social surroundings. In a society that believed that poverty resulted from the moral deficiency of the poor and that crime resulted from poverty, only a system of social congratulations for the givers (the prosperous) could have developed. The "categoric risk" of the poor has been confused with the cause of crime.

Attack against the Economic Conditions

Economic conditions as generating crime is one of the oldest beliefs concerning the cause of criminal lawbreaking. It engaged the attention of thinkers even before the rise of modern criminology. Xenophon, Plato, Aristotle, and the Romans Vergil and Horace all touched upon this subject.[3] Perhaps Thomas More was one of the first "sociologists"; in his *Utopia* he commented on the economic conditions of England as they related to crime as a social phenomenon. A poor man, he suggested, can spend only as much as he can steal or beg, and thus he may be hanged or will end up in a prison as a vagabond.[4] More and the other utopian writers over the millennia were not the only ones to relate economic conditions to criminality: it has been an aspiration of almost all who wanted to solve the crime problem. Hardly any of the thinkers of the causes of criminality omitted poverty or economic conditions from their catalogue of crime factors, and thus an endeavor to present those who have treated this issue would mean to list almost all who treated the problem of crime.

In the eighteenth century Cesare Beccaria, in *Dei delitti e delle pene,* suggested that theft arises out of economic misery and desperation.[5] K. F. Hommel, a Leipzig professor of criminal law, in a lecture in April 1765, a few months after Beccaria's work appeared, proposed a radical reform of criminal law. Among other proposals he suggested that the threat of punishment is useless and ineffective so long as economic misery impels to crime; to combat crime, economic conditions first have to be improved.[6] In the nineteenth century J. M. Charles Lucas, a French penal reformer and champion in the struggle against capital punishment, stated that the origin of crime is misery and that misery is the handmaiden of ignorance. In his work on the penal system in general[7] he states this as an axiom without statistical or other evidence to support it; in a later work on prison reform, published in 1836, Lucas suggested that want and destitution in the lower class make prevalent crimes against property.

The nineteenth century shows especially heavy references to the role of economic conditions in criminality, and even Morel and Lombroso bent their markedly biological theories to allow for poverty and misery as agents in crime causation. Enrico Ferri originally felt that "poverty and fatigue" were the main social factors of crime, but he did not advocate drastic changes; moreover, he polemicized against Filippo Turati's socialist understanding. Later he strongly leaned toward change in the economic system. Raffaele Garofalo, the third of the "holy three," in general denied the influence of poverty or economic conditions on crime and did not believe that property crimes were higher in the lower class. In Garofalo's example, highway robberies were fading out while robberies in Pullman cars were on the increase.

The early statisticians as a matter of course dealt with the relationship between economic conditions and crime. André Michel Guerry was ambivalent in his analysis. He did not recognize poverty as the principal cause of crime but admitted it was influential; he found much difficulty in forming a judgment.[8] Edouard Ducpetiaux, in his study of the physical and moral conditions of young workers[9] and in his *Mémoire,* on poverty in Flanders,[10] took a rather strong position on the effect of economic conditions and found criminality an "inseparable companion" of poverty. An increase in the number of poor, he argued statistically, results in an increase in crime. Georg von Mayr, in his *"Statistics of the Judicial Police in the Kingdom of Bavaria and in Some Other Territories"* (England, Wales, and France), pioneered in working with a number of new statistical aspects. Among others he used police statistics, as opposed to court and prison figures; he introduced the price of rye as his independent variable; and he reflected from crime the state of morality. He found that a drop in prices produced a comparable decrease in crimes against property but an increase in offenses against the person.[11] A. Corne contended that possession of property is a preventive factor against criminality, since property ownership develops a sense of responsibility; he also named family and education as preventive forces.[12] In his study on criminality in Prussia, the German prison warden H. von Valentini recognized social and economic conditions as basic causes of crime. In his view the overwhelming majority of crimes are "purely material" in origin, and he too suggested that possession of property serves as a preventive to crime.[13]

Adolphe Quetelet, perhaps the most remarkable social statistician of his time, did not concentrate his analyses on economic conditions. Climate, age, sex, and similar variables were related to trends of criminality, and poverty was only one of the issues to which he paid some attention.[14] He did not deny that poverty might also be a factor that may cause a man to violate the criminal law. The other outstanding statistician of this era, A. von Oettingen, in his study of the significance of moral statistics for a social ethics,[15] used other investigators' findings along with his own to present a sort of comparative analysis. He pointed to the fact that unfavorable economic conditions create beggars and vagabonds, and also suggested that rising food prices increase offenses against property. Similar results were presented by the Hungarian Béla Földes, whose work, published in Germany, was highly praised by Joseph Van Kan.[16] Földes compared agricultural conditions in France (1845–1864), Belgium (1841–1860), England (1811–1858), and Austria (1831–1850).

Oettingen's and Valentini's views were fully shared by L. Fuld, who found a positive connection between prices and crime rates.[17] His novel finding was that fluctuations in prices had a particularly severe effect on the criminality of the young and were more likely to produce first offenders than recidivists. By this, Fuld meant to indicate the criminogenous significance of "need." The same notion is expressed by B. Weiss in his statistical study of economic and moral issues, published at the same time as the statistical study of Földes.[18] Weiss contended that hunger is the most forceful crime factor, and if a hungry man cannot be satisfied by any other means he will turn to crime.

W. Starke's careful statistical analysis, notwithstanding severe criticism by Mittelstadt, Aschrott, Schmoller, and other contemporaries, was a significant contribution to the problem of economic conditions and crime.[19] As Bonger described it, Starke found that the food prices influenced marriage and birth rates, and also the prevalence of criminality. When the price of rye and potatoes rose, so did the crime rates. Starke also found that when winters were very severe (as in 1855, 1856, 1865, and 1871), the price of food soared and stayed inflated for the entire year, affecting crime patterns even in the following spring and summer. Starke correlated different crimes (mainly theft, fraud, embezzlement, falsification of documents, bankruptcy, "malicious mischief," and others) with the seasons, income, education, tax, development of manufacturing, and other factors. L. M. Moreau-Christophe, in his study on the problem of misery and its ancient and modern solutions, also referred to industrial progress.[20] He suggested that, for England at least, the growth of industrialism increased pauperism, which in turn increased crime. He gave examples of English cities, such as Newcastle, where in 1837 every twenty-fourth person was arrested; Leeds, where in a six-year period (1833–1838) one out of every thirty-two people was sentenced; and Manchester, where in 1841 one out of every twenty-one people had to go to the magistrate.

Industrial conditions were also in the center of the statistical argument of M. Tugan-Baranowsky, who analyzed the social impact of "commercial crises" in England in 1823–1850 and 1871–1896 as they affected criminality.[21] Tugan-Baranowsky arranged his data by agricultural areas (Cambridge, Essex, Norfolk, Suffolk, Oxford, Lincoln, and Wilts), and then by industrial areas (Lancaster and Chester), and then for all of England. He found the most important changes in criminality in the industrial districts, where "each crisis had a devastating effect on the ranks of the working-classes." As a result of the crises, he observed, workhouses were loaded with the unemployed and prisons filled with those who had committed "crimes of necessity."

Like Quetelet and Guerry, there were other nineteenth-century statisticians who did not find poverty or economic depressions decisive crime factors. H. Stursberg, in his study on the increase of crime and its causes, did not deny that "misery" is an important factor but felt that the fundamental cause is "irreligion" and the weakening of Christian sentiment in church and school.[22] In analyzing crime and social life in Russia, E. Tarnowski indicated doubts about the determining role of poor harvests in theft rates since the overwhelmingly agricultural population profited by the resultant high price of grain.[23] A. Meyer, in his extensive statistical study on crimes and their connection with the economic and social conditions in the Swiss canton Zurich, showed that crimes against property are closely correlated with living conditions. But, he argued, this is not the only cause of crime; criminality is a "product of history" and economic conditions is only one of the many relevant factors.[24]

Rettich, cited by Bonger,[25] conceding the relationship between crimes against property and economic conditions, could not accept "the favorite expression of the Social-Democrats," which suggested that property crimes would "disappear" if private property were abolished. They forget, he argued, that robbery is not confined to individual victims and that "under the new order" the state would be robbed by the same robbers. Rettich claimed that "the apostles of state-ownership" should offer evidence for the fact that property crimes are "entirely due to hunger and need." H. Müller, in his statistical "investigations of criminality in its connection with economic conditions," seemed to lean toward a socialist understanding. He presented Prussian statistical data for a high percentage of theft, fraud, embezzlement, and other crimes against property, which, he said, were due to the "degeneration" of industrial activities. Müller claimed that the economic crisis beginning in 1873 was accompanied by dissatisfaction with the existing economic, social, and political conditions; it "embittered people's minds" and developed the struggle of labor against capital.[26]

The effect of economic conditions on criminality was also emphasized by the so-called *terza scuola* (the "third school"), sometimes confused with the Italian positivist school of criminology. A few Italian writers established it in the last decade of the nineteenth century, under the leadership of E. Carnevale[27] and B. Alimena,[28] who took a stand against the Lombrosian anthropological approach and argued for the social and economic understanding of the crime problem. Enrico Ferri petulantly stated there was no reason for the existence of this "third school": "One cannot believe that mere disagreements of personal views are sufficient to make a school or a scientific movement."[29] Jenö Balogh agreed with Ferri, since the significance of social and economic factors was well known for years before the *terza scuola* came into existence (it was propounded by the

French school, mainly by Lacassagne and Tarde), and in other respects the "third school" did not really differ from the tenets of the positivist school.[30]

Filippo Poletti was not a member of the *terza scuola,* but was nevertheless attacked by Ferri, Tarde, Garofalo, Niceforo, and others. Poletti, in his work on the sentiment in the science of criminal law, made the point that economic conditions could not be held responsible for crime without qualification.[31] He proposed to compare the rise of criminality with the growth of commerce and industry. Poletti found that between the years 1826 and 1878 in Italy crime rose 254 percent while the economy grew 300 percent; thus, he argued, industrialization produced relatively less crime.

E. Fornasari de Verce presented one of the most extensive nineteenth-century studies on poverty and crime.[32] He investigated changes in economic conditions and criminality in Italy from 1873 to 1890, in Great Britain and Ireland between 1840 and 1890, and in New South Wales, Australia, between 1882 and 1891. He listed a number of crimes, such as theft, embezzlement, blackmail, offenses against the order of the family (e.g. adultery, child-killing), homicide, assault, rebellion and violence against the public authorities, offenses against the public administration, offenses against religion, sexual crime, arson, horse stealing, homosexuality, and others, and analyzed the effect of economic conditions on each crime separately. Agricultural vicissitudes, fluctuations in the price of food, industrial crises and strikes, and conditions of the working class are only examples of the several variables di Verce used in his numerous correlations. He expressed the degree of influence of economic conditions in general terms, such as "much," "moderate," "little," "only slightly," and "not at all." One of his many findings was that crime was higher in those regions where wealth was above average; his explanation was that where there is wealth there is also poverty, and poverty induces use of criminal opportunities. Yet, to Bonger's disappointment,[33] di Verce failed to take the final step of advocating change in the whole economic system.

Willem Adriaan Bonger also seemed disappointed with many others who treated the problem of economic conditions and crime. He found only "a small number" who agreed with his socialist theory.[34] Most authors, he wrote, mention poverty and wealth but fail to see that these phenomena need explanation and have "a great influence upon the whole social organization." Bonger contended that the structure of a capitalist society exerts different pressures on different social classes. This calls to mind Leon Radzinowicz's comment that Robert K. Merton's notion of class vulnerability, a dimension he added to Durkheim's anomie theory, was "in some ways curiously reminiscent of Bonger."[35] One may add that this is not the only facet of modern criminological thought that recalls Bonger or another thinker of the past. Corne's reference to areas of "opportunities for wrong-doing,"[36] Quetelet's allusion to the "inequality of fortune" that makes the members of the working-class "desperate,"[37] Fuld's relating crime to economic competition,[38] Weiss's description of "wants" that may be satisfied through illegitimate means if legitimate ones are not available,[39] and others' emphases on various blockades and oppressions and on the pressures of social and economic factors may be seen as the seeds of many present-day explanations of crime and delinquency. Bonger himself, he made it clear, constructed his explanations around the classic doctrines of Marx and Engels;[40] while most of those whom Bonger criticized attacked one or another economic inequity, he attacked the entire capitalist economic system.

Attack against the Economic System

Bonger certainly was not the first to seek the answer to the problem of crime in the problems of capitalist economies. The historical understanding of economic conditions, the significance of the class struggle, the idea of the surplus value, and other issues of the Marxist ideology were known in one form or another before Karl Marx and Freidrich Engels united them into a single formidable theory and delivered perhaps the most important contribution of all time to the world of philosophical, political, economic, and social ideas. While not directly addressing themselves to the crime problem, Marx and Engels laid the foundation of theoretical attacks against the capitalist economic system. This group of theories, many before Bonger, attempted to find the capitalist economic structure of society responsible for leading man against the criminal law.

Marx proposed that all social phenomena—political, religious, ethical, psychic, and material—are products of economic conditions. He assumed that man is guided not by his conscience but by his economic position, which, then, determines the nature of his conscience. All social life, therefore, must be submitted to the strict law of causality. As all human beings are largely dependent on the economic structure of society, their personal and social lives are merely a superstructure (*Überbau*) built upon the deterministic economic foundation.

Orthodox Marxism, which has been periodically reinterpreted and misinterpreted, shows in some of its segments an illusory logic and contradictory hypotheses. A basic contradiction may seem to exist, for example, between the strict law of causality and the sensual-existential empiricism. Since man's social and economic existence determines his moral development, causality can lead only to extreme fatalism. Crime, therefore, cannot be prevented. Although Marx's theory of values seems to point to some particular moral law, the principle of immoralism—which assumes that ethical views must be excluded because all phenomena should be understood only in terms of necessity—challenges the theory of values. In this respect the formulation of a criminal law and the definition of crimes would need some interpretation. The forming and shaping role of man's will too is in contradiction with the general principle of fatalism, which may obscure the concept of crime and the role of free will. According to the original theory, science represents a variable function of economic conditions; Marxism, therefore, could be interpreted as rejecting the objective validity of scientific truths in favor of dogmatic ideological assertions that would ultimately hinder research attempts. The thesis that assumes the possibility of promoting or retarding even necessary and inevitable developments also appears as a contradiction and may place insoluble difficulties in the way of scientific criminology.

Of the two partners, Engels contributed more directly to the crime problem by comparing the increased criminality in England with the depression of 1844 in *The Condition of the Working Class in England in 1844*.[41] He pointed out that the number of crimes increased sixfold between 1815 and 1842 and that crimes were higher in agricultural than in industrial areas. Engels concluded that crime depends on the economic position of the proletariat. He described a sort of "anomic" and "blocked" position of the working class, which carries "all the disadvantages of the social order without enjoying its advantages" and to which "the social system appears in purely hostile aspects." Engels contended that "under the brutal and brutalizing treatment of the bourgeoisie" the working man, of necessity, often becomes a criminal.

Filippo Turati, the first to fully delineate a Marxist theory of crime, in discussing crime and the social question proposed that economic factors are virtually the only causes of criminality.[42] Although strongly opposed by Ferri, Turati felt that Lombroso's "born criminal" hypothesis did not explain why only a small portion of the population committed crimes, since biological factors ought to affect all men equally. Personal factors leading to crime, Turati implied, account for less than 10 percent of the crime-producing factors, regardless of economic conditions. Crime, he suggested, is the "monopoly" of the poor and, instead of changing the offender, society should be changed. Turati's firm stand for a socialist criminology brought clearly into question the position of Enrico Ferri. Although Ferri proclaimed in his *Socialismo e criminalita* that Marx complements Darwin and Spencer, and "together they form the great scientific trinity of the nineteenth century,"[43] his polemic against Turati casts grave doubts on the belief in a "socialistic Ferri." Indeed, Ferri was not far from that, but perhaps his basic arguments for radical social reform and strong state control would better characterize his approach to the problem of criminality. He saw criminal sociology as a midpoint between the extremist socialist understanding, which attributes all crime to flaws in the social structure, and the extremist biological understanding, which can see only individual factors.

In his study on crime and economic conditions in Sicily, Alfredo Niceforo, somewhat like Ferri, also strongly leaned toward a socialist view of crime factors.[44] Niceforo pointed out that class conflict plays an important role in the "direct" causes of crime and that property owners, through their influential economic position, control the machinery of the police, which is directed against the poor. As "indirect" causes of crime, Niceforo mentioned the decline in altruism among the humiliated and exploited laborers and "organic degeneracy" among the poor, which, he said, is the result of an inferior economic position.

Close to the Marxist ideology is the thinking of Max Nordau, who in his "new biological theory of crime" proposed an idea later adopted by the socialist criminal law system of the Soviet Union.[45] He suggested that "human parasitism" may develop as a product of social maladjustment. Nordau explained that crime often equated with "parasitism," but he used this term in its analogical rather than its biological sense. In society there are men who wish to take away the fruit of other people's labor without compensation. "In short," Nordau said, "they are men who treat other men as raw material from which they satisfy their needs and appetites." Rafael Salillas called this a "fundamental theory of crime" and extended it with the factor of poverty;[46] however, C. Bernaldo de Quirós accepted it only in a restricted sense.[47] Nordau and Salillas used "parasites" to mean professional and habitual criminals; de Quirós thought it meant professional offenders, beggars, and prostitutes. The modern Soviet understanding of parasite refers to socially undesirable persons rather than to criminals, that is, those who avoid socially useful work and lead an antisocial way of life;[48] the "parasite law" of the U.S.S.R. is based on the thesis that those "who will not work shall not eat." Able-bodied adults who neglect their moral duty to work according to their best abilities, the parasites, represent "the marginal elements between the socially approved and the clearly criminal."[49] In the light of the dynamic goals of Soviet society, a judicial public warning or exile to compulsory labor may adjust them to society.

Achille Loria, in arguing for "the economic bases of the social system," attacked the capitalist economic structure even more heavily and emphasized the contradictions between the socialist and the anthropological-individualist approaches to crime.[50] Bruno Battaglia, in analyzing "the dynamics of crime," also refused to follow the tenets of the anthropological or biological explanations, although he conceded that anatomical and physiological characteristics are not unimportant.[51] Battaglia suggested that man is made criminal by his psychological qualities that make him unable to conform to the demands and conditions of his society. The criminal lacks the ability to adjust to the moral harmony between the individual and his group. However, Battaglia concluded, "Crime in itself is not a phenomenon that assumes the criminal character from its own nature," for "criminal character is affirmed or denied" by one's social relations.[52] These social relations are responsible for creating degeneracy, or any anatomical or physiological defects of the criminal. Battaglia takes a Marxist stance in the second part of his study; here he lists all the faults and disorders of society that are potential to the development of crime. Family, social position, education, religion, alcoholism, parenthood, prostitution, ignorance, immorality, plutocracy, and other issues are criticized, and the capitalist economic structure is blamed for all shortcomings and difficulties. Battaglia proposed only one effective remedy, to distribute the total production of labor among the workers, not among the capitalists.

Antonio Marro, in presenting the characteristics of criminals, found that poverty and the desperate financial status of the proletariat produces a faulty nervous system in some people, which in turn leads to deviant behavior.[53] In his work on "the woman and socialism," August Bebel also took a strong Marxist stand.[54] He proposed that an increase in any crime is due to social conditions. "Annihilation" of the criminal leads nowhere; "removal" of the causes of crime, that is, the capitalist economic system, would eliminate crime. Even stronger is the position of Paul Lafargue, who, in support of Quetelet and contrary to Lombroso, celebrated "the correctness of the historical theory of Karl Marx."[55] Lafargue found that an increase of criminality coincided with the increase of productive forces in France, and to him it was evident that there is a close correspondence between economic factors and crime.

H. Denis, the scholarly leader of the Belgian Socialist Party, arrived at more moderate conclusions than his Italian colleagues. He too thought that economic conditions are responsible for crime and urged "a normal equilibrium of collective function." But he did not believe that all crimes would be eradicated by "instilling justice into our economic institutions."[56] Contrary to Denis, H. Lux in his "social-political handbook" denounced the "degenerative influence of capitalism." He contended that crime is a normal byproduct in a capitalist society, as are prostitution and the destruction of countless people by economic exploitations.[57]

Perhaps the most towering figure among the nineteenth-century criminal socialists was Napoleone Colajanni, who in his monumental criminal sociology[58] placed himself solidly with the Marxists, without, however, subscribing to all doctrines of the original Marxism. He could not accept the thesis that the economic structure is the origin of all social phenomena. Colajanni strongly criticized the tenets of the Italian anthropological or biological school and turned to the analysis of social and economic factors of crime. Using comparative data from Ireland, Italy, Scotland, and England, Colajanni demonstrated the pathology of crime on economic bases: war, industry, family, marriage, revolution, education, political institutions, prostitution, vagrancy, and other factors may indirectly result in criminality, but they themselves are the resultants of economic and social forces. In the capitalist economic system, contended Colajanni, there are insufficient means of satisfying the wants of man. These wants irritate man and spur him to reach for gratification. If, Colajanni suggests, the honest, conventional way of gaining economic satisfaction is made difficult or impossible by the society, crime is the only rational alternative available. A dishonest person will be reinforced by the experience that honest labor is less advantageous and more dangerous than the dishonest way of living.

A milestone in the socialist perspective of crime was reached in 1899 when the law faculty of the University of Amsterdam offered a prize for an essay on "a systematic and critical review of the literature concerning the influence of economic conditions on criminality." Only two contestants, students of the university, submitted papers. Joseph Van Kan won the gold medal, with Willem Adriaan Bonger receiving honorable mention. Both published their own work, Van Kan in 1903[59] and Bonger in 1905.[60] Both were fundamental documents in the history of criminological thought, and many later authors drew much information from them. Both were committed to economic collectivism and a socialist order of society; neither sympathized with any system of dictatorship. To criminlogy it is quite unfortunate that Van Kan turned to Roman law and history; fortunately Bonger remained with criminology and sociology until his suicide on the eve of the German invasion of the Netherlands. J. M. Van Bemmelen justly claimed that Bonger deserves a place among the great criminologists and sociologists "because he fought against hypocrisy, untruthfulness, dilettantism," and had "a great influence on American and English authors."[31]

Defense of an Economic System

What Turati, Van Kan, and Bonger dreamed of became real in the twentieth century. In Russia a series of events that brought the Bolsheviks to power in October 1917 ended with the dethronement of capitalism. A "dictatorship of the proletariat and the poor peasantry," as Lenin described it at the Sixth Party Congress, began to change the economic structure and introduced an order under which the "exploitation of man by man" would come to an end. Revolutionary change in political and economic conditions, first transforming a number of societies to People's Democracies, developed a revolutionary change in the notion of dual responsibility. Both the responsibility with which the lawmaking power charged certain behaviors, and the responsibility of factors that guide man against the criminal law, became defined in terms of the defense of the new economic system. The individual's conforming or criminal functioning began to be reexamined in the light of the new socialist ideology; the individualist and even the universalistic understanding of the crime problem yielded to a suprauniversalist concept of criminal lawbreaking.

The individualistic understanding of crime is an eighteenth-century product. At that time it was a revolutionary change from the medieval arbitrariness of the judges. In this system, based upon a rather particularist criminal law, the criminal is viewed as an independent individual, the offender's individual rights are carefully safeguarded, and his crime is judged as merely an attack by one individual upon another. It is called individualist because it inflicts punishment for injury to an individual victim and in proportion to the individual injury.

The universalistic understanding of crime is a product of the nineteenth century. It struggles against the lack of our knowledge of causes and attempts to find a way to a better understanding of crime. It extends the safeguards of the individual to the safeguard of the "universe," that is, the protection of the society as a whole. It does not dissolve the individual in a sea of collectivity; nor is the universalist orientation in the crime problem intended to make the individual a medium for its anti-individualistic goals. But the universalist approach does propose a revision of the classic concept of individual guilt in crime; it tries to see the individual in the context of his social situation; and it stands for a stronger emphasis on the broader and more extensive concept of functional responsibility. For about a century the universalist orientation has been on its long, exciting, and multiform journey toward an answer to the problem of crime. Nevertheless, the theorists are still groping, and one must concede that the solution is not yet in sight.

"Recognition of the society" was the signal that heralded the decline of the formalist-individualistic understanding of crime and opened the way to a universalist approach. In past centuries justice was exercised in the name of society, but only the harm or injury to the individual victim was emphasized, and punishment was meted out according to the degree of wrong done by the individual criminal. In the universalist orientation, on the other hand, the normative organization and value structure of the society in which the criminal and his victim live—and their relationship to this organization and to other members of their group—are the central constructs. This orientation is concerned with what might be tentatively called the criminal's "functional responsibility" rather than with a discrete act or an isolated criminal conduct. The universalistic approach to the crime problem apparently grew out of a recognition that the individualist orientation might have favorable aspects but leads only to social confusion. The universalistic orientation views the criminal and his victim as social phenomena that can only be understood through their relations to their social environment and to each other. However, in a social structure like that of the Soviet Union and other socialist countries, where the political and economic system holds a crucially significant position and where a determined move toward an ideological goal represents the social dynamics, the merely social (but not ideological) universalist understanding of crime could not provide satisfactory protection of the system and its future developments.

Thus, a broader and stronger concept of responsibility is created, based on an ideological and often totalitarian interpretation or modification of the universalistic orientation. This might be called the suprauniversalistic understanding of the crime problem. In this interpretation a social (or, better, political) idea transcends individual and even conventional group interests in the society. It offers direct protection, care, and defense not only to individuals and their group but to the idea itself. This concept of crime extends the scope of judicial decision making to elements beyond the objective, formalistic guilt of the individual. The prime objective is to safeguard the ideology.

"A program of action" in the Soviet Union is "expected to improve the economic and political status of both peasants and workmen";[62] thus in the Soviet suprauniversalistic understanding of crime the norms of responsibility and the evaluation of crime factors have to yield to the supremacy of the governing political philosophy. "The Soviet distinction," writes Harold J. Berman, "between theft of personal and theft of state property is probably an essential feature of the socialist system."[63] In general, he continues, "Not merely the act but the 'whole man' is tried; at the same time, his crime is considered in the context of the 'whole community.' "[64] Because social control is based on ideology-directed social defense, the interpretation of responsibility is necessarily subjective. Crime and the doer-sufferer relationship is viewed from the angle of the ruling doctrines; responsibility is defined and distributed, and the degree of responsibility is evaluated according to the ideological-social value of the crime target.

Since the Soviet ideological understanding of crime emphasizes the broadest social aspects, social cohesion, and extensive social responsibility, its outlook on the crime problem may be mistaken for a universalistic orientation. However, it is suprauniversalistic in nature. There are profound differences in the historical development as well as in the social context and goals of the two orientations. While the universalistic orientation aims at a harmony among conflicting responsibilities and tries to see them in their functional operation, the suprauniversalistic view is reluctant to tolerate a conflict of responsibilities, is ideology directed, and for the sake of the ruling idea tends to disregard individualist crime factors. The "court is an instrument of state policy and by no means impartial," and the purpose of criminal law is the maintenance of order for the benefit of the aims of the revolution.[65] Not the personal drama of the criminal and his victim, and not the conflict between the criminal and his society, but the drama of the criminal and ideology is of paramount importance. The suprauniversalistic concept of crime substitutes for the personal victim the idea of a victimized ideology. The suprauniversalistic orientation gave rise to the idea of the metaphysical victim. In general, rethinking the concept of responsibility resulted in an increasing tendency to turn from an act-oriented to an actor-oriented view of criminality. The Soviet approach leans toward an ideology-oriented judgment of crime.

The Responsible Social Danger

In view of the supreme importance of defending the ruling ideology and so protect the political and economic system, the central issue of the Soviet conception of crime, common to all socialist societies, is the notion of "social danger." Although this term has been widely used from Enrico Ferri to modern criminologists, socialist criminology has changed its original meaning to serve ideological purposes. The Soviet understanding theorizes that "Crimes, without exception, mean the breach of the rules of socialistic life and of workshop discipline." While crimes are "relics of the past," they are also "actions of the people's enemies, foreign agents and their accomplices, wreckers and saboteurs, spies and traitors, and manifest forms of the open battle waged by the capitalistic world" against the socialist societies.[66] This is why "the consequence of a human action, and especially the socially dangerous consequence, occupies a central place in the system of Soviet criminal law."[67] Crime is a "social danger," meaning the harm, risk, or peril to which the political and economic institutions, as the representations of the ideology, are exposed. Logically enough, the criminal is viewed in the same context; according to M. D. Shargorodskii and N. A. Beliaev, guilt means a person's *otnoshenie:* his mental attitude toward his socially dangerous conduct.[68] The idea of "social danger," as F. J. Feldbrugge put it, is indeed a fundamental aspect of the Soviet understanding of crime and is "the pivot around which the whole system of Soviet criminal law is constructed."[69]

The first criminal code of the Soviet Union (*Ugolovnyi Kodeks* R.S.F.S.R.)[70] identified crimes with socially dangerous acts. However, the later "Principles of Criminal Legislation of the U.S.S.R. and the Union Republics" (*Osnovy Ugolovnogo Zakonodatelstva Soiuza S.S.R. i Soiuznykh Respublik*)[71] extended the concept to include some noncriminal conducts and deter-

mined which of the socially dangerous behaviors are to be classified as crimes. Feldbrugge suggests that the list of interests pro-
tected by criminal law may indicate what conducts are regarded
as criminal. On this basis "socially dangerous" is any act directed
against the Soviet social, political, or economic system; against
the socialist property or socialist legal order; or against the person, or the political, labor, property, or other rights of the citi-
zen.[72] Early in Soviet history no definitive criminal law existed,
and crime was generally determined by the concept of social
danger; only later developments made possible laws determining
what acts are to be labeled as socially dangerous.

The Soviet concept of social danger is not a rigid category, but
subjective and relative; thus, by being a changing element within
a changing law, it exposes the offender to the risk of a change in
his responsibility. A. A. Piontkovskii called attention to this
practical significance of the "material concept" of crime, although he did it in an indirect fashion by referring to Article 43
of the *Osnovy*.[73] This rule of the "Principles" frees the offender
from responsibility in case of changed circumstances: if in the
new circumstances the kind of behavior previously assessed as a
danger to the society is no longer regarded as such or if the
offender's personality has ceased to be of a dangerous nature.
Thus, social danger may be judged *ex nunc* rather than *ex tunc*,
that is, at the time the act is being judged, not at the time it took
place. This flexible nature of the concept of social danger, which
we may tentatively call the "risk of a double-decker responsibility," is an essential aspect of the Soviet understanding of crime.

As Feldbrugge pointed out, Soviet lawyers and politicians are
inclined to emphasize that law is an instrument of the ruling
classes and that therefore Soviet criminal law has to approximate
the political developments in the Soviet society.[74] The Soviet
outlook on crime and the Soviet criminal law at any given
moment reflects the changes, developments, goals, and political
decisions of the society and its ruling authorities. The dynamics

of the social and economic system require flexibility in the central element of criminal law, the notion of social danger.

Otnoshenie, the offender's attitude toward his social danger-ousness, reflects his "guilt." For a long time it was a dominating view of the Soviet criminal sciences that only this factor—the offender's psychic relationship with the socially dangerous nature of his act—determined his criminality. However, later it was recognized that the "content of guilt" is not exhausted by this single attitude. T. V. Cereteli and V. G. Makasvili state that guilt in the Soviet understanding is "in close connection with the ele-ment of moral censure" and that crime "always presents itself as something that must be condemned and disapproved from the point of view of the moral-political ideas of the socialist so-ciety."[75] This moral element, however, has nothing in common with the bourgeois normative notion;[76] the moral disapproval of crime is justified by the antisocial or asocial inclination of the criminal, the elements of necessity and expediency, and the moral ideas of the socialist society.

The Soviet ideas of social danger and moral censure are in-separable; they are categories presupposing each other.[77] "Who-ever recognizes the immorality of his act," suggested László Viski, "also recognizes the social dangerousness of the act."[78] Some contend this is contrary to the Western concept of guilt; as P. A. Sariia, in discussing "a few questions of the Communist morality," put it, "In the antagonistic class-society, naturally, not all those acts are immoral which violate the existing social or-der."[79] Indeed, the "damage to the society" or "damage to the public" as proposed by Reinhard Frank,[80] Edmund Mezger,[81] Arthur Kaufmann,[82] Wilhelm Sauer,[83] and others, is not neces-sarily immoral. In the Soviet approach, however, danger to so-ciety and immorality seem to merge. To comply with the develop-mental demands, the immorality of the act is also judged *ex nunc,* in other words, interpreted at the time of the judgment rather than as it was interpreted at the time of the act. The Soviet legal system, Harold Berman observed, "expresses in a most vivid and real way what a society stands for."[84] As Soviet society moves from its unfinished state to a higher stage of development, the transition necessarily brings about changes in what is deemed socially dangerous and what not and, at the same time, in what is moral and what immoral. V. D. Menishagin, N. D. Durmanov, P. S. Romashkin, and others stated that, contrary to bourgeois formalism, crime in the Soviet system is defined in a "material" way and that this indicates its political and class character.[85] In a changing political climate, crime itself becomes a variable.

A peril of the changing character of crime is how Soviet citizens, exposed to varying meanings of social danger and morality, can adapt to the prevailing consciousness. The rather frequent adaptations of socialist law to economic and social conditions is a historical fact. The creators of the Napoleonic Code thought that they had prepared a legal system that would last for centuries, and they were not wholly erroneous. Socialist lawmakers can have no similar long-range goals; inevitable developmental forces of the socialist system prevent making laws for generations, or even for a decade. As Imre Szabó explained it, "The increase of the circulation speed of the socialist laws mirrors the fact that under the conditions of socialism the speed of social development generally increases."[86] The character of the socialist law, so the argument runs, is to express the prevailing social conditions and to defend them, and thus it changes as the social conditions change: the socialist concept of crime is a kind of utilitarian notion.

The Communist Party makes strenuous efforts toward acquainting the whole of Soviet society with the law. In high school and college curricula, in political seminars for adults at their working places, in public lectures or organized Sunday visits to people's homes, through mass communications, and in all other possible ways, nearly everyone is exposed to the official understanding of the political and social situation. Through this inten-

sive and extensive political educational system—John Hazard
called it "radiating influence"[87]—the prevailing meaning of
social danger and the prevailing interpretation of morality reach
almost all members of the society. A. A. Piontkovskii contended
that there is no need to prove that the offender was aware of the
"social danger" of his act; in view of the elaborate informational
system it is presumed that everybody is aware of the quality of
his own conduct. In any case, proposed Piontkovskii, if consciousness of social danger was not a legal presumption, it would
then be only a privilege of those bourgeois elements who are
reluctant to make an acquaintance with the socialist law.[88] However, V. F. Kirichenko, in discussing "the meaning of error,"
suggested that a person may not be punished if he erroneously
assumed that his act was not socially dangerous, but only if his
error is excusable.[89]

The educational activity of the party does not stop at acquainting people with the law and its political and moral elements. As
Imre Szabó viewed it, activity aimed at informing about the law
is closely connected with attempts at persuading members of the
society as to the rightness and utility of the law. "The essential
purpose is that the law should not only be known to the citizens,
but also they should agree with it, they should make it a part of
their social consciousness, and they should direct their own conduct accordingly."[90] In the Soviet Union the educational role of
the law—the notion of the so-called parental law—has from the
beginning been central to the concept of justice itself.[91]

The Responsible Remnants

If the essential features of criminology are a desire to understand
the criminal and his crime and the systematic study of criminogenic factors, then Soviet criminology does not seriously differ
from Western criminal sciences. Yet Soviet criminology insis-
tently claims that its theoretical orientation is completely different

and fully rejects premises originating in other parts of the globe. Socialist criminology contends that it offers the only viable thinking and that the Western social science will not, because it cannot, ever solve the crime problem.

In his lectures on "the study and prevention of criminality" before the Scientific Council of the Soviet Scientific Research Institute of Criminalistics,[92] A. A. Gertsenzon listed a number of Western criminologists (among them Harry Elmer Barnes, Negley K. Teeters, Walter C. Reckless, Donald R. Taft, the Austrian Ernst Seelig, and the German Franz Exner and Edmund Mezger, whom he called "the newest biocriminologists") who "obviously lost their hope in finding the way of prevention of criminality in social measures, therefore they turned away from sociology and seek the solution of the problem of crime prevention in the field of biosociology."[93] As Gertsenzon said, he was not surprised that most bourgeois criminologists still discuss "criminal personalities"; after all, they do so "in order to avoid touching the real roots of criminality." "Just what sort of preventive recipes are given by the bourgeois criminologists," asked Gertsenzon, "when the whole capitalist form of life directly determines the increase of child criminality and deepens the moral corruption of the society and family?"[94] It is no wonder that crime occupies such an important place in the bourgeois criminological, sociological, and psychological literature. Gertsenzon concluded that "Most of the bourgeois criminologists utilize the problem of crime prevention only for apologetic purposes [and] hide the real causes of crime."[95]

M. I. Kovaljov shared Gertsenzon's views. In discussing "the Soviet criminology and its place," Kovaljov maintained that the bourgeois criminology is characterized by efforts "to arrange things so that crime would appear to be the product of social and biological factors." But, Kovaljov suggested, to put the question in this context is "unscientific, and the faulty methodology is obvious"; all definitions of the bourgeois criminology are "formalistic," and "the empirical investigation of the phenomena is superficial."[96] He concluded that "the bourgeois criminology completely devours the criminal science."[97]

In the Soviet Union Gertsenzon wrote that

"Material foundations of crime prevention are secured by the development of building Communism in the economic, political, and cultural fields. For the very reason that in the character of the socialist society there is nothing which could generate criminality, in the Soviet Union the basic social causes of crime have already ceased to exist, and in the course of the development of building Communism every step forward promotes the full extermination of criminality."[98]

For the "remnants" of criminality (crime-producing elements not yet eliminated by the system) Gertsenzon proposed study of the criminal's personality, however not in the bourgeois social-biological fashion ("which has nothing to do with science"). He suggested that "the reasons and endeavors, which result in the violation of law or the commission of crime, have to be revealed; also, it is important to characterize with adequate care the social dangerousness of the person in question, by revealing his past, his way of life and customs, his relation to the collectivity of workers, his abilities and his readiness to work."[99] M. Benjamin added to this list the offender's vocational training, his discipline in the course of his education, his cultural life, the influence of the workers' collectivity on him, and his class and family origin.[100]

Most socialist criminologists and criminal lawyers emphasize it would be a mistake to assume that, just because the basic social causes of crime have been eradicated, no factors exist that might produce criminality. It is a common assertion in socialist studies of crime that "the remnants of the bourgeois way of thinking" have the major responsibility for leading some men against the socialist criminal law. It has been explained many times by many socialist commentators[101] that in a short period of history it is impossible to eliminate all those ideas and habits that operate against Communist morality and that, after all, piled up in the course of centuries. Such ideas and habits remain viable even for those who live in a socialist society. Man, as Gertsenzon explained,[102] is not born to violate the social order or to become a criminal, or even to be a carrier of the "remnants" of the past; however, under certain conditions it is possible that a person's consciousness and conduct may react to these dormant remnants and he will violate the law. In the Soviet Union in recent years, 30 percent of all homicides were committed under the pressure of anger, 24 percent as a result of "rough disorderly behavior," 8 percent due to greed, and 8 percent because of jealousy.[103]

It is often said that survival of "the capitalist ideological and moral remnants" of the past ruling class hinders the development of a socialist consciousness. Their antisocial frame of mind, József Vigh stated, often leads to the open or camouflaged expression of their views.[104] The capitalist environment, which is active through "hostile" radio and press reports, and the subversive activity of foreign agents are often mentioned as major factors preserving capitalist remnants. G. M. Minkovskii, in discussing "the prevention of crimes"[105] and A. B. Saharov, in analyzing "the personality of the criminal and the causes of crime in the Soviet Union,"[106] contend that remnants of the past have an impact ideologically, psychologically, and socioeconomically. They emphasize that in the Soviet Union there are no economic conditions that could conceivably lead to antisocial views. But, they suggest, there are some "existing social difficulties and contradictions" that in themselves would not generate antisocial conduct but may help fortify and vitalize these remnants of the consciousness.

In their study on "the investigation of the personality of the criminal on the basis of criminological research data," S. S. Ostromov and V. J. Tsugunov analyzed in a relatively small geographical area the sex and age of the offenders, their income and housing conditions, educational and family circumstances, interest in sport activities, and participation in self-education and socialist work. They found that "The causes of criminality are the antisocial views, traditions, and customs." They go on to say that "The viability of such past remnants can be explained by the fact that the consciousness is lagging behind the social existence, also by the existence of a hostile capitalist world, and then again by the still prevailing deficiencies in the citizens' material, cultural, and educational supplies and provisions." "The past remnants," continued Ostromov and Tsugunov, "are deeply rooted there in the existence and consciousness of the millions of people, for a long time even after the material conditions of these remnants disappeared."[107]

Remnants of the bourgeois past are not always blamed as the only cause of crime. A. S. Sliapochnikov, in discussing "questions in connection with the investigation of the causes of criminality," suggested that "the past remnants which make their way into the consciousness of people" is typical to the "old world." He proposed that the remnants illuminate only the character of antisocial factors "alien to the socialist order," but this "does not consider the degree of development of the socialist system in its relation to Communism."[108] The Czech Miroslav Veverka was even stronger in his opposition to the "remnants" theory. He proposed that this "unscientific thesis must be liquidated," since it is "the product of dogmatism [and is] idealistic and speculative of nature." "The structure of the socialist society has to be examined for the causes of crime; this is as important as the remnants." "It is a logical conclusion," Veverka continued, "that the success of the struggle against criminality is dependent not so much on education as on changes in the course of building the society."[109]

The keynote, however, always seems to be the "social danger." Even in the rare examples of socialist criminal typologies the element of social danger plays a decisive role. M. I. Kovaljov proposed, "Criminal types have to be classified according to the social danger generated by the capitalist remnants in the consciousness."[110] Veverka catalogued crime and delinquency types that reach the courts and delinquencies that are not within the courts' jurisdiction. Juvenile delinquency, disciplinary delinquency, and negligent delinquency are listed under delinquencies that reach the court. Under crimes he classified psychopathic criminality, situational crimes, crimes committed under the influence of alcohol, and counterrevolutionary crimes, which represent the gravest attack against the socialist economic order and are motivated by "hatred of the class enemy." All, however, are unquestionably socially dangerous.[111]

The Soviet Union's unparalleled attempt to transform a society could not have succeeded without the assistance of a utilitarian criminal law. To protect this transforming process the lawmaking power (the "sovereign") charges with responsibility all those who stand against the goal of transformation. It is for the sovereign to decide how promising this goal is and how the transformation should take place. Whether Plato, Hobbes, Bentham, or anyone else can be cited here in a modified and adjusted shape, is open to argument; in any case, in the socialist approach to the understanding of crime one part of the "dual responsibility" is seen here as "the command of the sovereign." The other part is open to argument.

NOTES

1. Georg Simmel, "The Poor," Claire Jacobson (tr.), *Soziologie: Untersuchugen über die Formen der Vergesellschaftung* (Leipzig, 1908), pp. 454–493; *Social Problems*, 13 (Fall 1965), 138; the same view expressed by Lewis A. Coser in "The Sociology of Poverty," *Social Problems*, 13 (Fall 1965), 140–148.

2. A. Corne, "La criminalité, sur ses causes, sur les moyens d'y

remédier," *Journal des Economistes*, IX (January 1868), 63–93.

3. Ernst Roesner, "Wirtschaftslage und Straffälligkeit," in Alexander Elster and Heinrich Lingemann (eds.), *Handwörterbuch der Kriminologie und der anderen strafrechtlichen Hilfswissenschaften* (Berlin and Leipzig, 1933), pp. 1079–1116.

4. Sir Thomas More, *De optimo reipublicae statu sive de nova insula Utopia*. The first edition in the original Latin was probably published in 1516 in Louvain; one of the modernized texts (New York, 1947), p. 34 and *infra*.

5. Bonesana Cesare Marquis de Beccaria, *Dei delitti e delle pene* (Haarlem, 1764).

6. Hommel's lecture is cited in Jenö Balogh, *Nyomor és büntettek* (Budapest, 1908), pp. 31–32.

7. J. M. Charles Lucas, *Du Système pénal et du système répressif en général, de la peine de mort en particulier* (Paris, 1827).

8. André Michel Guerry, *Essai sur la statistique morale* (Paris, 1833).

9. Edouard Ducpetiaux, *De la condition physique et morale des jeunes ouvriers* (Brussels, 1843).

10. Edouard Ducpetiaux, *Mémoire sur le paupérisme dans les Flandres* (Brussels, 1850).

11. Georg von Mayr, *Moralstatistik mit Einschluss der Kriminalstatistik* (Tübingen, 1917).

12. A. Corne, "La criminalité, sur ses causes, sur les moyens d'y remédier," *Journal des Economistes*, IX (January 1868), 63–93.

13. H. von Valentini, *Das Verbrecherthum im preussischem Staat* (Leipzig, 1869).

14. Adolphe Quetelet, *Sur l'homme et la développement de ses facultés ou essai de physique sociale* (Paris, 1835).

15. Alexander V. Oettingen, *Die Moralstatistik in ihrer Bedeutung für eine Sozialethik* (3rd ed., Erlangen, 1882).

16. Béla Földes, "Über einige wirtschaftliche und moralische Wirkungen hoher Getreidepreise," *Jahrbücher für National-ökonomie und Statistik* (Leipzig, 1881), p. 80 and *infra*.

17. L. Fuld, *Der Einfluss der Lebensmittelpreise auf die Bewegung der strafbaren Handlungen* (Mainz, 1881).

18. B. Weiss, "Über einige wirtschaftliche und moralische Wirkungen hoher Getreidepreise," *Jahrbücher für Nationalökonomie und Statistik* (Leipzig, 1881).

19. W. Starke, *Verbrechen und Verbrecher in Preussen 1854–1878* (Berlin, 1884).

20. L. M. Moreau-Christophe, *Du problème de la misère et de la solution chez les peuples anciens et modernes* (Paris, 1851); *Le monde des coquins* (Paris, 1863).

21. M. Tugan-Baranowsky, *Studien zur Theorie und Geschichte der Handelskrisen in England* (Jena, 1901).

22. H. Stursberg, *Die Zunahme der Vergehen und Verbrechen und ihre Ursachen* (Düsseldorf, 1878).

23. E. Tarnowski, "La delinquenza e la vita sociale in Russia," *Rivista Italiana di Sociologia,* 1898. (Bonger, in error, misspelled his name Tarnowsky. Pauline Tarnowsky was a different person; she wrote on female murderers: *Les femmes homicides* [Paris, 1908]).

24. A. Meyer, *Die Verbrechen in ihrem Zusammenhang mit dem wirtschaftlichen und sozialen Verhältnissen in Kanton Zürich, Abhängigkeit von tellurischen Faktoren* (Jena, 1895).

25. Rettich, "Die Würtembergische Kriminalität," *Würtembergische Jahrbücher,* 1894, cited in Bonger, *Criminality and Economic Conditions* (New York, 1967), pp. 66–68.

26. H. Müller, *Untersuchungen über die Bewegung der Kriminalität in ihrem Zusammenhang mit dem wirtschaftlichen Verhältnissen* (Halle, 1899).

27. E. Carnevale, "Una terza scuola di diritto penale in Italia," *Rivista Carceraris,* July 1891; "La nuova tendenza nelle discipline criminali," *Antologia Giuridica,* 1892.

28. B. Alimena, *Naturalismo critico e diritto penale* (Rome, 1892); *La scuola critica di diritto penale* (Naples, 1894).

29. Enrico Ferri, *Criminal Sociology,* Joseph I. Kelly and John Lisle (trs.) (New York, 1967), p. 23.

30. Jenö Balogh, *Nyomor és büntettek* (Budapest, 1908), pp. 41–42.

31. Filippo Poletti, *Del sentimento nella scienza del diritto penale* (Udine, 1882).

32. E. Fornasari di Verce, *La criminalita e le vicende economiche d'Italia dal 1873 al 1890 e osservazioni sommarie per il Regno Unito della Gran Bretagna e Irlanda (1840–1890) e per la Nova Galles del Sud (1882–1891)*, (Turin, 1894).

33. Willem Adriaan Bonger, *Criminality and Economic Conditions*, Henry P. Horton (tr.) (New York, 1967), p. 145.

34. *Ibid.*, pp. 244–246.

35. Leon Radzinowicz, *Ideology and Crime* (New York, 1966), p. 90.

36. Corne, *op. cit.*, Part II.

37. Quetelet, *op. cit.*, p. 279.

38. Fuld, *op. cit.*

39. B. Weiss, "Über einige wirtschaftliche und moralische Wirkungen hoher Getreidepreise," *Jahrbücher für Nationalökonomie und Statistik* (Leipzig, 1881).

40. Bonger, *op. cit.*, p. 244.

41. Friedrich Engels, *Die Lage der Arbeitenden Klasse in England* (Stuttgart, 1892).

42. Filippo Turati, *Il delitto e la questione sociale* (Milan, 1883).

43. Enrico Ferri, *Socialismo e criminalita* (Turin, 1883), cited in C. Bernaldo de Quirós, *Modern Theories of Criminality*, Alfonso de Salvio (tr.) (New York, 1967), p. 67.

44. Alfredo Niceforo, "Criminalita e condizioni economiche in Sicilia," *Rivista di scient. di diritto*, 1897.

45. Max Nordau, "Une nouvelle théorie biologique du crime," *La Revue*, 1902, cited in de Quirós, *Modern Theories*, *op. cit.*, pp. 64–65.

46. Rafael Salillas, "Hampa," in *Estudios de Derecho penal preventivo* (Madrid, 1901), cited in de Quirós, *Modern Theories*, *op. cit.*, pp. 65–66.

47. C. Bernaldo de Quirós, *La mala vida en Madrid* (Madrid, 1901).

48. R. Beermann, "The Parasite Law in the Soviet Union," *The British Journal of Criminology*, 3 (July 1962), 71–80.

49. *Ibid.*, p. 79.

50. Achille Loria, *Les bases économiques de la constitution sociale* (Paris, 1894).

51. Bruno Battaglia, *La dinamica del delitto* (Naples, 1886).

52. *Ibid.*, p. 201.

53. Antonio Marro, *I caratteri dei delinquenti* (Turin, 1887).

54. August Bebel, *Die Frau und der Sozialismus* (Stuttgart, 1899).

55. Paul Lafargue, *Der wirtschaftliche Materialismus* (Zurich, 1886); "Die Kriminalität in Frankreich 1840–1886," *Neue Zeit*, 1889.

56. H. Denis, "La criminalité et la crise économique," *Actes du III Congr. d'anthropologie criminelle* (Brussels, 1893); "Le socialisme et les causes économiques et sociales du crime," *Compte rendu V Congr. d'anthropologie criminelle* (Amsterdam, 1901).

57. H. Lux, *Sozialpolitisches Handbuch* (Berlin, 1892).

58. Napoleone Colajanni, *Sociologia Criminale* (Catania, 1889).

59. Joseph Van Kan, *Les causes économiques de la criminalité* (Paris, 1903).

60. Bonger, *op. cit.* His original essay has been extended in the published form.

61. J. M. Van Bemmelen, "Willem Adriaan Bonger," in Hermann Mannheim (ed.), *Pioneers in Criminology* (London, 1960), pp. 349–363.

62. John N. Hazard, *The Soviet System of Government* (Chicago, 1964), p. 2.

63. Harold J. Berman, *Justice in the U.S.S.R.* (rev. ed., New York, 1963), p. 163.

64. *Ibid.*, p. 257.

65. Hazard, *op. cit.*, p. 168.

66. V. D. Menshagin, A. A. Gertsenzon, M. M. Ishaiev, A. A. Piontovskii, and B. S. Utevskii, *Szovjet Büntetöjog, Egyetemi Tankönyv*, official edition of the University textbook of the Soviet criminal law, in Hungarian (Budapest, 1951), p. 247.

67. F. J. Feldbrugge, *Soviet Criminal Law, General Part* (Leyden, 1964), p. 101.

68. M. D. Shargorodskii and N. A. Beliaev (eds.), *Sovetskoe Ugolovnoe Pravo, Obshchaia Chast* (Moscow, 1960), p. 313.

69. Feldbrugge, *op. cit.*, p. 169.

70. Enacted May 24, 1922.

71. Enacted December 25, 1958.

72. Feldbrugge, *op. cit.*, p. 89.

73. A. A. Piontkovskii, "A büntetöjogi felelösség alapja," originally published in *Sovetskoe Gosudarstvo i Pravo*, 1959, No. 11, and in *Jogtudományi Közlöny*, April 1960, XV: 4, 237–238.

74. Feldbrugge, *op. cit.*, p. 26.

75. T. V. Cereteli and V. G. Makasvili, "A bünfelelösség elvének fejlödése a szovjet büntetöjogban," *Jogtudományi Közlöny*, January 1967, XXII:1, 13–14.

76. *Ibid.*, p. 14.

77. Similar analysis expressed by László Viski, *Szándékosság és társadalomra veszélyesség* (Budapest, 1959), p. 84.

78. *Ibid.*, p. 109.

79. P. A. Sariia, *A Kommunista erkölcs néhány kérdése* (Budapest, 1951), p. 71.

80. Reinhard Frank, *Über die Aufgabe des Schuldbegriffs* (Giessen, 1907), p. 187.

81. Edmund Mezger, *Strafrecht* (Munich, 1948), I, 330.

82. Artur Kaufmann, *Das Unrechtsbewusstsein in der Schuldlehre des Strafrechts* (Mainz, n.d.), cited in Theodor Rittler, "Der böse Vorsatz," *Österreichische Juristenzeitung*, 1954, p. 554.

83. Wilhelm Sauer, *Allgemeine Strafrechtslehre* (Berlin, 1949), pp. 143–148.

84. Berman, *op. cit.*, p. 4.

85. V. D. Menishagin, N. D. Durmanov, and P. S. Romashkin (eds.), *Sovetskoe Ugolovnoe Pravo, Chast Obshchaia* (Moscow, 1962), p. 64. See also F. C. Schroeder, *Die Grundsätze der Strafgesetzgebung der UdSSR und der Unionsrepubliken* (Herrenalb, 1960), pp. 26–39; cited by Feldbrugge, *op. cit.*, p. 95.

86. Imre Szabó, *Társadalom és jog* (Budapest, 1964), p. 73.

87. *Ibid.*, pp. 35–48.

88. A. A. Piontkovskii, *Uchenie o prestuplenii po sovetskomu ugolovnomu pravu* (Moscow, 1961), p. 401 and *infra.*; Viski, *op. cit.*, pp. 217–218.

89. V. F. Kirichenko, *Znachenie oshibki po sovetskomu ugolovnomu pravu* (Moscow, 1952), pp. 32–34.

90. Szabó, *Társadalom és jog, op. cit.*, p. 41.

91. Berman, *op. cit.*, pp. 282–284.

92. For "criminology" the socialist literature sometimes use "criminalistics," which in our understanding means the police sciences, mainly the technical, scientific, and administrative aspects of crime detection and investigation.

93. A. A. Gertsenzon, "A bünözés tanulmányozásáról és megelözéséröl," originally published in *Sovetskoe Gosudarstvo i Pravo*, (1960), 77–88; trans. into Hungarian Gyula Alapy in *Jogtudományi Közlöny*, January–February 1961, XVI:1–2, 24–30.

94. *Ibid.*, p. 25.

95. *Ibid.*, pp. 24–25.

96. M. I. Kovaljov, "A szovjet kriminológia és helye a jogtudományok rendszerében," *Pravovedieniie*, 1965, No. 1; and *Külföldi Jogi Cikkgyüjtemény*, 4 (1965), 554–562.

97. *Ibid.*, p. 554.

98. Gertsenzon, *op. cit.*, p. 25.

99. *Ibid.*, p. 29.

100. M. Benjamin, "Wie Können die Ursachen der Kriminalität erforscht werden," *Neue Justiz*, 2 (1962), 48.

101. See e.g., Piontkovskii, *op. cit.;* Shargorodskii and Beliaev, *op. cit.;* Gertsenzon, *op. cit.;* Kirichenko, *op. cit.;* Kovaljov, *op. cit.*

102. Gertsenzon, *op. cit.*, p. 27.

103. *Ibid.*, p. 27.

104. József Vigh, "A bünözés okainak problémái," *Jogtudományi Közlöny*, XVIII:9, 497. How the past capitalist ruling class could survive almost half a century, from the birth of the Soviet Union to the publication of the article, was not explained by the author.

105. G. M. Minkovskii, *A büncselekmények megelözése* (Moscow, 1962), p. 10; cited by Vigh, *op. cit.*, p. 499.

106. A. B. Saharov, *A Bünözö személyéröl és a bünözés okairól a*

Szovjetunióban (Moscow, 1961), p. 76.; cited by Vigh, *op. cit.*, p. 499.

107. S. S. Ostromov and V. J. Tsugunov, "A bünözö személyének vizsgálata a kriminológiai kutatások adatai alapján," *Sovetskoe Gosudarstvo i Pravo*, 9 (1965); and *Külföldi Jogi Cikkgyüjtemény*, 1 (1966), 65–73.

108. A. S. Sliapochnikov, "A bünözés okainak kutatásával kapcsolatos kérdések," *Voprosi Filosofii*, 1 (1966); and *Külföldi Jogi Cikkgyüjtemény*, 3 (1966), 472–482.

109. Miroslav Veverka, "A bünözés okairól," *Filosofický Casopis*, 6 (1964); and Külföldi Jogi Cikkgyüjtemény, 4 (1965), 540–553.

110. Kovaljov, *op. cit.*, p. 555.

111. Veverka, *op. cit.*, pp. 548–552.

XIV

The Enforcement
of Responsibility

The Justification of Punishment

If there was ever living proof that the work of centuries does not necessarily develop a reassuring answer to a problem, it is the problem of punishment. Criminologists are trying to change the old punitive formulas to "correction," "reform," and "rehabilitation," and many are ready to extrapolate known processes into hypotheses the viability of which remains unknown. Yet, strangely, not too much consolation has been reached by the interminable speculation about what we are doing wrong and what we ought to be doing instead. Even the so-called operational approaches, which extrapolate an unknown into the known, do not offer much; statistics are cold comfort. The problem of punishment causes constant, anguished reassessment, not only because we keep speculating on what the effective consequence of crime should be, but also because there is a confusion of ends and means. We are still far from the answer to the ultimate questions: What is the right punishment? and On what grounds do we punish others?

The search for the justification of punishment is as old as the philosophy of law. If Herbert Hart is correct in suggesting that the "general interest in the topic of punishment has never been greater than it is at present," this may be due to the increasing crime rate and to the increased membership in the ranks of criminological thinkers. How much can be attributed to this factor is not measurable; however, Hart follows up by indicating that public discussion of the problem has never been more confused.[1] There can be little doubt that the disagreement among legal philosophies on the one hand and among the criminological theories on the other, and above all the disagreement between the legal philosophies and criminological theories, represent one of the major reasons why the problem of crime remains unanswered.

Punishment is the enforcement of responsibility. The responsibility with which the lawmaking power charges certain conducts reaches the enforcement stage when man defies the criminal-law command. How this responsibility should be enforced, and why, and on what grounds it can be enforced are questions of the right punishment and the justification of punishment and therefore refer the thinker to some of the basic issues of the philosophy of law and criminological theories. Enforcement of responsibility is ordered and administered by the ruling social power, by human beings against other human beings, and it is generally agreed that it involves "pain or other consequences normally considered unpleasant."[2] It is not necessarily a "disadvantage"[3] because it is at least formally assumed that the enforcement of responsibility is applied in the best interest of the one upon whom it is inflicted; indeed, there are instances where the "punished" person (for example, the so-called prison aspirant) does not feel it is a disadvantage. Oetker differentiates a "rewarding criminal law" (*Lohnstrafrecht*) and a "rewarding retribution" (*Lohnweiser Vergeltung*),[4] he points to the absence of disadvantage experienced by some offenders and the retributive disadvantage suffered by others. Nevertheless, the question of physical or psychic pain caused by the enforcement of responsibility is at the crux of the problem: How much relationship is there between the crime and the factors responsible for leading man against the responsibility-charging command? To what degree and in what manner does the lawmaking power try to influence these crime factors by enforcing responsibility against the criminal? And what justifies the lawmaking power to enforce this responsibility at all?

The lawmaking power's conceptualization of crime will depend in large measure on the philosophical and criminological theories it adopts.

The theories approaching the problem of grounds and justification for punishment are usually classified into three general groups. The absolute theories call for "justice" as the grounds for penal consequences. The relative theories suggest that punishment serves utility. The compromissual theories try to combine the other two.

The Absolute Responsibility

The absolute theories find justification for punishment in the idea of "justice" and assume responsibility as a pure and independent concept. They represent a legalistic orientation and recognize the grounds for punishment in the committed crime according to Seneca's axiom, *Quia peccatum est.* This group is ethically oriented; they believe in the freedom of will and thus propose that punishment should express a societal reproach, a retribution. Their penal philosophy is one of retributive punishment. It logically follows that these theories pay minimal attention to the other end of the dual responsibility—what is responsible for guiding man against the criminal law. In general, the absolute theories can be catalogued into the following two categories:[5]

1. The theories of moral or divine retribution (main representative Herbart and perhaps also Trendelenburg, Merkel, Binding, Nagler, Brusa, Luchini, Stahl, and Bekker). This orientation

contends that punishment is the expression of justice because it restores the moral balance or the divine order that was disturbed by the criminal. Punishment, then, is an ethical necessity.

2. The theories of legal retribution, which branch in two directions. The "talio" theories (main representatives Kant, Stammler, Dohna, Birkmeyer) suggest that punishment is the postulate of justice, that it is a "categorical imperative" and therefore does not need justification. Punishments are based on equality; ideally, they are uniformly inflicted. The dialectic theories (main representatives Hegel, Berner, Halschner) suggest that crime is a negation of law. Since punishment is supposed to control crime, punishment is the negation of the negation of law; it therefore restores the reign of law and serves the idea of justice.

The Relative Responsibility

The relative theories find justification for punishment in the idea of usefulness and refer responsibility to an expressed or implied antecedent. They may represent a sociological, psychological, or biological orientation, and they find the grounds for punishment in the criminal's social, psychic, or physical state according to Seneca's *Nemo prudens punit, quia peccatum est, sed ne peccatur*. This group is naturalistically oriented; they believe that all human behavior, including crime, operates within the law of causality. Thus man can be made responsible if the causes of crime are realized in him. They maintain that punishment must be applied in order to prevent future crimes; prevention makes the punishment useful. Their proposed penal consequence is "purposeful punishment" (*Zweckstrafe*). As opposed to the absolute theories of punishment, the relative theories pay maximum attention to the other end of the dual responsibility—what social, psychic, or biological factors are responsible for leading man against the criminal law—and propose that these factors should be attacked through punishment.

In general, the relative philosophies may be classified into the following main categories:

1. The *theories of prevention*, which, according to their theoretical orientation toward exercising influence on the total society or only on the individual, fall into two categories: theories of general prevention and theories of special prevention.

Among the theories of general prevention, the hypotheses of deterrence (main representatives Filangieri, Gmelin, Mittelstädt) suggest that severe, retributive punishments influence members of the society. Some of the exponents of retributive punishment (interestingly, one of them is Adolf Merkel[6]) lean toward a concept of purposive retribution. The theories of psychic pressure (main representative Feuerbach) propose to threaten with sensual punishment, and this will serve as a counteracting motive against the motive of crime. The theories of warning (main representative Bauer) are different from the theories of psychic pressure only in the target of the threat: the pressure should be exerted on the moral sensibilities of the society rather than on its "sensual sensitivity."

Among the theories of special prevention, the hypotheses of retention (main representative Grollman) contend that the criminal must be deterred from crime by controlling his activities. The theories of reformation (main representatives Ahrens, Krause) would fortify and redirect the internal moral strength of the criminal to enable him to use his moral forces for the right conduct; this, however, can be achieved only by punishment, primarily deprivation of liberty.

2. The *theories of social defense* (main representatives Schulze, Romagnosi, Martin), which argue that crime attacks the state and therefore society must defend itself against this danger. The instrument of defense is punishment.

3. The *theories of satisfaction* (main representative Welcker), which seek justification for punishment in the idea of reparation. According to their argument, crime causes not only material

damages (which, after all, may be remedied through civil legal proceedings), but also "intellectual damage" in three directions. First, the criminal himself, by his stand against the law, suffers intellectual impairment. Second, there is intellectual damage caused to the society by the criminal's bad example. And third, the rights of the victim are curtailed by the crime. Punishment is justified because it repairs this threefold damage: punishment fortifies repect for the law, and it restores the rights of the victim.

4. The *theories of contract* (main representatives Hobbes, Rousseau, Fichte), which are based on natural law and which contend that at the establishment of the state the members of the society "signed" a contract of chastisement agreeing that those who violate the law would not be excluded from the state but would be punished.

5. The *utilitarian theories* (main representative Bentham), which maintain that the purpose of punishment is to secure the greatest happiness for the greatest number of people, and that this is sufficient justification for it.

6. The *theories of necessity* (main representatives Jhering, Liszt, Gerland), which have in common the belief that attacks against society can be deterred only by punishment. Punishment is therefore justified because it is a "social necessity" (*soziale Notwendigkeit*).

7. The *theories of protection* (main representative Vargha), which state that punishment may bring satisfaction and reparation but that its main purpose is the protection of society.

The Compromissual Responsibility

Many theorists hypothesizing a justification for punishment are those who first developed a theory on crime itself. However, far from all who meditated on the problem of crime took the next logical step, that is, speculating on the grounds for and the consequences of crime. Many stepped over the crime problem altogether and, by using others' theories (or none at all) as their premise, simply expressed their thoughts on the problem of punishment. Among those who advocated the compromissual notion of responsibility (main representatives Abegg, Rossi, Carrara, Vámbéry, Angyal, and many others) all three groups are represented.

Adherents of the compromissual understanding of responsibility settle the justification and grounds for punishment through concession and compromise of conflicting views. In general, they lean toward the absolute theories for justification for punishment and toward the relative theories for the nature of punishment. Indeed, the justice of the punishment and the usefulness of punishment indicate essentially the same problem viewed from two different angles. If the question is asked, What justifies the state in inflicting punishment upon the criminal members of the society? the answer may be that the state hopes to prevent the criminal and others from engaging in future crimes. If the question is then asked, What entitles the state to apply punishment? the answer may be that punishment prevents crimes and is thus useful; also that the maintenance of law and order is the supreme responsibility of the state and that punishment is necessary to accomplish this.

Defensive punishment (*Schutzstrafe*) is their proposition.

In other words, the exponents of the compromissual theories contend that justice demands retribution, which, then, is regulated and moderated by the idea of purpose. In their thinking the "contents" of punishment are retribution and deterrence and its effect is prevention. Modern penological theorists are making substantial efforts to appear as "relativists" and propose only protective and preventive measures for the criminal lawbreaker. In fact, however, they should be catalogued among the "compromissualists"; as yet, no protective or preventive measure has succeeded in eliminating retributive and deterrent punishment.

Slaves to the Law

Both "justice" and "usefulness" may justify the "sovereign" in issuing commands that charge certain conducts with responsibility, so long as he has the power to decide right from wrong and useful from useless. Regardless of whether the sovereign takes the form of dictator, a presidium, or a democratic parliament, the supreme and ultimate social power is the one that defines justice, that has the authoritative word about what is useful to ensure the undisturbed functioning of the commands. The history of mankind presents a considerable variety of sovereigns and, accordingly, a variety of definitions of what "justice" and "useful" are.

The recurrent failures of enforcing responsibility are evidenced by the history of crime with merciless clarity, and thus leave us with doubts about the usefulness of punishment. The forms and volume of crime as well as methods for enforcing obedience may have changed, but the trend of failures is constant throughout history. Evidently something went wrong at some point in the evolution of *homo sapiens* or, maybe, with the sovereigns and their societies. But when we ask what is it that has gone wrong, we can get only obscure answers or promising propositions that soon cease to live up to their promise.

James Fitzjames Stephen's view, that "the meaning of responsibility is liability to punishment,"[8] is depressing. Barbara Wootton's hope that the *mens rea* will wither away and the day will come when we no longer will think in terms of punishment[9] is encouraging but seems to oversimplify a highly complex issue. No analysis of the punishment is possible without a comparable analysis of the crime; even a practical or operational approach to punishment is only a *posterior* to an understanding of the violation of criminal law. In any view of crime, it would be hard to deny that crime is a disapproved conduct; after all, this is why the sovereign charges the carrier of such conduct with responsibility. It may be easy to imagine the contrary statement, that the whole criminal law should wither away, but even the Marxist utopians do not see our arrival in such a social paradise until the very end of our developmental wandering.

Although criminological research is expending gigantic efforts to find the crucial factors responsible for pushing or pulling man against the criminal law, there is no indication from the investigators that these factors have been found. Even should the crime factors be found (whether they be social or psychic or physical in nature) crime will continue to be disapproved, and no social response to crime can make this disapproval disappear.

The traditional term "punishment" may be replaced by other terms, such as "treatment," "reform," "rehabilitation," or "correction," but this will not change their implying disapproval of criminal conduct. The official-social consequences of crime, whether they be named punishment or by another term, will still be punitive and expiatory (as it was in the earliest form of retribution for the sins against the divine power) or deterrent and preventive (as it became later for the violation of the terrestrial criminal act). Even Lady Wootton's proposed measures for social hygiene (which were actually visualized by Garraud in 1910 at the meeting of the Société Générale des Prisons and not much later by Angyal in their imaginary *code d'éducation* and *code de curation*) are responses to a disapproved conduct. Crime has always been disapproved and probably will remain so in the future, even if it is the product of, say, social injustice or the sick mind of the criminal. The controversial aphorism *Tout comprendre est tout pardonner* may have gained some credence, but no one has proposed *Tout pardonner est tout approuver*.

Disapproval is the crucial element of "punishment," in whatever form it is applied, with whatever motive it is reasoned, and for whatever conduct it is meted out. Most crimes, and particularly serious crimes, are acts that, as Morris Ginsberg put it, are "condemned by the moral sense of the community and from which every man knows, or is presumed to know, he ought to refrain."[10] This is why the most essential feature of punishment is that it expresses to the criminal and all others in the society that the conduct to be "punished" is reprehensible. And this is why social-moral disapproval brings us back to the problem of the "justice" and "usefulness" of penal consequences to the ethics of punishment. Patrick Devlin proposed, "The question is not how a person is to ascertain the morality which he adopts and follows, but how the law is to ascertain the morality which it enforces."[11] The problem of punishment is that "moral rules are obligatory"; as Nicholas Timasheff put it, these rules are not "recommended statements, which may be recognized or not recognized by group-members" but are "social commands which must be carried out, even if they run counter to individual interest or desires"; thus, "if this rule is transgressed, a social reaction generally takes place."[12] In the case of crime, the social reaction is punishment.

The punishment appears, in Georg Jellinek's words, as the "normative force of the actual" (*normative Kraft des Faktischen*).[13] If a member of the society comprehends the society's concept of "wrong," he responds adequately to the prevailing ethical rules; if, however, he does not grasp the society's morality and transgresses on the ethical law to the degree regarded as criminal, the sovereign power must show its disapproval in the form of punishment, for he and everybody else needs to be condemned for his conduct.

When the supreme social power charges certain conducts with responsibility and is ready to enforce that responsibility against any violator, it distinctly pronounces the moral or value system to be followed. When a punishment is applied, it articulates the sovereign's disapproval of attacks against the system. If there were an "absolute" morality, there would be no difficulty in defining and declaring it. Indeed, this difficulty has led to voices in favor of eliminating moral judgments from charging and enforcing responsibility; they propose instead to strive toward social objectives.[14] However, many disagreements and misunderstandings arise because morality is often identified with theological doctrines or confused with natural law. Morality, as used here, is the compound of the socioethical values as professed by the social power. And, as Patrick Devlin indicates, "A man who concedes that morality is necessary to society must support the use of those instruments without which morality cannot be maintained."[15] Hart complements this by suggesting that though the role responsibility might take either legal or moral form, it is not necessary to treat them separately: "The word 'moral' is unilluminatingly used simply to exclude legal responsibility."[16] As a matter of fact, distinguishing law from morality in this context is close to impossible,[17] and punishment expresses both legal and moral, or better, the socioethical, disapproval.[18]

Justification for punishment cannot be found in anything but the law itself; and the law, with its responsibility-charging command, represents the socioethical value system for which the sovereign stands and which he is determined to enforce. Law and socioethical values cannot rationally be separated. Devlin gives this example:

If one can imagine a judge dividing a sentence into parts and sentencing a man to three months for the harm he has done to his victim and six months for his wickedness in doing it, the result would be just the same as if he had been separately charged under two separate sections of a statute, one which made the act an offense if done without any intent and another which made it a graver offense if done with a wicked intent.[19]

The supreme social power, the "sovereign," may or may not take into consideration the factors responsible for guiding man against the law (not to mention that these factors may not be known, or if known they may change according to the changing criminal law, its changing socioethical content—and the changing sovereign). Regardless of the changes, however, man has to follow the command actually in force, for that is what defines his conformity or criminality. To betoken this fate of man more emphatically, the author quotes Cicero when he spoke for Cluventio: *Legum ministri magistratus, legum interpretes iudices, legum denique idcirco omnes servi sumus ut liberi esse possimus.*[20] Indeed, "In the end, we all are slaves to the law, because this is the condition of our freedom." But Beccaria's view may soften this pessimistic truth: "No lasting advantage is to be hoped for from political morality if it is not founded upon the ineradicable feelings of mankind."[21]

NOTES

1. H. L. A. Hart, *Punishment and Responsibility* (Oxford, 1968), p. 1.
2. See among others: A. Flew, "The Justification of Punishment," *Philosophy*, 1954, p. 291; K. Baier, "Is Punishment Retributive?" *Analysis*, 1955, p. 25; S. I. Benn, "An Approach to the Problems of Punishment," *Philosophy*, 1958, pp. 325–326; Hart, *Punishment and Responsibility, op. cit.*, pp. 4–5.
3. Rusztem Vámbéry, *Büntetöjog* (Budapest, 1913), II, 1–2.
4. Fr. Oetker, "Strafe und Lohn," *Rektoratsrede* (Würzburg, 1907).
5. This classification, in its outline, follows Pál Angyal's categories; see his *A magyar büntetöjog tankönyve* (Budapest, 1920), pp. 41–43.
6. Adolf Merkel, *Vergeltungsidee und Zweckgedanke im Strafrecht* (Leipzig, 1892).
7. Angyal, *op. cit.*, p. 43.
8. James Fitzjames Stephen, *A History of the Criminal Law of England* (London, 1883), II, 183.
9. Barbara Wootton, *Social Science and Social Pathology* (London, 1959); "Diminished Responsibility: A Layman's View," *Law Quarterly Review*, Vol. 76 (1960); *Crime and Criminal Law* (London, 1963).

10. Morris Ginsberg, *On Justice in Society* (Harmondsworth, Eng., 1965), p. 164.

11. Patrick Devlin, *The Enforcement of Morals* (London, 1968), p. x.

12. Nicholas S. Timasheff, *An Introduction to the Sociology of Law* (Cambridge, Mass., 1939), pp. 143–144.

13. G. Jellinek, *Das Recht des modernen Staates* (Berlin, 1900), pp. 308–314.

14. Marc Ancel, "Social Defence," *Law Quarterly Review*, Vol. 78, (1962), p. 491.

15. Devlin, *op. cit.*, p. 25.

16. Hart, *op. cit.*, pp. 214–215.

17. Gustav Radbruch, *Rechtsphilosophie* (3rd ed., Berlin, 1932).

18. The problem of morals, laws, and social realities, from Mill and Stephen to contemporary thinkers, has a vast literature.

19. Devlin, *op. cit.*, p. 130.

20. Cicero, *Pro A. Cluventio oratio*, book 53 line 146.

21. Bonesana Cesare, Marquis de Beccaria, *On Crimes and Punishments*, Henry Paloucci (tr.) (New York, 1963), p. 10.

Selected Bibliography

Abrahamsen, David. *The Psychology of Crime*. New York, 1960.

Aichorn, August. *Wayward Youth*. New York, 1935.

Alexander, Franz, and Hugo Staub. *The Criminal, the Judge, and the Public*. Gregory Zilboorg (tr.). Glencoe, 1956.

———, and Louis B. Shapiro. "Neuroses, Behavior Disorders, and Perversions," in Franz Alexander and Helen Ross (eds.), *Dynamic Psychiatry*. Chicago, 1952.

Alimena, B. *Naturalismo critico e diritto penale*. Rome, 1892.

———. *La scuola critica di diritto penale*. Naples, 1894.

Allen, Francis A. "Raffaele Garofalo," in Hermann Mannheim (ed.), *Pioneers in Criminology*. London, 1960.

Ancel, Marc. "Social Defence," *Law Quarterly Review*, Vol. 78 (1962).

Andrews, W. *Punishments in the Olden Times*. London, 1881.

Angyal, Pál. *A magyar büntetöjog tankönyve*. Budapest, 1920.

Aschaffenburg, Gustav. *Das Verbrechen und seine Bekämpfung*. Heidelberg, 1903.

Atlas, Nicholas. "Criminal Law and Procedure," in Vernon C. Branham and Samuel B. Kutash (eds.), *Encyclopedia of Criminology*. New York, 1949.

Aubry, P. *La contagion du meurtre*. Paris, 1894.

Austin, John. *Lectures on Jurisprudence or the Philosophy of Positive Law*. London, 1861.

Baer, A. *Der Verbrecher in Anthropologischer Beziehung*. Leipzig, 1893.

Baets, de M. *L'école d'anthropologie criminelle*. Gand, 1893.

———. *Les influences de la misère sur la criminalité*. Gand, 1895.

Baier, K. "Is Punishment Retributive?" *Analysis*, 1955.

Balogh, Jenö. *Nyomor és büntettek*. Budapest, 1908.

Barnes, Harry Elmer, and Negley K. Teeters. *New Horizons in Criminology.* New York, 1944.

Batchelor, John. *The Ainu of Japan.* London, 1892.

Battaglia, Bruno. *La dinamica del delitto.* Naples, 1886.

Bebel, August. *Die Frau und der Sozialismus.* Stuttgart, 1899.

Beccaria, Bonesana Cesare Marquis de. *Dei delitti e delle pene.* Haarlem, 1764; in English: *An Essay on Crime and Punishments,* 5th ed., with commentary by Voltaire. London, 1804.

Becker, Howard S. *Outsiders, Studies in the Sociology of Deviance.* New York, 1963.

Beermann, R. "The Parasite Law in the Soviet Union," *The British Journal of Criminology,* 3 (July 1962).

Bemmelen, J. M. van. "Willem Adriaan Bonger," in Hermann Mannheim (ed.), *Pioneers in Criminology.* London, 1960.

Benedikt, M. "Biologie und Kriminalistik," *Zeitschrift für d. ges. Strafrechtswissenschaft.* Vol. VII.

―――. *Anatomical Studies upon Brains of Criminals.* New York, 1881.

Benjamin, M. "Wie können die Ursachen der Kriminalität erforscht werden," *Neue Justiz,* No. 2, 1962.

Benn, Stanley. "An Approach to the Problems of Punishment," *Philosophy,* 1958.

―――, and Richard S. Peters. *The Principles of Political Thought.* London and New York, 1965.

Bentham, Jeremy. *Principles of Penal Law.* Edinburgh, 1843.

Bergbohm, Karl. *Jurisprudenz und Rechtsphilosophie.* Leipzig, 1892.

Berman, Harold J. *Justice in the U.S.S.R.* Rev. ed. New York, 1963.

Bierling, Rudolf Ernst. *Zur Kritik der juristischen Grundbegriffe.* 2 vols. Leipzig, 1877–1893.

―――. *Juristische Prinzipienlehre.* 5 vols. Leipzig and Freiburg, 1894–1917.

Binding, Karl. *Die Entstehung der öffentlichen Strafe in germanisch-deutschem Recht.* Leipzig, 1908.

Birnbaum, Karl. *Kriminalpsychopathologie und Psychobiologische Verbrecherkunde.* Berlin, 1931.

Bockelman, Paul. *Studien zum Täterstrafrecht.* Berlin, 1940.

Bodenheimer, Edgar. *Jurisprudence, the Philosophy and Method of the Law.* Cambridge, Mass., 1962.

Böhmer, G. M. *Handbuch der Litteratur des Kriminalrechts.* 1816.

Boies, Henry M. *The Science of Penology.* New York, 1901.

Bonger, Willem Adriaan. *Criminality and Economic Conditions.* Henry P. Horton (tr.). New York, 1967.

Bosco, A. *La statistica civile e penale.* Rome, 1898.

Bowring, John (ed.), *The Works of Jeremy Bentham.* Edinburgh, 1843.

Branham, Vernon C., and Samuel B. Kutash (eds.). *Encyclopedia of Criminology.* New York, 1949.

Breckenridge, Sophonisba, and Edith Abbott. *The Delinquent Child and the Home.* New York, 1912.

Bromberg, W. *The Mind of Man: The Story of Man's Conquest of Mental Illness.* New York, 1937.

Burchardt, H. H. *Kriminalität in Stadt und Land.* Berlin, 1936.

Bürger-Prinz, H. *Motiv und Motivation.* Berlin, 1950.

Burt, Cyril. *The Young Delinquent.* London, 1925.

Caldwell, Charles. *Elements of Phrenology.* New York, 1824.

Camp, M. du. "Paris, ses organes, ses fonctions et sa vie," *Revue des Deux Mondes,* 1869.

Cardozo, Benjamin Nathan. *The Nature of the Judicial Process.* New Haven, 1921.

———. *The Growth of the Law.* New Haven, 1924.

———. *The Paradoxes of Legal Science.* New York, 1928.

Carnevale, E. "Una terza scuola di diritto penale in Italia," *Rivista Carceraria,* July 1891.

———. "La nuova tendenza nelle discipline criminali," *Antologia Giuridica,* 1892.

Carpzov, Benedict. *Practica nova imperialis saxonica rerum criminalium,* 1635; "new" edition with various observations edited by Johannes Samuel Fridericus Böhmer in 1758, Frankfurt-am-Main.

Carrara, F. "Il diritto penale e la procedura penale," *Opuscoli di diritto criminale,* Vol. V, 1874.

Carus, N. *Grundzüge einer neuen und wissenschaftlichen Kranioscopie.* Stuttgart, 1840.

Casey, M. D., L. J. Segall, D. R. K. Street, and C. E. Blank. "Sex Chromosome Abnormalities in Two State Hospitals for Patients Requiring Special Security," *Nature* (London), 1966, 209.

———, C. E. Blank, D. R. K. Street, L. J. Segall, J. H. McDougall, P. J. McGrath, and J. S. Skinner, "YY Chromosomes and Antisocial Behaviour," *Lancet,* 1966, 2.

Castiglioni, A. *Adventures of the Mind.* New York, 1946.

Cavan, Ruth Shonle. *Criminology.* 2nd ed. New York, 1957.

Cereteli, T. V., and V. G. Makasvili. "A bünfelelösség elvének fejlödése a szovjet büntetöjogban," *Jogtudományi Közlöny,* XXII:1, January 1967.

Chilton, Roland J. "Continuity in Delinquency Area Research: A Comparison of Studies for Baltimore, Detroit, and Indianapolis," *American Sociological Review,* Vol. 29, (February 1964).

Christiansen, Karl O. "Kriminologie (Grundlagen)," in Rudolf Sieverts (ed.), *Handwörterbuch der Kriminologie*. Vol. II. 2nd ed. Berlin, 1968.

Cicero, Marcus Tullius. *De republica*.

————. *Pro A. Cluventio oratio*.

Clinard, Marshall B. *Sociology of Deviant Behavior*. Rev. ed. New York, 1963.

————, and Richard Quinney. *Criminal Behavior Systems: A Typology*. New York, 1967.

Cloward, Richard A., and Lloyd E. Ohlin. *Delinquency and Opportunity: A Theory of Delinquent Gangs*. Glencoe, 1960.

Cohen, Albert K. *Delinquent Boys: The Culture of the Gang*. New York, 1955.

————. "Multiple Factor Approaches," in Marvin E. Wolfgang, Leonard Savitz, and Norman Johnston (eds.), *The Sociology of Crime and Delinquency*. New York, 1962.

————. *Deviance and Control*. Englewood Cliffs, N.J., 1966.

Cohen, Morris Raphael. *Reason and Law*. New York, 1961.

Colajanni, Napoleone. *Sociologia Criminale*. Catania, 1889.

Coleman, James C. *Abnormal Psychology and Modern Life*. 3rd ed. Chicago, 1964.

Corne, A. "La criminalité, sur ses causes, sur les moyens d'y remédier," *Journal des Economistes*, Vol. 9 (January 1868).

————. *Les criminels*. Paris, 1889.

Coser, Lewis A. "The Sociology of Poverty," *Social Problems*, Vol. 13 (Fall 1965).

Court-Brown, W. M. "Studies on the Human Y Chromosome," *Medical Research Council Annual Report: April 1966–March 1967*. London, 1967.

————. "Genetics and Crime: The problem of XXY, XY/XXY, XXYY and XYY males," *Journal of the Royal College of Physicians*, 1967.

Cressey, Donald R. *Other People's Money: A Study in the Social Psychology of Embezzlement*. Glencoe, 1953.

————. "Criminological Research and the Definition of Crime," *American Journal of Sociology*, May 1951.

————. "Crime," in Robert K. Merton and Robert A. Nisbet (eds.), *Contemporary Social Problems*, 2nd ed. New York, 1966.

Dahm, Georg. "Die Erneuerung der Ehrenstrafe," *Deutsche Juristenzeitung*, 1934.

————. *Der Tätertyp im Strafrecht*. Leipzig, 1940.

Davenport, C. B. "Hereditary Crime," *American Journal of Sociology*, November 1907.

Denis, H. "Criminalité et la crise économique," *Actes du II Congr. d'anthropologie criminelle*. Brussels, 1893.

————. "Le socialisme et les causes économiques et sociales du crime," *Compte rendu V. Congr. d'anthropologie criminelle.* Amsterdam, 1901.

Despine, Prosper. *Psychologie naturelle, essai sur les facultés intellectuelles et morales dans leur état normal et dans leurs manifestations anormales chez les aliénés et chez les criminels.* Paris, 1868.

Devlin, Patrick. *The Enforcement of Morals.* London, 1968.

Diamond, A. S. *Primitive Law.* London, 1935.

Dijck, T. V. Van. *Bijdragen tot de psychologie van den misdadiger.* Groningen, 1906.

Drähms, August. *The Criminal: His Personnel and Environment.* New York, 1900.

Driver, Edwin D. "Charles Buckman Goring," in Hermann Mannheim (ed.), *Pioneers in Criminology.* London, 1960.

Drobisch, M. W. *Die Moralische Statistik und die Willensfreiheit.* Leipzig, 1867.

Ducpetiaux, Edouard. *De la condition physique et morale des jeunes ouvriers.* Brussels, 1843.

————. *Mémoire sur le paupérisme dans les Flandres.* Brussels, 1850.

Dugdale, Richard Louis. *The Jukes, A Study in Crime, Pauperism, Disease, and Heredity.* New York, 1895.

Duguit, Léon. *L'Etat, le droit objectif et la loi positive.* Paris, 1901.

Dunning, William Archibald. *A History of Political Theories from Luther to Montesquieu.* New York, 1902.

Durkheim, Emile. *De la division du travail social.* Paris, 1893.

————. *Le Suicide.* Paris, 1897.

————. *Rules of Sociological Method.* Glencoe, 1950.

East, Norwood. *Society and the Criminal.* Springfield, Ill., 1951.

Ehrlich, Eugen. *The Fundamental Principles of the Sociology of Law.* Cambridge, Mass., 1936.

————. "The Sociology of Law," *Harvard Law Review,* Vol. 36 (1922–23).

Eissler, Kurt R. *Searchlights on Delinquency.* New York, 1949.

Ellis, Havelock. *The Criminal.* 2nd ed. New York, 1900.

Elster, Alexander, and Heinrich Lingemann (eds.), *Handwörterbuch der Kriminologie und der anderen strafrechtlichen Hilfswissenschaften.* Berlin and Leipzig, 1933.

Emerton, Ephraim. *Introduction to the History of the Middle Ages.* Boston, 1888.

Engels, Friedrich. *Die Lage der Arbeitenden Klasse in England.* Stuttgart, 1892.

Estabrook, Arthur H., *The Jukes in 1915.* New York, 1916.

Exner, Franz. *Kriminologie.* Berlin, 1949.

Eysenck, H. J. *Uses and Abuses of Psychology.* Harmondsworth, Eng., 1953.

Feldbrugge, F. J. *Soviet Criminal Law, General Part.* Leyden, 1964.

Feré, Charles. *Dégénérescence et criminalité.* Paris, 1888.

Ferri, Enrico. *I nuovi orizzonti del diritto e della procedura penale.* Turin, 1881.

————. *La sociologia criminale.* Turin, 1884.

————. *Criminal Sociology.* Joseph I. Kelly and John Lisle (trs.). New York, 1967.

————. *Socialismo e criminalità.* Turin, 1883.

————. "Variations thermométriques et criminalité," *Archives d'anthropologie criminelle et des sciences pénales,* 1886.

————. *L'omicidio-suicidio.* Rome, 1884.

Ferriani, L. *Delinquenti scaltri e fortunati.* Como, 1897.

Fink, Arthur E. *The Causes of Crime: Biological Theories in the United States 1800–1915.* Philadelphia, 1938.

Finkey, Ferenc. *A magyar büntetöjog tankönyve.* Budapest, 1914.

————. *Adatok a büntettesek jellem csoportjainak megállapitásához.* Budapest, 1933.

Fitzgerald, P. J. *Criminal Law and Punishment.* Oxford, 1962.

Fletcher, Joseph. "Moral and Educational Statistics of England and Wales," *Journal of the Statistical Society of London,* 15, March 1855.

Flew, A. "The Justification of Punishment," *Philosophy,* 1954.

Földes, Béla. "Über einige wirtschaftliche und moralische Wirkungen hoher Getreidepreise," *Jahrbücher für Nationalökonomie und Statistik.* Leipzig, 1881.

————. *A bünügy statisztikája.* Budapest, 1889.

Forel, Auguste, and Albert Mahaim. *Crime et anomalies mentales constitutionelles, la plouie sociale des déséquilibrés à responsabilité diminuée.* Geneva, 1902.

Forsyth, J. *The Highlands of Central India.* London, 1871.

Franck, Ad. *Philosophie du droit pénal.* Paris, 1864.

Frank, Jerome. *Law and the Modern Mind.* New York, 1931.

Frank, Reinhard. *Über die Aufgabe des Schuldbegriffs.* Giessen, 1907.

Frégier, H. A. *Des classes dangereuses de la population dans les grandes villes et des moyens de les rendre meilleures.* Paris, 1840.

Freud, Sigmund. *A General Introduction to Psychoanalysis.* New York, 1920.

————. *Hemmung, Symptom und Angst.* Vienna, 1926.

————. *Das Ich und das Es.* Vienna, 1923.

————. *An Outline of Psychoanalysis.* New York, 1949.

Frey, Erwin. *Der frühkriminelle Rückfallsverbrecher.* Basel, 1959.

Friedlander, Kate. *The Psychoanalytical Approach to Juvenile Delinquency.* New York, 1947.

Friedmann, Wolfgang. *Law in a Changing Society.* Baltimore, 1964.

Friedrich, Carl Joachim. *The Philosophy of Law in Historical Perspective.* 2nd ed. Chicago and London, 1963.

Fuld, L. *Der Einfluss der Lebensmittelpreise auf die Bewegung der strafbaren Handlungen.* Mainz, 1881.

Fuller, Lon L. *The Morality of Law.* New Haven and London, 1964.

Gaedeken, P. "Contribution statistique à la réaction de l'organisme sous l'influence physico-chimique des agents météorologiques." *Archives d'anthropologie criminelle et de médecine légale.* Vol. 24 (1909).

Gall, Franz Joseph. *Sur les fonctions du cerveau.* Paris, 1825.

Galton, F. *Hereditary Genius.* London, 1892.

————. *Inquiries into Human Faculty and Its Development.* London, 1883.

Gareis, Karl. *Rechtsenzyklopädie und Methodologie.* 2nd ed. Stuttgart, 1900.

Garofalo, Raffaele. *Riparazione alle vittime del delitto.* Turin, 1887.

————. *La superstition socialiste.* Paris, 1895.

————. *De la solidarité des nations dans la lutte contre la criminalité.* Paris, 1909.

————. *Criminology.* Robert Wyness Millar (tr.). Boston, 1914.

Garraud, E. *Traité théorique et pratique du droit pénal français.* 3rd ed. Paris, 1913.

Gault, Robert H. *Criminology.* New York, 1932.

Gény, François. *Science et technique du droit privé positif.* Paris, 1914–1922.

————. *Méthodes d'interprétation et sources du droit positif.* Paris, 1919.

Gerard, Margaret W. "Emotional Disorders of Childhood," in Franz Alexander and Helen Ross (eds.), *Dynamic Psychiatry.* Chicago, 1952.

Gertsenzon, A. A. *"A bűnözés tanulmányozásáról és megelözéséröl"*; originally published in *Sovetskoe Gosudarstvo i Pravo,* 7 (1960); trans. into Hungarian, Gyula Alapy in *Jogtudományi Közlöny,* XVI (January–February 1961), 1–2.

Gibbons, Don C. *Changing the Lawbreaker.* Englewood Cliffs, N.J., 1965.

Gillin, John Lewis. *Criminology and Penology.* New York, 1926.

Ginsberg, Morris. *On Justice in Society.* Harmondsworth, Eng., 1965.

Glaser, Daniel. *The Effectiveness of a Prison and Parole System.* New York, 1964.

Glueck, Sheldon. "Roscoe Pound and Criminal Justice," *Crime and Delinquency,* Vol. 10 (October 1964).

————, and Eleanor Glueck. *Unraveling Juvenile Delinquency.* New York, 1950.

————. *Physique and Delinquency.* New York, 1956.

Goddard, Henry Herbert. *The Kallikak Family, A Study in the Heredity of Feeblemindedness.* New York, 1913.

————. *Feeblemindedness, Its Causes and Consequences.* New York, 1914.

Golding, M. P. (ed.). *The Nature of Law, Readings in Legal Philosophy.* New York, 1966.

Golunskii, S. A., and M. S. Strogovich. *Teorija gosudarstva i prava.* Moscow, 1940.

Goring, Charles B. *The English Convict: A Statistical Study.* London, 1913.

Grazia, Alfred de. *The Elements of Political Science.* London and New York, 1965.

Gross, Hans. *Criminal Investigation.* London, 1962.

Guerry, André Michel. *Essai sur la statistique morale.* Paris, 1833.

————. *Statistique morale de l'Angleterre comparée avec la statistique morale de la France.* Paris, 1864.

Gurvitch, Georges, *Sociology of Law.* New York, 1942.

Halleck, Seymour L. *Psychiatry and the Dilemmas of Crime, A Study of Causes, Punishment and Treatment.* New York, 1967.

Hanon, A. *De la définition du crime.* Paris, 1893.

Hart, Herbert Lionel Adolphus. *The Concept of Law.* Oxford, 1961.

————. *Law, Liberty, and Morality.* New York, 1963.

————. *Punishment and Responsibility.* Oxford, 1968.

Hauriou, Maurice. *Science sociale traditionelle.* Paris, 1896.

————. *Principes de droit public.* 2nd ed. Paris, 1916.

Hazard, John N. *The Soviet System of Government.* Chicago, 1964.

Healy, William. *The Individual Delinquent.* Boston, 1915.

————, and Augusta F. Bronner. *New Light on Delinquency and Its Treatment.* New Haven, 1936.

Hentig, Hans von. "Gustav Aschaffenburg," in Hermann Mannheim (ed.), *Pioneers in Criminology.* London, 1960.

Hippel, Robert von. *Deutsches Strafrecht.* Berlin, 1960.

Hobhouse, L. J., G. C. Wheeler, and N. Ginsberg. *The Material Culture and Social Institutions of the Simpler Peoples.* London, 1915.

Hoebel, E. Adamson. *The Law of Primitive Man, A Study in Comparative Legal Dynamics.* Cambridge, Mass., 1954.

Hoegel, Hugo. *Die Einteilung der Verbrecher in Klassen.* Leipzig, 1908.

Holdsworth, W. S. *A History of English Law.* London, 1903–1909.

Holmes, Oliver Wendell. *The Common Law.* Boston, 1881.

————. *Collected Legal Papers.* New York, 1921.

Hook, Sidney. *Marx and the Marxists, The Ambiguous Legacy.* Princeton, 1955.

Hooton, Ernest A. *The American Criminal: An Anthropological Study.* Cambridge, Mass., 1939.

———. *Crime and the Man.* Cambridge, 1939.

Horváth, Barna. *Angol jogelmélet.* Budapest, 1943.

Hunt, Robert Nigel Carew. *The Theory and Practice of Communism.* Baltimore, 1963.

Im Thurn, E. F. *Among the Indians of Guiana.* London, 1883.

Ives, George. *A History of Penal Methods.* London, 1914.

Jacobs, P. A., and J. A. Strong. "A Case of Human Intersexuality Having a Possible XXY Sex-Determining Mechanism," *Nature* (London), 1959.

Jacobs, P. A., M. Brunton, M. M. Melville, R. P. Brittain, and W. F. McClemont. "Aggressive Behaviour, Mental Subnormality and the XYY Male," *Nature* (London), 1965, 208.

Jaensch, E. R. *Zur Eidetik und Intergrationspsychologie.* Leipzig, 1941.

Janka, Karl. *Der Strafrechtliche Nothstand.* Vienna, 1878.

Jelgersma, G. "De geboren misdadiger," *Tijdschrift v. Strafrecht,* 1891.

Jellinek, Georg. *Die Sozialethische Bedeutung von Recht, Unrecht und Strafe.* Vienna, 1878.

———. *Allgemeine Staatslehre.* Berlin, 1900.

———. *Das Recht des modernen Staaten.* Berlin, 1900.

Jhering, Rudolf. *Kampf ums Recht.* Vienna, 1872.

———. *Der Zweck im Recht.* Leipzig, 1877–1883.

———. *Geist des römischen Rechts.* Leipzig, 1873.

Joffe, O. S., and M. D. Shargorodskii. *Voprosy teorii prava.* Moscow, 1961.

Joly, Henri. *Le Crime.* Paris, 1888.

———. *La France Criminelle.* Paris, 1889.

Jonnés, Moreau de. *Statistique de la Grande Bretagne et de l'Irlande.* Paris, 1838.

Jung, Carl G. *Modern Man in Search of a Soul.* New York, 1933.

———. *Psychology and Religion.* New Haven, 1938.

Kan, Joseph Van. *Les causes économiques de la criminalité.* Paris, 1903.

Kantorowicz, Hermann. *Rechtswissenschaft und Soziologie.* Tübingen, 1911.

———. *Die Aufgabe der Soziologie.* Leipzig, 1923.

———. *Aus der Vorgeschichte der Freirechtslehre.* Mannheim, 1925.

———. "Some Rationalism about Realism," *Yale Law Journal,* Vol. 43 (1933–34).

———. *Tat und Schuld.* Zurich, 1933.

Kareva, M. P., and Fedjkin, G. I. (eds.). *Teorija gosudarstva i prava.* Moscow, 1955.

Kaufmann, Arthur. *Das Unrechtsbewusstsein in der Schuldlehre des Strafrechts.* Mainz, no date.

Kaufmann, M. *Die Psychologie des Verbrechers.* Vienna, 1912.

Kellor, Frances. *Experimental Sociology.* New York, 1901.

Kelsen, Hans. *Allgemeine Staatslehre.* Berlin, 1925.

———. *Reine Rechtslehre.* Leipzig and Vienna, 1934.

———. *Der juristische und der soziologische Staatsbegriff.* Tübingen, 1922.

———. *Hauptprobleme der Staatsrechtslehre entwickelt aus der Lehre vom Rechtssatze.* Tübingen, 1911.

———. *Das Problem der Souveränität und die theorie des Völkerrechts.* Tübingen, 1920.

———. "The Pure Theory of Law: Its Methods and Fundamental Concepts," *The Law Quarterly Review*, Vol. 50 (October 1934).

———. "The Metamorphoses of the Idea of Justice," in Paul Sayre (ed.), *Interpretations of Modern Legal Philosophies, Essays in Honor of Roscoe Pound.* New York, 1947.

Kerimov, D. A., A. J. Koroliev, and M. D. Shargorodskii. *Obshchaia teorija gosudarstva i prava.* Leningrad, 1961.

Kinberg, Olaf. *Basic Problems of Criminology.* Copenhagen, 1935.

Kinch, John W. "Continuities in the Study of Delinquent Types," *The Journal of Criminal Law, Criminology and Police Science*, Vol. 53 (September 1962).

Kirichenko, V. F. *Znachenie oshibki po sovetskomu ugolovnomu pravu.* Moscow, 1952.

Kitsuse, John J., and David C. Dietrich. "Delinquent Boys: A Critique," *American Sociological Review*, April 1959.

Klineberg, Otto. "Mental Tests," *Encyclopedia of the Social Sciences.* New York, 1933.

Kohler, Josef. *Shakespeare vor den Forum der Jurisprudenz.* Berlin, 1884.

———. *Verbrecher-Typen.* Berlin, 1903.

Kovalevsky, P. *La psychologie criminelle.* Paris, 1903.

Kovaljov, M. I. "A szovjet kriminológia és helye a jogtudományok rendszerében," *Pravovedieniie*, 1965, No. 1; and *Külföldi Jogi Cikkgyüjtemény*, 1965, No. 4.

Kraepelin, Emil. *Psychiatrie.* Leipzig, 1883.

Kranz, Heinrich. *Lebensschicksale Krimineller Zwillinge.* Berlin, 1936.

Krauss, A. *Psychologie des Verbrechers.* Tübingen, 1884.

Kretschmer, Ernst. *Körperbau und Charakter.* Berlin, 1921; in English, *Physique and Character*, W. J. H. Sprott (tr.). London, 1925.

Kurella, Hans. *Cesare Lombroso, A Modern Man of Science.* M. Eden Paul (tr.). New York, 1910.

———. *Die Grenzen der Zurechnungsfähigkeit und die Kriminalanthropologie.* Halle, 1903.

———. *Lombroso als Mensch und Forscher.* Wiesbaden, 1913.

———. *Naturgeschichte des Verbrechers: Grundzüge der Kriminellen Anthropologie und Kriminalpsychologie.* Stuttgart, 1893.

Lacassagne, A. "Marche de la criminalité en France de 1825 à 1880," *Revue scientifique,* May 28, 1881.

———. *Peine de mort et criminalité.* Paris, 1908.

———. *Précis de Médecine légale.* Paris, 1906.

Lafargue, Paul. *Der wirtschaftliche Materialismus.* Zurich, 1886.

———. "Die Kriminalität in Frankreich 1840–1886," *Neue Zeit,* 1889.

Lander, Bernard. *Toward an Understanding of Juvenile Delinquency.* New York, 1954.

Lange, Johannes. *Verbrechen als Schicksal.* Leipzig, 1919; in English, *Crime and Destiny,* Charlotte Haldane (tr.). New York, 1930.

Laski, Harold J. *Studies in the Problem of Sovereignty.* New Haven, 1917.

———. *A Grammar of Politics.* London, 1925.

———. *Studies in Law and Politics.* London, 1932.

———. *The State in Theory and Practice.* London, 1936.

Laurent, E. *Le criminel.* Paris, 1908.

Lauvergne, H. *Les forcats considerés sous le rapport physique, morale et intellectuel observés au bagne de Toulon.* Paris, 1844.

Lavater, John Casper. *Physiognomical Fragments.* Zurich, 1775.

Legras, A. M. *Psychose en Criminaliteit bei Twellingen.* Utrecht, 1932.

Lenz, Adolf. *Grundriss der Kriminalbiologie.* Berlin and Vienna, 1927.

———. "Der Kriminalbiologische Untersuchungsbogen des Grazer Institutes und der Wiener Polizeidirection," *Mitteilunger der Kriminalbiologischen Gesellschaft,* 1929.

———. *Mörder, Die Untersuchung der Persönlichkeit als Beitrag zur Kriminalbiologischen Kasuistik und Methodik.* Graz, 1931.

———. "Die Bedeutung der Kriminalbiologie," *Archiv für Kriminalbiologie,* 88, 1931.

Lindesmith, Alfred R., and H. Warren Dunham. "Some Principles of Criminal Typology," *Social Forces,* March 1941.

Liszt, Franz von. *Lehrbuch des deutschen Strafrechts.* Berlin, 1881.

———. *Das Verbrechen als Sozialpathologische Erscheinung.* Dresden, 1899.

———. *Strafrechtliche Aufsätze und Vorträge.* Berlin, 1905.

Llewellyn, Karl N. *The Bramble Bush.* New York, 1930.

———. *Jurisprudence: Realism in Theory and Practice*. New York, 1962.

Lloyd, Dennis. *The Idea of Law*. Baltimore, 1964.

Lombroso, Cesare. *L'Uomo delinquente*. Milan, 1876.

———. *Crime: Its Causes and Remedies*. Henry P. Horton (tr.). Boston, 1912.

———. *Delitti vecchi e delitti nuovi*. Turin, 1902.

———, with G. Ferrero. *La donna delinquente, la prostituta e la donna normale*. Turin, 1893.

———. *Genio e follia*. Milan, 1864.

Loria, Achille. *Les bases économiques de la constitution sociale*. Paris, 1894.

Lottier, Stuart. "Distribution of Criminal Offenses in Metropolitan Regions," *The Journal of Criminal Law, Criminology and Police Science*, Vol. 29 (1939).

Lucas, J. M. Charles. *Du système pénal et du système répressif en général, de la peine de mort en particulier*. Paris, 1827.

Lux, H. *Sozialpolitisches Handbuch*. Berlin, 1892.

Mádl, Ferenc. *A deliktuális felelösség*. Budapest, 1964.

Maine, Sir Henry Sumner. *Ancient Law, Its Connection with the Early History of Society and Its Relation to Modern Ideas*. London, 1861; with Introduction and notes by Sir Frederick Pollock, London, 1906.

Makarewicz, J. *Einführung in die Philosophie des Strafrechts auf entwicklungsgeschichtlicher Grundlage*. Stuttgart, 1906; Amsterdam, 1967.

Malone, Wex S. "Nature of Proof of Cause-In-Fact," in Richard C. Donnelly, Joseph Goldstein, and Richard D. Schwartz (eds.), *Criminal Law*. New York, 1962.

Mannheim, Hermann (ed.). *Pioneers in Criminology*. London, 1960.

Mannheim, Karl. *Systematic Sociology: An Introduction to the Study of Society*. J. S. Erös and W. A. C. Stewart (eds.). New York, 1957.

Manouvrier, Léonce. "La genèse normal du crime," *Bulletins de la Société d'Anthropologie de Paris*, Vol. 4 (1893).

Mariner, William. *An Account of the Natives of the Tonga Islands*. London, 1817.

Marro, Antonio. *I caratteri dei delinquenti*. Turin, 1887.

———. *La puberta studiata nell'uomo e nella donna*. Turin, 1898.

Maudsley, Henry. *Body and Mind*. London, 1870.

———. *The Physiology of Mind*. London, 1867.

———. *The Pathology of Mind*. London, 1867.

———. *Responsibility in Mental Disease*. London, 1874.

———. *Natural Causes and Supernatural Seemings*. London, 1886.

Maxwell, J. *Le criminel et la société*. Paris, 1909.

———. *Le concept social du crime et son évolution*. Paris, 1914.

Mayhew, H., and J. Binney. *The Criminal Prisons of London.* London, 1862.

Mayr, Georg von. *Statistik der gerichtlichen Polizei im Königreiche Bayern und in einigen anderen Ländern.* Munich, 1867.

———. *Moralstatistik mit Einschluss der Kriminalstatistik.* Tübingen, 1917.

Mead, Georg Herbert. "The Psychology of Punitive Justice," *American Journal of Sociology,* Vol. 23 (1928).

Menshagin, V. D., N. D. Durmanov, and P. S. Romashkin (eds.). *Sovetskoe Ugolovnoe Pravo, Chast Obshchaia.* Moscow, 1962.

———, A. A. Gertsenzon, M. M. Ishaiev, A. A. Piontovskii, and B. S. Utevskii. *Szovjet Büntetöjog, Egyetemi Tankönyv.* Budapest, 1951. Official University textbook of Soviet criminal law, in Hungarian.

Merkel, Adolf. *Vergeltungsidee und Zweckgedanke im Strafrecht.* Leipzig, 1892.

———. *Juristische Encyclopädie.* 7th ed. Leipzig, 1922.

Merton, Robert K. "Social Structure and Anomie," *American Sociological Review,* Vol. 3 (1938).

———. *Social Theory and Social Structure.* New York, 1957.

Meyer, A. *Die Verbrechen in ihrem Zusammenhang mit dem wirtschaftlichen und socialen Verhältnissen in Kanton Zürich, Abhängigkeit von tellurischen Faktoren.* Jena, 1895.

Mezger, Edmund. *Deutsches Strafrecht: Ein Grundriss.* Berlin, 1938.

———. *Kriminalpolitik und ihre Kriminologischen Grundlagen.* 3rd ed. Stuttgart, 1944.

———. *Kriminologie, Ein Studienbuch.* Berlin, 1951.

———. *Strafrecht.* Munich, 1948.

Miller, Walter B. "Lower Class Culture as a Generating Milieu of Gang Delinquency," *Journal of Social Issues,* Vol. 14 (1958).

Minkovskii, G. M. *A büncselekmények megelözése.* Moscow, 1962.

Mommsen, Theodor. *Römisches Strafrecht.* Leipzig, 1899.

———. *Zum ältesten strafrecht der Kulturvölker.* Leipzig, 1905.

Monachesi, Elio. "Cesare Beccaria," in Hermann Mannheim (ed.), *Pioneers in Criminology.* London, 1960.

Montyel, Marandon de. "Contribution à l'étude clinique des rapports de la criminalité et de la dégénérescence," *Archives d'anthropologie criminelle,* 1892.

Moór, Gyula. *Bevezetés a jogfilozófiába.* Budapest, 1922.

———. *Macht, Recht, Moral.* Szeged, 1922.

More, Sir Thomas. *De optimo reipublicae statu sive de nova insula Utopia.* Louvain, 1516. There are many English editions.

Moreau-Christophe, L. M. *Du problème de la misère et de la solution chez les peuples anciens et modernes.* Paris, 1851.

―――. *Le monde des coquins.* Paris, 1863.

Moreau, G. *Souvenirs de la petite et de la grande roquette.* Paris, 1888.

Morel, Benoit Augustin. *De la contagion morale: du danger que présente pour la moralité et securité publique la relation des crimes donnée par les journaux.* Marseille, 1870.

Morris, Terence. *The Criminal Area.* London, 1958.

Morrison, William Douglas. *Crime and Its Causes.* London, 1891.

Muldal, S., and C. H. Ockey. "The 'Double' Male: A New Chromosome Constitution in Klinefelter Syndrome," *Lancet,* Vol. 2 (1960).

Müller, H. *Untersuchungen über die Bewegung der Kriminalität in ihrem Zusammenhang mit dem wirschaftlichen Verhältnissen.* Halle, 1899.

Müller-Freinfels, Richard. *Philosophie der Individualität.* Berlin, 1921.

Murchison, Carl. *Criminal Intelligence.* Worcester, Mass., 1926.

Näcke, P. *Verbrechen und Wahnsinn beim Weibe.* Leipzig, 1894.

Niceforo, Alfredo. "Criminalita e condizioni economiche in Sicilia," *Rivista di scient. di diritto,* 1897.

Nordau, Max, "Une nouvelle théorie biologique du crime," *La Revue,* 1902.

Nordenshiöld, Erik. *The History of Biology.* New York, 1928.

Oetker, Fr. *Strafe und Lohn, "Rektoratsrede,"* Würzburg, 1907.

Oettingen, Alexander von. *Die Moralstatistik in ihrer Bedeutung für eine Sozialethic.* 3rd ed. Erlangen, 1882.

Olrik, Eyvind. "Über die Einteilung der Verbrecher," *Zeitschrift für die gesamte Strafrechtswissenschaft,* XIV: 73.

―――. *Strafgesetzgebung der Gegenwart in rechtsvergleichender Darstellung.* Berlin, 1894.

Oppenheimer, H. *The Rationale of Punishment.* London, 1913.

Ostromov, S. S., and V. J. Tsugunov. "A Bünözö személyének vizsgálata a kriminologiai kutatások adatai alapján," *Sovetskoe Gosudarstvo i Pravo,* 1965, No. 9; and *Külföldi Jogi Cikkgyüjtemény,* 1966, No. 1.

Overholser, Winfred. "Isaac Ray," in Hermann Mannheim (ed.), *Pioneers in Criminology.* London, 1960.

Pareto, Vilfredo. *Sociological Writings.* Derick Mirfin (tr.). Introduction by S. E. Finer. New York, 1966.

Park, Robert E., Ernest W. Burgess, and Roderick D. McKenzie. *The City, The Ecological Approach to the Study of the Human Community.* Chicago, 1925.

Parmelee, Maurice. *Criminology.* New York, 1918.

Parsons, P. A. *Responsibility for Crime.* New York, 1909.

Parsons, Talcott. "The Law and Social Control," in William M. Evan (ed.), *Law and Sociology, Exploratory Essays.* New York, 1962.

———. "Comment" to L. Gross, "Preface to a Metatheoretical Framework," *American Journal of Sociology,* 67 (September, 1961).

———. "Introduction" to Max Weber, *The Sociology of Religion.* Ephraim Fischoff (tr.). Boston, 1963.

———. *The Structure of Social Action.* New York, 1968.

Paschukanis, E. B. *Obshchaia teoriia prava i marksism.* 2nd ed. Moscow, 1926.

———. "Foreword," *Allgemeine Rechtslehre und Marxismus.* Berlin, 1929.

Petrazhitsky, L. *Theory of Law and State.* St. Petersburg, 1909.

Phillipson, Coleman. *Three Criminal Law Reformers: Beccaria, Bentham, and Romilly.* New York, 1923.

Pike, L. O. *A History of Crime in England.* London, 1873–1876.

Piontkovskii, A. A. "A büntetöjogi felelösség alapja," originally published in *Sovetskoe Gosudarstvo i Pravo,* 1959, No. 11; *Jogtudományi Közlöny,* Vol. 15 (April 1960).

———. *Uchenie o prestuplenii po sovetskomu ugolovnomu pravu.* Moscow, 1961.

Poletti, Filippo. *Del sentimento nella scienza del diritto penale.* Udine, 1882.

Pollock, Frederick, and William Frederick Maitland. *The History of English Law.* 2nd ed. Cambridge, Mass., 1898.

Porte, J. Baptiste della. *The Human Physiognomy.* 1586.

Post, A. H. *Bausteine für eine Rechtswissenschaft auf vergleichend ethnologischer Grundlage.* Oldenburg, 1880.

———. *Die Grundlagen des Rechts, Leitfaden für den aufbau einer allgemeinen Rechtswissenschaft auf soziologischer Basis.* Oldenburg, 1884.

Pound, Roscoe. *An Introduction to the Philosophy of Law.* New Haven and London, 1965.

———. *Interpretations of Legal History.* Cambridge, Mass., 1923.

———. *The Spirit of the Common Law.* Boston, 1921.

———. *Laws and Morals.* 2nd ed. Chapel Hill, N.C., 1924.

———. *Outlines of Lectures on Jurisprudence.* 4th ed. Cambridge, Mass., 1928.

Price, W. H., and P. P. Whatmore, "Behaviour Disorders and Pattern of Crime among XYY Males Identified at a Maximum Security Hospital," *British Medical Journal,* 1, 1967.

Prins, Adolphe. *Criminalité et répression.* Brussels, 1886.

———. *La défense sociale et les transformations du droit pénal.* Brussels, 1910.

Proal, L. *Le crime et la peine.* Paris, 1892.

Quetelet, Adolphe. *Sur l'homme et la développement de ses facultés ou essai de physique sociale.* Paris, 1835.

Quirós, C. Bernaldo de. *Modern Theories of Criminality.* New York, 1967.

———. *La mala vida en Madrid.* Madrid, 1901.

———. "Enrico Ferri," in *Encyclopedia of the Social Sciences.* New York, 1931.

Radbruch, Gustav. *Rechtsphilosophie.* 3rd ed. Berlin, 1932.

Radloff, W. *Das Schamanenthum.* Leipzig, 1885.

Radzinowicz, Leon. *A History of English Criminal Law and Its Administration from 1750.* London, 1948–1956.

———. *Ideology and Crime.* New York, 1966.

Ray, Isaac. *A Treatise on the Medical Jurisprudence of Insanity.* 3rd ed. 1855.

———. *Contributions to Mental Pathology.* Boston, 1873.

Reckless, Walter C. *The Crime Problem.* 4th ed. New York, 1967.

———. "Halttheorie," *Monatschrift für Kriminologie und Strafrechtsreform,* Vol. 44 (June 1961).

Rickert, Heinrich. *System der Philosophie.* Tübingen, 1921.

Rittler, Theodor. "Der böse Vorsatz," *Österreichische Juristenzeitung,* 1954.

Roesner, Ernst. "Wirtschaftslage und Straffälligkeit" and "Kriminalstatistik," in Alexander Elster and Heinrich Lingemann (eds.), *Handwörterbuch der Kriminologie und der anderen strafrechtlichen Hilfswissenschaften.* Berlin, 1933.

Romashkin, P. S., M. S. Strogovich, and V. A. Tumanov (eds.). *Teorija gosudarstva i prava.* Moscow, 1962.

Rosanoff, A. J., Keva M. Handy, and Isabel A. Rosanoff. "Etiology of Child Behavior Difficulties, Juvenile Delinquency, and Adult Criminality," *Psychiatric Monographs.* Department of Institutions, California, 1941, No. 1.

Ross, E. *Social Control.* New York, 1901.

Rostow, W. W. *The Dynamics of Soviet Society.* New York, 1960.

Rowe, Allan W., and Miriam Van Waters, "Physical Associations and Behavior Problems," *Endocrinology,* 19, 1935.

Rusche, Georg, and Otto Kircheimer, *Punishment and the Social Structure.* New York, 1939.

Saharov, A. B. *A bünöző személyéről és a bünözés okairól a Szovjetunióban.* Moscow, 1961.

Sallillas, Rafael. "Hampa," in *Estudios de Derecho penal preventio.* Madrid, 1901.

Sariia, P. A. *A Kommunista erkölcs néhány kérdése.* Budapest, 1951.

Sartre, Jean Paul. *Being and Nothingness.* Hazel E. Barnes (tr.). New York, 1956.

Sauer, Wilhelm. *Allgemeine Strafrechtslehre.* Berlin, 1949.

Schafer, Stephen. "On the Proportions of the Criminality of Women," *The Journal of Criminal Law and Criminology,* 39, May–June 1948.

———. *The Victim and His Criminal: A Study in Functional Responsibility.* New York, 1968.

———. "Juvenile Delinquents in 'Convictional' Crime." *International Annals of Criminology,* 1962, Vol. I.

Scheff, Thomas J. "Introduction," *Mental Illness and Social Processes.* New York, 1967.

Schlapp, M. G., and E. H. Smith. *The New Criminology.* New York, 1928.

Schmid, Calvin F. *Social Saga of Two Cities, An Ecological and Statistical Study of the Social Trends in Minneapolis and St. Paul.* Minneapolis, 1937.

Schmidt, A. B. *Die Grundsätze über den Schadenersatz in den Volksrechten.* Leipzig, 1885.

Schroeder, F. C. *Die Grundsätze der Strafgesetzgebung der UdSSR und Unionsrepubliken.* Herrenalb, 1960.

Schuessler, Karl F., and Donald R. Cressey. "Personality Characteristics of Criminals," *American Journal of Sociology,* March 1950.

Seelig, Ernst. "Die Gliederung der Vebrecher," in Ernst Seelig and Karl Weindler (eds.), *Die Typen der Kriminellen.* Berlin, 1949.

———. "Das Typenproblem in der Kriminalbiologie," *Journal für Psychologie und Neurologie,* 1931.

Sellin, Thorsten. "Enrico Ferri," in Hermann Mannheim (ed.), *Pioneers in Criminology.* London, 1960.

———. "The Lombrosian Myth in Criminology," *The American Journal of Sociology,* May 1937.

———. *Culture Conflict and Crime.* Social Science Research Council, Bulletin 41. New York, 1938.

———, and Marvin E. Wolfgang. *The Measurement of Delinquency.* New York, 1964.

Sethna, Minocher J. *Jurisprudence.* 2nd ed. Girgaon-Bombay, 1959.

Shargorodskii, M. D., and N. A. Beliaev (eds.). *Sovetskoe Ugolovnoe Pravo Obshchaia Chast.* Moscow, 1960.

Shaw, Clifford R. *Delinquency Areas.* Chicago, 1929.

———, and Henry D. McKay. *Social Factors in Juvenile Delinquency.* National Commission of Law Observance and Enforcement, Report on the Causes of Crime, Vol. 2, No. 13. Washington, D.C., 1931.

———. *Juvenile Delinquency and Urban Areas, A Study of Rates of*

Delinquents in Relation to Different Characteristics of Local Communities in American Cities. Chicago, 1942.

Sheldon, William H. *Atlas of Man.* New York, 1954.

——. *Varieties of Delinquent Youth: An Introduction to Constitutional Psychiatry.* New York, 1949.

Shulman, Harry M. "Intelligence and Delinquency," *The Journal of Criminal Law, Criminology and Police Science,* Vol. 41 (March–April 1951).

Sieverts, Rudolf (ed.). *Handwörterbuch der Kriminologie.* 2nd ed. Berlin, 1967–1968.

Sighele, S. *La foule criminelle.* 2nd ed. Paris, 1901.

——. *Littérature et criminalité.* Paris, 1908.

——. *Le crime à deux.* 2nd ed. Paris, 1910.

Simmel, Georg. "The Poor." Translated by Claire Jacobson from "Der Arme," *Soziologie: Untersuchungen über die Formen der Vergesellschaftung.* Leipzig, 1908.

Sliapochnikov, A. S. "A bünözés okainak kutatásával kapcsolatos kérdések," *Voprossi filsofii,* 1966, No. 1; and *Külföldi Jogi Cikkgyüjtémény,* 1966, No. 3.

Söderman, Harry, and John J. O'Connell, *Modern Criminal Investigation.* 5th ed. Revised by Charles E. O'Hara. New York, 1962.

Sorley, W. R. *A History of English Philosophy.* Cambridge, England, 1920.

Sorokin, Pitirim A. *Social and Cultural Dynamics.* New York, 1937.

——. "Sociology of Yesterday, Today, and Tomorrow," *American Sociological Review,* Vol. 30 (December 1965).

Spranger, Eduard. *Lebensformen Geisteswissenschaftliche Psychologie und Ethik der Persönlichkeit.* Berlin, 1914.

Stammler, Rudolf. *Die Lehre von dem richtigen Rechte.* Halle, 1902.

——. *Wirtschaft und Recht nach der materialistischen Geschichtsanfassung.* 5th ed. Leipzig, 1924.

Starke, Wolfgang. *Verbrechen und Verbrecher in Preussen, 1854–1878.* Berlin, 1884.

——. *Die Entschädigung des Verletzten nach deutschen Recht unter besonderer Berücksichtigung der Wiedergutmachung nach geltendem Strafrecht.* Freiburg, 1959.

Steinmetz, S. R. *Ethnologische Studien zur ersten Entwicklung der Strafe.* Leiden, 1894.

Stephen, James Fitzjames. *A History of the Criminal Law of England.* London, 1883.

Strauss, Leo. *The Political Philosophy of Hobbes, Its Basis and Its Genesis.* Chicago, 1963.

——. *Natural Right and History.* Chicago and London, 1965.

Stumpfl, Friedrich. *Die Ursprünge des Verbrechens, dargestellt am Lebenslauf vom Zwillingen.* Leipzig, 1936.

Stursberg, H. *Die Zunahme der Vergehen und Verbrechen und ihre Ursachen.* Düsseldorf, 1878.

Sumner, William Graham. *Folkways.* Boston, 1906.

Sutherland, A. *The Origin and Growth of the Moral Instinct.* London, 1898.

Sutherland, Edwin H. *Principles of Criminology.* 4th ed. New York, 1947.

————. "Mental Deficiency and Crime," in Kimball Young (ed.), *Social Attitudes.* New York, 1931.

————, and Donald R. Cressey. *Principles of Criminology.* 7th ed. Philadelphia, 1966.

Sykes, Gresham M., and David Matza. "Techniques of Neutralization: A Theory of Delinquency," *American Sociological Review*, Vol. 22 (December 1957).

Szabó, Imre. *Társadalom és jog.* Budapest, 1964.

————. *Szocialista jogelmélet, népi demokratikus jog.* Budapest, 1967.

Taft, Donald R. *Criminology.* 3rd ed. New York, 1956.

————, and Ralph W. England, Jr. *Criminology.* 4th ed. New York, 1964.

Tappan, Paul W. *Juvenile Delinquency.* New York, 1949.

————. *Crime, Justice, and Correction.* New York, 1960.

Tarde, Gabriel. *La criminalité comparée.* Paris, 1890.

————. *La philosophie pénale.* Paris, 1890.

————. "Misère et criminalité," *Revue Philosophique*, Vol. 29 (1890).

Tarnowski, E. "La delinquenza e la vita sociale in Russia," *Rivista Italiana di Sociologia*, 1898.

Tarnowsky, Pauline. *Les femmes homicides.* Paris, 1908.

Tesar, Ottokar. *Die symptomatische Bedeutung des verbrecherischen Verhaltens: ein Betrag zur Wertungslehre in Strafrecht.* Berlin, 1904.

Thomas, W. I., and F. Znaniecki. *The Polish Peasant in Europe and America.* New York, 1927.

Thomasius, Christian. *Fundamenta Iuris Naturae et Gentium.* Halle, 1705.

Thrasher, Frederic M. *The Gang.* "Introduction" by James F. Short, Jr. Chicago, 1963.

Timasheff, Nicholas S. *An Introduction to the Sociology of Law.* Cambridge. Mass., 1939.

————. *Sociological Theory, Its Nature and Growth.* 3rd ed. New York, 1967.

Tönnies, Ferdinand. "Moralstatistik," in *Handwörterbuch der Staatswiss.* 4th ed. Jena, 1925.

Tugan-Baranowsky, M. *Studien zur Theorie und Geschichte der Handelskrisen in England.* Jena, 1901.

Tulchin, Simon H. *Intelligence and Crime.* Chicago, 1939.

Turati, Filippo. *Il delitto e la questione sociale.* Milan, 1883.

Vaccaro, M. A. *Genesie funzioni delle leggi penali.* Rome, 1889.

———. *Basi del diritto e dello stato.* Turin, 1893.

Valentini, H. von. *Das Verbrecherthum im preussischem Staat.* Leipzig, 1869.

Vámbéry, Rusztem. *Büntetöjog.* Budapest, 1913.

———. *Büntetöjog és ethika.* Budapest, 1907.

Vecchio, Giorgio del. *Philosophy of Law.* T. O. Martin (tr.). Washington, D.C., 1953.

Verce, E. Fornasari di. *La criminalita e le vicende economiche d'Italia dal 1873 al 1890 e osservazioni sommarie per il Regno Unito della Gran Bretagna e Irlanda (1840–1890) e par la Nova Galles del Sud (1882–1891).* Turin, 1894.

Vervaeck, Louis. *Syllabus du cours d'anthropologie criminelle donné à la prison de Forest.* Brussells, 1926.

Veverka, Miroslav. "A bünözés okairól," *Filosoficky casopis,* 1964, No. 6; and *Külföldi Jogi Cikkgyütemény,* 1965, No. 4.

Vigh, József. "A bünözés okainak problémái," *Jogtudományi Közlöny,* XVIII:9.

Viski, László. *Szándekosság és társadalomra veszélyesség.* Budapest, 1959.

Vold, George B. *Theoretical Criminology.* New York, 1958.

Vurpas, Vaschide Y. "Qu'est ce qu'un dégénéré?" *Archives d'anthropologie criminelle,* Vol. 12 (1902).

Vyshinsky, A. Ia. *Voprosy teorii gosudarstva i prava.* 2nd ed. Moscow, 1949.

———. *The Law of the Soviet State.* New York, 1948.

Wahlberg. W. E. *Das Prinzip der Individualisierung.* Vienna, 1869.

Wake, C. S. *The Evolution of Morality.* London, 1878.

Waldo, Gordon P., and Simon Dinitz, "Personality Attributes of the Criminal: An Analysis of Research Studies, 1950–65," *Journal of Research in Crime and Delinquency,* July 1967.

Walker, Nigel. *Crime and Punishment in Britain.* London, 1965.

Ward, L. *Dynamic Sociology.* New York, 1883.

Weber, Max. *Grundriss der Sozialökonomie, III Abteilung, Wirtschaft und Gesellschaft.* Tübingen, 1922.

Weiss, B. "Über einige wirtschaftliche und moralische Wirkungen hoher Getreidepreise," *Jahrbücher für Nationalökonomie und Statistik.* Leipzig, 1881.

Westermarck, Edward. *The Origin and Development of the Moral Ideas.* 2nd ed. London, 1912.

Wey, Hamilton D. *Criminal Anthropology.* New York, 1890.

Wilkins, Leslie T. "Operational Research and Administrative Problems," reprint from *O and M Bulletin,* Vol. 14, No. 6, London, no date.

―――. *Social Deviance, Social Policy, Action, and Research.* Englewood Cliffs, N.J., 1965.

Willenbücher, N. "Die Strafrechtsphilosophischen Anschauungen Friedrichs des Grosen," *Breslauer Abhandlunger,* Vol. 56 (1904).

Windelband, Wilhelm. *Die Geschichte der neureren Philosophie.* 6th ed. Leipzig. 1919.

Wines, Frederick H. *Punishment and Reformation.* New York, 1895.

Wolf, Eric. *Vom Wesen des Täters.* Berlin, 1932.

―――. "Richtiges Recht im nationalsozialistischen Staat," *Freiburger Universitätsreden,* Vol. 13 (1934).

Wolfgang, Marvin E. "Cesare Lombroso," in Hermann Mannheim (ed.), *Pioneers in Criminology.* London, 1960.

―――, and Franco Ferracuti. *The Subculture of Violence, Towards an Integrated Theory in Criminology.* London, 1967.

Woodward, Mary. "The Role of Low Intelligence in Delinquency," *British Journal of Delinquency,* Vol. 5 (April 1955).

Wootton, Barbara. *Social Science and Social Pathology.* London, 1959.

―――. "Diminished Responsibility: A Layman's View," *Law Quarterly Review,* Vol. 76 (1960).

―――. *Crime and Criminal Law.* London, 1963.

Wulffen, Erich. *Der Sexualverbrecher.* Berlin, 1911.

―――. *Psychologie des Verbrechers.* Berlin, 1908.

―――. *Gauner- und Verbrecher-Typen.* Berlin, 1910.

Zeleny, L. D. "Feeble-mindedness and Criminal Conduct," *American Journal of Sociology,* Vol. 38 (January 1933).

Zilboorg, Gregory. "Psychoanalysis and Criminology," in Vernon C. Branham and Samuel B. Kutash (eds.), *Encyclopedia of Criminology.* New York, 1949.

―――, and G. W. Henry. *A History of Medical Psychology.* New York, 1941.

Name Index

Subject Index